The World Ec

Yann Fitt, Alexandre Faire,
Jean-Pierre Vigier

The World Economic Crisis

U.S. Imperialism at Bay

Yann Fitt, Alexandre Faire, Jean-Pierre Vigier

Translated by Michael Pallis

Zed Press, 57 Caledonian Road, London N1 9DN

The World Economic Crisis was first published by Francois Maspero, 1 Place Paul-Painleve, Paris 5, in 1976 under the title *La crise d'imperialisme et la troisieme guerre mondiale.* First published in English, with a new Postscript to Part II, by Zed Press, 57 Caledonian Road, London N1 9DN in April 1980.

ISBN Hb 0 905762 53 3
Pb 0 905762 54 1

Typed by Gill Bussell
Designed by Mayblin/Shaw
Copy-edited by Bev Brown
Typeset by Lyn Caldwell
Proofed by Sarah Onions and Penelope Fryxell
Printed in Great Britain by Redwood Burn Limited
Trowbridge & Esher

Contents

List of Tables and Figures

Tables

Figures

Foreword: The Cornerstone of the American System

In April 1973, Henry Kissinger grandly announced the 'Year of Europe'. International society was to be reordered on the basis of certain 'new realities'. These new realities, which resulted from the success of the policies of the past generation, posed certain problems that must be confronted. As Kissinger explained 'the problems in Atlantic relationships', the United States had thought that 'a unified Europe working cooperatively with us in an Atlantic partnership would ease many of our international burdens,' but these expectations were not being satisfactorily fulfilled. At a still deeper level, problems arose from a fundamental disparity in the roles of the partners. The United States, Kissinger explained, 'has global interests and responsibilities,' while 'our European allies have regional interests.' While 'in economic relations, the European Community has increasingly stressed its regional personality,' the United States plays a fundamentally different role in world affairs: in particular, 'the United States . . . must act as part of, and be responsible for, a wider international trade and monetary system.' Our task, in the Year of Europe, was to 'reconcile these two perspectives.'

Five years earlier, Kissinger had developed a similar point. In his conception, 'regional groupings supported by the United States will have to take over major responsibility for their immediate areas, with the United States being concerned more with the overall framework of order than with the management of every regional enterprise.' Similarly, one could not expect the top management of General Motors to settle disputes on the shop floor in some plant manufacturing spark plugs for Chevrolet. So much for 'multipolarity'. Furthermore, the underlying U.S.-Soviet 'bipolar' structure was not to be a truly symmetric one. Rather, the junior partner must be made to understand that there will be a 'penalty for intransigence'. Any other attitude 'hardly serves the cause of peace.'[1]

Europe's failure to 'ease our international burdens' was, in fact, becoming something of a problem in 1973. Particularly significant was European reluctance to share the burden of maintaining the American client regime in South Vietnam. The vast and unanticipated costs of the American wars in South-East Asia were contributing to a relative decline in American power *vis-a-vis* its capitalist rivals. This was the major factor that turned ruling circles against the war, or more precisely, against the 'labour-intensive' tactics by which the war was being fought. Such was particularly the case after the Tet offensive of 1968 shattered the web of illusion spun by the propagandists. The historic achievement of the American peace movement was that it made a true national mobilization impossible. It became necessary to disguise the costs of the war, and, as Vietnamese resistance was miraculously sustained, the bill came due, bringing on an economic crisis. By 1968 Europe was no longer willing to cooperate fully in abetting American aggression in South-East Asia, let alone to take on the still greater share of the burden assigned to it under the Nixon-Kissinger doctrine. One goal of the Year of Europe was to remedy such defects in 'Atlantic relationships'.

The Year of Europe came to an end with the petroleum crisis following the fourth Arab-Israel war. The 'First World' of industrial state capitalism faced a serious internal crisis as European powers and Japan began to explore bilateral relationships with the oil-producing countries. They were quickly called to heel. There must be a 'united front', they were informed, led by the United States, which is unique in its 'global interests and responsibilities' and its responsibility for the 'wider trade and monetary system'. The distribution and marketing of petroleum must remain effectively in the hands of the multinational energy corporations, primarily U.S.-based. Since the Second World War control over energy had functioned as a highly effective device to ensure America's dominance over its allies, who were put on notice that no major change in this system would be tolerated.

To a significant extent, the oil crisis served to overcome the problems in Atlantic relationships that had so troubled Kissinger. As oil prices rose, Europe and Japan were, in effect, compelled to subsidize American industrial recovery. The energy companies benefited directly, and by early 1975 the United States was enjoying a favourable trade balance with the Middle Eastern countries (including Egypt, excluding Israel), substantially improving over the satisfactory performance of 1974. The major oil producers remain loyal client states. American business is jubilant over the vast opportunities opening throughout Iran and the Arab world, including even Iraq, which, they happily report, is behaving much like its more orthodox neighbours. Trade, construction, investment, and arms sales all promise a glorious future for American business in the region. Europe and Japan, in the words of *Business Week*, 'are footing most of the bill for the area's prosperity' while 'petrodollars coming back to the U.S. through trade offset this country's outlays for Middle Eastern oil.' American businessmen report a 'marked preference for American products', and the region is 'one of the few places in the world where private enterprise is making a comeback' – primarily American enterprise.

Meanwhile, Arab oil profits flow to the international economic institutions that will continue, as in the past, to work for the construction of a world that is open to American economic penetration and political control. Oil importing states are, in effect, taxed through the rise of oil prices and in this fashion, compelled to contribute to the American-dominated international institutions. A new economic order is taking shape in which American hegemony, threatened by the South-East Asian debacle, will, it is hoped, be restored, while the junior partners will limit themselves, once again, to developing their 'regional personality'.

In short, the Year of Europe proved to be a considerable success.

Kissinger's concept of 'multipolarity' defines the United States as the dominant world power, now compelled to accept the *detente* that had been offered by the Soviet Union in earlier years. According to Kissinger, in his earlier studies, the United States lost its opportunity to construct the stable world order of its choice through excessive timidity and misguided moral scruples, nurtured by Communist propaganda. It is now necessary to come to terms with the ensuing realities. The Nixon-Kissinger diplomacy constituted a break with the past in that these unpleasant realities were finally recognized. The hope of 'liberating' Eastern Europe so that it could attain the happy status of another Latin America was abandoned. The iron rule of Russian totalitarianism in Eastern Europe is now explicitly sanctioned, as Stalin and his successors had demanded. The expectation that China might collapse, held by State Department analysts through the late 1960s, was also reluctantly put to rest. The United States will no longer entertain the hope, in the short run at least, that China may again enjoy the benefits of rule by the Kuomintang. Rather, the United States will try to exploit to its advantage the Sino-Soviet rivalry, which can be traced to Stalin's deep-seated antagonism to the Chinese revolution. China is expected to play a conservative role in world affairs, supporting such American clients as Marcos and the Shah. So far, it has obliged.

To be sure, the matter is not put in quite these terms by Kissinger and other ideologists. The interpretation they prefer is that Russia and China have finally come to understand, under the careful tutelage of Kissinger (and, before he was demoted for his excesses, Nixon), that they must moderate the 'revolutionary' and 'aggressive' behaviour that was so threatening world peace in earlier years, according to official history, and must join the peace-loving countries led by the United States. Pronouncements to this effect do not evoke the scorn that they deserve. One must bear in mind the astonishing power of ideological controls in the United States, a matter of some importance.

Though American aspirations have been somewhat reduced, the general conception of the structure of international society developed during the Second World War continues to provide the guiding principles for American foreign policy. American planners confidently expected that the United States would emerge as the dominant world power. The United States would henceforth 'enforce the peace of the world,' as Harry Truman stated in October 1945, since 'we have learned the bitter lesson that the weakness of this great Republic invites men of ill-will to shake the very foundations of civilization all over the world.' As for the character of the civilization to be maintained by United States force, future events would show, though Latin Americans and Filipinos could have easily provided edifying testimony from their own history.

One should not suppose that later events have led to any serious erosion of the propaganda system promulgated in the universities and the media. Thus, at the height of the Vietnam war, the editor of 'a collection of scientific papers by students of society', 'peace researchers', explained that application of the tools of social science to the 'game of world domination' would improve the decision-making capacities of 'good-intentioned leaders and policy makers – as has characterized the foreign policy of U.S. and many other nations'.[2] And retrospective accounts of the Vietnam war by liberal analysts, academic or others, keep close to this basic tenet of the ideological system.

An interesting insight into the vision of the post-war world is provided by the deliberations of the Council on Foreign Relations from 1939-44.[3] A 1940 memorandum outlines the policy needs of the United States 'in a world in which it proposes to hold unquestioned power'. The memorandum outlines the 'component parts of an integrated policy to achieve military and economic supremacy for the United States within the non-German world,' including the Western hemisphere, the British Empire and the Far East. This U.S.-led non-German world, later called the 'Grand Area', was 'not regarded by the Group as more desirable than a world economy, nor as an entirely satisfactory substitute' (1941). Nevertheless, the Grand Area was to be developed in its own right and as a nucleus for the post-war world economy which, it was hoped, would result from the defeat of the Axis powers. Specifically, it was expected that 'the institutions developed for the integration of the Grand Area would yield useful experience in meeting European problems, and perhaps it would be possible simply to interweave the economies of European countries into that of the Grand Area,' which, crucially, was to be dominated by the United States and organized in such a manner as to satisfy American economic and strategic interests. There is much discussion of the problem of guaranteeing markets and access to raw materials, so that the American socio-economic system can be preserved without essential modification, as the world-dominant system.

The purpose of the Council's planning for the Grand Area, it was stressed, was 'to discover what "elbow room" the American economy needed to survive without major readjustments'. In April 1941 the Group did recognize, however, that the statement of war aims 'would have a better propaganda effect' if it stressed 'the interests of other peoples' instead of appearing to be 'concerned solely with Anglo-American imperialism'. A few months later, the Atlantic Charter was announced.

A crucial feature of all such plans was that Europe must not become an independent economic actor on a par with the United States. Similarly, the imperial systems had to be dismantled if there was to be a world economy or even a Grand Area. During the Second World War, the United States carefully regulated lend-lease assistance to Great Britain so that British reserves would remain between $600 million and $1 billion. The effect – and, one may rationally assume, the intent as well – was to keep Britain in the war, but without the power that would permit it to maintain independence and imperial control. The United States succeeded in taking over a dominant role in crucial areas of British power and influence in the Middle East and Latin America, in preparation for the U.S.-dominated Grand Area or, preferably, the full world economy.

The more realistic Nixon-Kissinger diplomacy, in effect, marks the abandonment of the hope for a true world economy in favour of the less satisfactory substitute, a Grand Area under American control (sorrowfully, without China). Britain was effectively reduced, materially and in part culturally as well, to the status of a satellite. Western Europe as a whole has surrendered a significant share of sovereignty to the United States, in part, through economic penetration. In Latin America, Cuba was lost but elsewhere imperial control is generally well-established. The Middle East is unstable but the energy reserves are largely in the hands of United States clients, and the major military powers, Israel and Egypt, are increasingly dependent on the United States, while Iran remains a loyal ally. Indochina has separated itself from the Grand Area. The United States is expending considerable efforts to ensure that the dominoes do not totter beyond. While the world of 1975 is not exactly what the planners had in mind, still, in something like the Grand Area extended to Western Europe, American corporations have thrived, foreign investment having increased by a factor of 10, and an integrated global economy has developed – to a substantial degree under the control of U.S.-based multinational corporations.

In the memoranda and reports of the Council on Foreign Relations and various study groups that represent ruling elites, global planning motivated by the needs of American business and the economy it owns is a constant and unvarying theme. The same is true of reports of the National Security Council and other significant decision-making segments of the state executive, quite generally. It is only in academic history that such considerations are regularly discounted, while stress is laid on pronouncements that 'have a better propaganda effect'; for example, the alleged commitment of the United States to 'Wilsonian principles' of independence and self-determination. More realistic historians do take note of the fact that the American commitment to such principles is revealed most clearly in rhetoric concerning the lands beyond the Iron Curtain, while somehow they are regularly ignored in the vast domains where American power prevails. This fact, duly noted, is described as 'ironic', but mere fact cannot shake the basic principles of the state religion, as put forth by the secular priesthood of subservient intellectuals.

The fragmentation of Europe into a system of Russian colonies and American dependencies was more or less inevitable, given the American goal of creating a U.S.-dominated world economy and Russian insistence on maintaining client ('friendly') regimes in the region conquered by the Red Army. For the United States, the optimal solution would have been to incorporate a united Europe, concerned solely with its 'regional personality', within the Grand Area. This being impossible, a divided Europe is preferable to an independent and unified region which might very well become a real competitor in the global system. It is not surprising, then, that tentative Russian moves in the early 1950s to explore the possibility of a unified and independent European system were ignored or rebuffed – for example, the proposal to unify Germany outside the framework of the Western military alliance. It is unlikely that these moves would have amounted to very much in any event. Russia shares with the United States an overriding antipathy towards an independent Europe, no matter what its political and social structure. A particular danger is that such a unified Europe might even develop genuine socialist institutions in a free society: workers' control under conditions of intellectual and cultural freedom and political and economic democracy. Such an outcome would be no less abhorrent to the Soviet Union than the United States.

When a society escapes somehow from the Grand Area, the United States, if unable to reintegrate it by force, must seek to impose barriers to its successful development. China, Cuba, Allende's Chile, and now Indochina and revolutionary Portugal (where the battle to maintain the dominance of international capital is by no means lost), must be subjected to blockade and other forms of harassment in the hope that the economy will collapse and a harsh and authoritarian regime will be established. The great fear that unites the superpowers is that genuine socialism will develop somewhere, serving as a model for other societies and winning what the Pentagon planners sometimes called 'ideological successes'. The rational version of the domino theory was largely based on such fears. Pentagon planners did not really expect the Viet Minh to conquer Thailand or set sail for Indonesia and San Francisco – such stories were designed only to terrorize domestic public opinion. They did fear, and perhaps with some reason, that the revolutionary nationalists of Indochina might achieve social gains that would seem impressive to peasant societies subjected to the preferred 'trickle down' model of development, their resources devoted to serving the needs of the capitalist industrial world dominated by the United States.

On occasion, the basic principles of order and stability are expressed rather frankly. A study sponsored by the Woodrow Wilson Foundation and the National Planning Association (1955) identifies the primary threat of Communism as the economic transformation of the Communist powers 'in ways which reduce their willingness and ability to complement the industrial economies of the West.' The threat, in short, is the refusal of these powers to play their proper role in the global economy. What is more, genuine socialism might threaten stability and order in the imperial power itself. It is possible, after all, to raise certain questions about the use and control of productive resources or the distribution of wealth in a society where many suffer hunger and want as they watch television commercials advertising new products for overweight dogs. For comparable reasons, the Kremlin can hardly be expected to tolerate socialist stirrings in Czechoslovakia, which are far more dangerous than, say, a fascist movement supported from outside.

The Second World War made it possible for the United States to organize an expanded Grand Area, approaching but never achieving a world capitalist economy. It also brought the Great Depression to an end. Earlier New Deal measures were not successful, though they did succeed in smoothing some of the rough edges. The corporate managers who flocked to Washington to run the wartime economy learned the lesson that Germany and Japan had discovered without the benefit of Keynes. Government-induced production of armaments, on a massive scale, can – temporarily – overcome the crisis of capitalist institutions.

In the post-war world, the lesson was taken to heart. The state maintained its central role in stimulating industrial production and sponsoring research. It was, of course, constrained to do so in a way that would not interfere with the interests of monopoly capital but would, rather, enhance these interests where possible. Armaments, a massive highway programme, and, for a time, the enormously expensive and quite pointless manned space programme were natural directions to pursue. Meanwhile, production of useful goods began to be transferred elsewhere in the Grand Area, where wages were lower, 'externalities' (e.g. pollution) could be ignored, and the work force more easily controlled.

In the United States, one result has been an inexorable deterioration in the material basis for a functioning industrial society; for example, the gradual decline of the machine tools industry. Meanwhile, government support for agribusiness and the mechanization of agriculture induced a massive migration to the cities. In an economy geared to high technology production, this 'internal immigration' could not be absorbed as were earlier waves from abroad. One enduring result is the current urban race problems and the general crisis of the cities, which must provide services but cannot offer employment. The problem is exacerbated by the flight of wealth to the suburbs, with the tax burden for maintaining the urban centre falling on the poor. In a profoundly inegalitarian society, virtually any programme will be administered in practice in such a way as to favour the wealthy and powerful over the defenceless poor. 'Urban renewal' became a device to subsidize upper and middle income groups. Funds for higher education are so distributed that the higher a person's socio-economic status, the more tax funds are spent on his education. Programmes to integrate public education (for example, forced bussing) are designed to exclude suburban areas, again imposing severe problems on the poor, whose neighbourhoods – virtually the only source of a degree of personal fulfillment in a world of meaningless work, cultural barrenness, and limited opportunity – are destroyed. For those trapped in the declining cities, such 'Ulsterization' raises new and insurmountable barriers to the kind of mass popular organization that might permit the urban poor to resist the economic processes that are grinding them down. A stagnant domestic economy breeds urban crime. The cities are caught in a 'debt trap', not unlike that of the 'developing' countries of the neo-colonial system, New York City being the most dramatic example. Under current conditions, the problem can only worsen.

Furthermore, as the business press constantly warns, there is a severe liquidity crisis. The federal government commands a huge share of capital, which is in part dedicated to the production of waste and the fulfillment of 'global interests and responsibilities', as in South-East Asia. Corporations are faced with debt and shortage of capital for investment. The consequence can only be an acceleration of the process of concentration, as weaker sectors give way to powerful monopolies, leading to what *Business Week* describes as a *Zaibatsu* system: a few conglomerates linked to a powerful state. To guarantee capital for investment, the state must find a way to curtail services and impose a wage squeeze (through inflation, if in no other way). The reaction of the federal government to the crisis of New York City is instructive. New York pays far more to the federal government than it receives in services, in contrast to such states as California and Texas which have benefited, for example, from government-induced production in aerospace and armaments. The federal government does not propose measures to redress the balance, but instead, the President announces, will intervene to subsidize 'essential services' such as police and fire protection – one cannot, after all, have people robbing the Chase Manhattan Bank in desperation. Health and education, however, are no more 'essential' than the opportunity for meaningful work, or for that matter, any work. As New York City slowly collapses, and with it the market for municipal bonds, the cost of running other towns and cities must correspondingly increase. The great corporations and their representatives in the national government will not tolerate a serious decline in the federal armaments budget, but local municipal services are another matter.

It is now widely assumed that national planning must be instituted on a far more extensive scale than heretofore. Under an emerging *Zaibatsu* system, this can only mean that those who already control the central economic institutions and thus monopolize the planning function will use their power to manipulate the state executive still more systematically, in their own interest. The pre-war crisis of capitalist institutions led to the rise of fascism in parts of the industrial world and to the strengthening of state capitalist institutions elsewhere. The current crisis will carry the process a step further, particularly, in a society such as the United States which is atomized and in an important sense, depoliticized. There are no mass reformist parties to defend the rights of worke[rs] or the 'underclass' of unemployables. Many have warned that some kind of 'friendly fascism' – fascist-style institutional structure without excesses of police state terror – may well be a result.

Revolutionary stirrings in the periphery of the Grand Area will be met with force, as in the past. Unless dramatic changes take place in the centre of world capitalism – changes that do not now seem very likely – the incomparable military and economic power of the United States will be deployed to crush those benighted elements of world society that struggle to gain control of their human and material resources and direct them to internal needs, instead of continuing to 'complement the industrial powers of the West.' The results no doubt will be mixed, as in past years, and in part dependent on the national mood in the United States.

In this context, it is important to pay careful attention to ideological currents in the United States. During the 1960s, a popular movement to end the war achieved a quite unprecedented scale. The resistance of American youth to the war against Vietnam – and Laos, and Cambodia – has no historical parallel, to my knowledge. There are widespread illusions about this movement. Thus, it is widely believed that the universities and the liberal media launched a crusade against the war, entering into an adversary relation to state power. This is gross nonsense. From the earliest stages of the war until the very end, the media faithfully repeated government lies and rarely strayed from official interpretation of events. And university resources were devoted to the imperial enterprise at every level: training of police and colonial administration, design of counterinsurgency technology, study and analysis of 'pacification' programmes, and so on. Students came to oppose the war *en masse,* as did some faculty, but the submissiveness of the universities as institutions to state power never really ended. Studies of the 'American intellectual elite', largely university- based, reveal that they finally opposed the war, but on 'pragmatic grounds', turning against it at about the same time that conservative business circles did so, and for essentially the same reasons. Furthermore, they pride themselves on this 'pragmatic attitude', that is, the conviction that the war was wrong because the United States could not win. Principled opposition to the war was generally foreign to the 'intellectual elite'.

The popular movement of the 1960s, which ultimately placed serious restrictions on the war planners while leading to the collapse of the conscript army in the field, developed out of the control of its 'natural leaders', a matter of some consequence that deeply troubles intellectual ideologists. For the imperial venture to be pursued, it will be necessary to restore the ideological controls that were swept aside by this popular movement. It is interesting to see how the task is being carried out. Particularly revealing is the debate over the 'lessons of Vietnam' as conducted by liberal ideologists. Almost without exception, the war is described as 'a mistake'. Good motives and benevolent intentions were transmuted, in some mysterious way, into bad policy. The *New York Times* recounts the cosmic battle between 'the hawks', who urged that we could win with a full application of our power, and 'the doves', who countered that victory was beyond our grasp. There was, of course, a third position: the United States had no right to win or to intervene by force in the first place. This position, typical of the genuine peace movement, must be excluded from debate and has, by now, been effectively eliminated from the mass media and journals of opinion. At the same time, the custodians of history are at work recasting the past in the terms that they prefer. The 'pragmatic doves' were the true advocates of peace, hampered in their task by the irresponsible, violent, totalitarian left.

Given the control over ideological institutions exercised by the liberal intelligentsia, there is little doubt that the reconstruction of history will prevail.

It is particularly important to eliminate any moral issue from the debate over the lessons of Vietnam. The public came to regard the war, with much justice, as the liberals' war. The resulting loss of moral legitimacy is a serious matter for the guardians of ideology. If the population is to bear the not inconsiderable costs of empire with willingness or at least resignation, if Camelot is to be rebuilt, the loss of legitimacy must be overcome and the moral dimension eliminated from consciousness. Tens of thousands of resisters and deserters are a constant reproach, intolerable to the liberal ideologues who supported American aggression as long as it seemed to promise success and who, to this day, reject with incomprehension or contempt the idea that the United States has no right to impose its will by force.

Consequences of these ideological imperatives are everywhere apparent. When the American U.N. Ambassador castigates Uganda's Idi Amin as a 'racist murderer', no doubt correctly, liberal commentators are overcome with admiration for his honesty and courage. No one would be so vulgar as to recall that this same person was a minor flunkey in the Johnson Administration, which was guilty of racist murder on a scale that exceeds Amin's wildest fantasies.

Or consider the recent Solzhenitsyn affair. Evidently, liberal intellectuals are unable openly to endorse his religious mysticism, his plea for reaction and autocracy, his hatred of democracy, his perverse account of much of recent history. But with rare exceptions, his critics describe him as a 'moral giant', a visionary and prophet who speaks in tones that we can scarcely comprehend. In our society, according to the constant refrain, one cannot conceive of such heights of moral grandeur.

A curious spectacle, when one recalls the many thousands of young Americans who were willing to suffer severe punishment and exile to save the peasants of Indochina from destruction and massacre. In many thousands of cases, their sacrifice was purely altruistic, on an incomparably higher moral level than that of someone who fights courageously for his own rights and the rights of others like him. What is more, it is ludicrous to apply the term 'moral giant' to a man who urged the United States to greater heights of violence and terror in its Indochina crusade. By any reasonable standard of moral judgement, Solzhenitsyn stands on a par with someone who struggles courageously in defence of the oppressed in the United States, while supporting the Russian invasion of Czechoslovakia and Stalin's slave labour camps. But these elementary truths cannot be expressed. It is necessary to gaze in awe and wonder upon this paragon of morality, however misguided, who speaks in terms of moral values that are so foreign to our society and its problems. For if the real truth is to be faced, if the moral issues of the American war are to be honestly confronted, then how will history judge the 'pragmatic' intellectual elite of the United States? Better to pretend that moral issues simply do not arise, cannot even be conceived, from our mean and petty view.

This travesty is of no small importance. It is an integral part of the effort to rebuild the shattered framework of belief in preparation for the day when we will, once again, have to shoulder our 'global responsibilities'. While the defeat in South-East Asia was no doubt a setback to American global strategy, it would be an error to regard it as a truly serious blow. Rather, it is a failed venture, unwisely undertaken, to be liquidated and forgotten as quickly as possible so that the main enterprise can proceed. For the goals of this enterprise, Europe, Japan, and the Middle East are incomparably more important than the fate of some far off peasant society in South-East Asia, and the more rational imperialists have therefore urged – quite rightly, from their point of view – that global affairs must be restored to a more reasonable perspective.

Putting polysyllabic obfuscation to one side, 'multipolarity' reveals itself to be just another version of the familiar doctrine. The United States will work to construct a global economy organized in such a way as to fulfil the needs of international capital, largely American-based. Economic concentration will continue and the state will play an increasing role in serving its demands, at home and abroad. Countervailing forces within the United States are weak and scattered, and generally well controlled. The United States retains its capacity to impose an 'over-all framework of order' within which our European allies may pursue the management of their 'regional' enterprise, taking care not to exceed the limits set by the one effective international authority. The junior partners in *detente* are to contribute to international order in the prescribed way, while the United States will permit, and even assist them, to manage their internal problems. The world of the next generation should not be markedly different from what has come before. This seems a reasonable, if far from certain, prospect.

In the last days of the Vietnam war, there was some trepidation that trouble was looming. The problems were discussed quite frankly in the business press. Thus, *Business Week* (7 April 1975) commented editorially on the 'jarring foreign policy failures that have hit the U.S.' and expressed concern that 'President Ford and Secretary of State Henry Kissinger seem unable to cope with a pattern of growing world disorder.' The editorial described briefly and accurately 'the international economic structure, under which U.S. companies have flourished since the end of the Second World War', a structure which is now 'in jeopardy', as follows: 'Fuelled initially by the dollars of the Marshall Plan, American business prospered and expanded on overseas orders despite the cold war, the end of colonialism, and the creation of militant and often anti-capitalistic new countries. No matter how negative a development, there was always the umbrella of American power to contain it . . . The rise of the multinational corporation was the economic expression of [the post-war] political framework.'

But 'now, this stable world order for business operations is falling apart.' Some of the problems are reviewed. 'Even in Western Europe – the keystone of the American international framework – there are increasing threats to stability', specifically, failure to cooperate in the oil crisis. Furthermore, there is fear 'that the Portuguese illness will spread to Spain.' In addition to these 'crushing blows' there is a potential problem 'if Japan cannot continue to export a third of its products to South-East Asia' – the editors do not add that a major goal of the American intervention in Vietnam, from the earliest days, was to ensure Japanese access to South-East Asia so that Japan would not be tempted to 'accommodate' mainland Communism. Congress was adding to the problems through its failure, in Kissinger's words, to come to an understanding 'about the proper relationship between the executive and the legislative functions,' that is, to leave the executive a free hand in global management.

The fears expressed were unwarranted. It would be a serious misunderstanding of the American political system to believe that Congress might act in such a way as to undermine 'the international economic structure, under which U.S. companies have flourished,' or to shackle the American power that must be at hand to 'contain negative developments'. After the first shock passed, it became clear, as I am sure the editors would agree, that Congress will cooperate, as in the past. The distribution of power within American society permits nothing else. The world has not become ungovernable as a result of U.S. failures in South-East Asia. The 'stable world order for business operations' is not falling apart. Effective reserves of power, economic and military, are in place to make the world safe for American business, despite the threats to order and civilization on every side.

Noam Chomsky
Cambridge Massachusetts
5 November 1975

References

1. Henry A. Kissinger, *American Foreign Policy*, expanded edition, Norton, N.Y., 1974.
2. Walter Isard, ed., *Vietnam: Some Basic Issues and Alternatives,* Peace Research Society (International), Schenkman, Cambridge, Mass., 1969.
3. Lawrence H. Shoup, 'Shaping the Post-war World', *The Insurgent Sociologist,* Vol. V, Spring 1975. Shoup appears to be the first to have undertaken a careful and serious study of the deliberations of the extremely influential Council on Foreign Relations. Avoidance of crucial topics in the formation of foreign policy, such as the influence of corporate interests and their representatives is, not surprisingly, a characteristic feature of the academic literature.

PART I

Two Tools for Domination: Industry and Agriculture

by Yann Fitt

1. Introduction

The possibility of an end to American hegemony is an idea which has been much at issue since the withdrawal of American troops from Vietnam. Yet there is no shortage of signs disproving the proposition that American world domination is in decline.

Thanks to the 'cold war', the United States has managed to secure considerable influence over European industry and agriculture. These means of domination are still relevant, although they have had to be constantly adapted to the changing circumstances of the last few years, especially in these times of *'detente'* and economic crisis. Having contributed very considerably to the growth of the crisis which has developed since the end of 1973, the United States now seeks to rally its allies behind the effort to impose a 'new international economic order' on the rest of the world, a 'new economic order' which is obviously not the one desired by the countries of the Third World. The American desire for power is all the more intense because of the crisis which the American economy and, in a broader sense, American society, is going through. And whilst American leadership may well turn out to be less prominent a feature of the coming years than it has been for the two decades which followed the Second World War, the underlying goals will remain the same.

Agriculture is an important but often overlooked element of America's ability to dominate the rest of the world. It has become one of the main trump cards in the new American strategy. Expert opinion predicts that the imbalance in the distribution of world food supplies will persist and even increase over the next thirty years; American agriculture is thus a very effective instrument for blackmail. The United States would not seek hegemony so avidly were it not for the American multinational companies which have installed themselves all over the planet. It is to defend the actions and the development of these companies that American power is brought to bear (as in Chile, for example). Conversely, these companies are imperialism's pawns. Subtly and almost irresistibly, like gigantic squids, they spread their tentacles.

The first victims of this terrible machine are the countries and peoples of the Third World. The process is fuelled by the pillage of natural and mineral resources. The Third World's attempts to counteract the disequilibrium in its relations with the industrialized West have usually been abortive. The United States is not willing to undermine a situation which is a significant basis for its power, even though America, as the world's largest producer of raw materials, has interests similar to other producers of certain raw materials.

Washington has done everything it can to convince its allies to resolve the crisis collectively, it being understood that they must, of course, always recognize American leadership. The voice from across the Atlantic is listened to with an attentive ear, as the disruption of the system has affected the United States itself; all the Western leaders are well aware that the health of the economies they control is dependent on the health of the American economy. However, even the staunchest defenders of American policy were taken aback when the State Department admitted its duplicity over oil policies.

The State Department had made a great fuss about its desire for a drop in oil prices, and had even brandished the threat of a military occupation of the oil fields from time to time. At the end of 1974, however, it admitted that it favoured a price of $11 a barrel,[1] a slightly higher price than the one set by OPEC! It was obvious that, for both internal and external reasons, the United States had facilitated the acceleration of the rise in oil prices. The internal reason was that, according to expert opinion, only a high price for oil would enable the U.S. to regain the independence in energy matters crucial to its security as a great power. The external one was that the European and Japanese economies, which had become too competitive *vis-a-vis* the American economy, would be hit four-square by the high price. Despite all this, the European and Japanese leaders, once they had recovered from their surprise, preferred to retain the advantages of American 'protection' to taking a courageous and possibly even dangerous decision in favour of independence. There is a widespread belief today that the difficulties facing the U.S. domestic economy herald the end of the hegemony exercised by the world economy's number one power. In our opinion, such a conclusion is too hasty. After a brief description of the cracks appearing in the edifice of world capitalism, we will show that they are the result of adjustments made inevitable by radical changes in the fundamentals of the world economy. It is American imperialism itself which has brought these changes about, in order to halt a decline caused by its own internal lack of economic vitality, by European and Japanese competition, by the upsurge of Third World demands and by the end of the great military adventures abroad.

Ever since the beginning of the decade, the U.S. has been remodelling the world with a view to imposing a new order. This new system will rely less on B52s and more on complex mechanisms of economic domination. In order to achieve this, the U.S. is integrating all the elements of its power. The U.S. will not hesitate to use the threat of a withdrawal of military protection or of petro-dollars in its effort to maintain a path for its products. Kissinger has made it clear that 'staying in NATO is not a favour granted to the United States'. But American capitalism's desire for expansion does not exclude flexibility and adaptability. The need of developed and developing states to be associated with the ventures of American capitalism is no longer treated as incompatible with its dominant ethic, just as it is now considered preferable to spread the risks in 'unstable' countries, namely in the Third World, rather than to go it alone. The development of raw material extraction is increasingly a matter for international capitalism. The way ownership of African mineral resources has been carved up is particularly instructive in this regard.[2]

In other words, American capitalism is not pursuing the same strategy in the developed countries as in the Third World, where the unity of international capitalism is seen as essential to the survival of the system. It is actually far more important to block the developing countries' efforts at repossession of their mineral wealth than to indulge in some merciless inter-capitalist struggle in which capitalism as a whole would be the loser.

The rationalization of the new economic order which America is in the process of imposing, is liberalism presented as a factor in the general progress of humanity; world-wide integration of production is possible only if every form of protectionism disappears or diminishes considerably. The American Government has, over the last few years, been doing everything it can to enable its companies to impose a new world division of labour, whose primary dynamism would be the rational exploitation of inequalities. We will deal with the law of unequal development at greater length later on. For the moment, let us just say that the 'American project' consists essentially in ensuring that American companies can effectively corner the market for certain very sophisticated products (aeronautics, nuclear energy, computer science, chemicals), for services and for some agricultural products, leaving the Third World to serve as a reservoir of raw materials, as a source of semi-finished goods, and even as a possible site for the setting up of simple manufacturing industry. Rearguard actions are still being fought within the developed world over the demarcation of zones of activity, but the outcome of the struggle is practically a foregone conclusion: one only has to examine the structure of the key Western industrial sectors. Alongside the (military) Atlantic Alliance, there is an economic alliance. The crack troops of this new alliance are the so-called 'multinationals', whose 'secret weapon' is the fact that they have a faster growth rate than the national economies. We shall therefore take great pains to outline the basis of their particular dynamism and its consequences. These firms, which are constantly conquering new markets and gaining access to new sources of raw materials operate beyond the economic level as the vectors of a 'world-wide', and hence American, culture and ideology.

The American Crisis

The United States is not immune to the repercussions of the crisis which it, far more than any other country, has brought about. We will mention only certain aspects of the problem.

The United States' share of the Western world's production has fallen considerably since 1950. It has gone down from 70% to less than 50%. This relative decline is fairly striking, but does not take into account production carried out abroad by American companies. Taking the dominant nationality of companies rather than the locus of production as one's criterion, the American share of the Western world's production is still over 60%.

This relative decline in American economic power is due to the fact that the U.S. has a slower growth rate than its main competitors. This phenomenon, particularly marked since 1965, is partly explained by the drop in American productivity, and the consequent drop in American competitiveness. From the beginning of the '70s, the U.S. has been handicapped in world markets by the relatively high prices of its products, despite the fact that the standard of living of American employees has remained almost stagnant. Another important factor is that in the U.S. there has been far less productive investment than amongst its major Western competitors. Between 1967 and 1971, the rate of productive investment in the U.S. was only 7%, compared with 31.3% in Japan, 11.8% in Germany and 11.7% in France over the same period. The position of the U.S. in world trade has suffered from this economic sluggishness. Between 1960 and 1970 the growth rate of U.S. exports was about three points lower than that of European exports and more than nine points below that of Japanese exports.

The American trade balance started deteriorating considerably in 1968; by 1971 it was $4,000 million in deficit and in 1972 it stood at $6,400 million in the red. Analysis of the international balance of trade during the period casts the U.S. in a surprising role – the only areas in which exports rose more sharply than imports were raw materials and foodstuffs. Furthermore there were only three sectors where the U.S. enjoyed a positive balance of trade: products incorporating a very high level of technology (notably products of the aeronautics and arms industries), chemicals, and agricultural products.

These are the sectors in which the U.S. reconquest of the world will be the most violent. On the other hand, there has been a steady decline in the industries concerned with clothing, textiles, shoes, cars, lorries, components for assembly, minerals, petroleum products and finally even in the steel industry. This decline has mainly benefited *Japan, Canada and, to a lesser extent, the E.E.C. countries,* notably Germany.

Another important source of concern for the U.S. administration is that the sources of raw materials within the dollar zone are rapidly being exhausted, so that the U.S. has to rely on countries which are considered unstable. From 1970 onwards, the security angle has been stressed, again and again, in a variety of contexts. Indeed it would seem that, in order to drive the point home as quickly as possible and to stimulate some effective action on the subject, a particularly black picture has quite deliberately been painted.

The deterioration in the trade balance was accompanied by a similar deficit in the other sectors of the balance of payments. U.S. foreign indebtedness doubled from 1967 to 1972, financed by the rest of the world accepting the dollar as a reserve currency (see Part II, 'The Reign of the Dollar'). The U.S. balance of payments situation has two noteworthy features. Firstly, 'political' operations have involved an expenditure of $143,000 million since 1945, a sum which has been distributed not without hope of a good return; nearly 80% of this money has helped to keep American industry turning over, especially the arms and agricultural industries. This apparent largesse can therefore be treated as mainly a subsidy for the home economy. Secondly, there is the fact that long-term capital investment programmes have resulted in an outflow of U.S. capital amounting to $66,000 million since the Second World War, which has been handsomely compensated for by returns in the form of interest, transfers, royalties, etc., amounting to $101,000 million.

It was under President Nixon, in 1971, that a fundamental shift in American economic policy was decided upon.

The New Strategy

The new American policy emerged gradually, attaining its final form in 1973. Its main characteristic was to integrate the economy into a global strategy aimed at establishing the basis for a new world order, in which American leadership, while less visible than it was following the Second World War, would be just as efficacious. The avowed goal was to re-establish America's position on the world chessboard. The first step was taken on 15 August 1971 – the dollar was declared non-convertible. Nixon then spoke quite straightforwardly about the links existing between commercial, monetary and military problems. The partners of the United States were being told that they were to heed the American *diktat.* Starting from the postulate that 'economic conflicts increase political tension and weaken security ties,' Nixon set out to eliminate these conflicts. How? By eliminating all customs barriers; by a return to the sort of economic liberalism which, it was hoped, would act as a magic tonic for the American economy. In other words, the point was to break agricultural Europe and to hinder the development of industrial Europe. As far as the developed countries were concerned, America's action was geared to gain access to an important market for its agricultural products and to prevent a powerful European industry from competing too effectively with the major American firms.

The reinforcement of the United States' position abroad, aimed at re-establishing the balance of trade and the balance of payments on a healthy footing, was to be financed by drawing on the rest of the world's wealth.

The process was given another boost in 1972 with the devaluation of the dollar. Without going into the details of the financial manipulations involved (these are dealt with in Part II of the present volume) we can nonetheless list some of their consequences:

1. Inflation enabled companies to accumulate capital in order to finance future development. American firms had seen their ability to finance themselves levelling off and even diminishing ever since 1965. From 1971 to 1973 company profits rose sharply, by 59% in fact, during a period when the gross

national product grew by only 23%.

2. The effects of a slight deterioration of the terms of exchange combined with a significantly faster fall in the value of the dollar had a very favourable effect on the balance of trade and hence on the balance of payments, without changing the structure of the American economy. From 1971-72 onwards, exports soared.

3. Inflation, which rose much faster amongst the U.S.'s main partners (except Germany), was thus, in relative terms, helpful to the competitiveness of American products; the U.S. level of inflation was 11% in 1974, as against 24.5% in Japan, 16% in the United Kingdom, 19.1% in Italy . . .

4. The penalization of rival economies was reinforced by the abrupt increases in raw material prices. The most striking of these was the rise in the price of oil, which quadrupled at the end of 1973. This staggering jump was due not only to an accident of history (the October War) but also to the conjoined intent of both the oil majors and the U.S. administration, as well as to a real desire on the part of the producing countries to make up for the drop in their real income resulting from the declining value of the dollar.

This abrupt increase in oil prices did not have identical results in each of the importing countries. The U.S. depends on imports for only 15% of its energy needs. In Europe, over 65% of energy requirements have to be met from abroad, and in Japan the level of imports is of the order of 90%. Europe and Japan were thus penalized as against the U.S.

In the Third World the new oil prices, combined with the huge increase in the prices of agricultural products to the greater benefit of the U.S. (the price of wheat almost tripled between 1972 and 1974; the price of fertilisers doubled), meant a substantial drop in real income. Inequalities sharpened considerably within humanity's largest family, the poor. They were the ones who suffered most from the U.S.'s efforts to reassert itself. European incomes may have remained static or increased only slightly; African and Asian incomes, already barely enough for subsistence, fell dramatically. And the American companies set about reshuffling their interests throughout the world. Despite pressure from the trade unions and from a significant body of opinion in Congress, multinational corporations continued to be favoured by U.S. fiscal legislation. As Nixon put it in his address to Congress on 10 April 1973, 'an open system of international investment, a system which does away with artificial stimulants and barriers, both at home and abroad, offers the greatest hope for greater prosperity throughout the world.' He was careful to add that not only did these investments not take jobs away from Americans on the contrary, they meant that they would have more jobs and *more interesting* ones at that. 'Interesting' refers to the setting up of a new division of labour which leaves all the menial tasks to the rest of the world while America keeps the more 'noble' jobs for itself. In order to give an inside view of the new American strategy, we have included in an appendix some extracts from a document published in July 1973 by the assistant to Peter Peterson, the former Secretary of State for Trade. The two key phrases of this document are as follows:

> The linkage strategy recognizes the weaknesses in the U.S. bargaining position on trade, and seeks to offset it by tying the talks to other issues, where U.S. negotiating leverage is greater . . .
>
> If the linkage strategy is followed, the trade delegation will be only one section in an orchestra of negotiations under the overall direction of Henry Kissinger. Kissinger's job would be to coordinate the play of all sections – including those on security, monetary reform and energy – to ensure that they complement one another and that successes in one area were not achieved at the expense of another. (See Appendix to Part I)

We will examine just how the United States set about developing this strategy.

America's agriculture is now one of its most important trump cards. Integrated as it is into the world capitalist system, it enables the U.S. to play on world hunger, thus becoming a powerful means of blackmail.

Mobilized on every front, the multinationals constitute a great American army which shapes and enslaves the world for the greater prosperity of the U.S. A notable feature of this assault is the robbery of a Third World which grows increasingly poorer and has few means to defend itself. Will the application of this economic strategy inevitably lead to a reinforcement of American hegemony? The U.S. has already won some important victories.

2. Agriculture in the Service of American Hegemony

> *Food resources are a new form of power. They are wealth. They are a new asset in our diplomacy.*
> Senator Hubert Humphrey

In an effort to explain the upsurge in food prices to puzzled Americans, the 15 March 1973 issue of the U.S. journal *Forbes* drew a connection between this phenomenon and the rise in oil prices. The article's attempt to square the circle went like this: given that the U.S. no longer has a technological lead over Europe and Japan, and given that imported oil is more and more expensive, how can one pay for the oil at a time when exports of manufactured products continue to fall? As a way out of the problem, 'the United States has at its disposal an unlimited natural resource: arable land . . . [it] can become the "granary" of the world.' And the article goes on to say that 'the Nixon administration is banking on agriculture to save the dollar.'

That it is possible for American agriculture to play such a role is no accident for, thanks to systematic modernization, it was the first to integrate itself into the capitalist market. Its great advantage is the comparatively weak degree of integration characteristic of the agricultural sectors of other countries. American agricultural imperialism stems from this fact. It will continue to grow for several reasons:

1. Agriculture is from now on part of the overall strategy of reconquest.

2. Agricultural production still has enormous potential for expansion. Even in 1974 the U.S.'s position as 'granary of the world' was already striking as Table I.1 clearly demonstrates.

3. The population boom in the developing countries will in effect heighten the importance of American agriculture.

4. The agricultural policy of the U.S.S.R. has proved to be a failure.

Capitalism's penetration of the countryside started by doing away with archaic forms of production. The products of modern enterprises were gradually integrated into the distribution system. American agribusiness then extended its network beyond the confines of the U.S. This rationalization of structures was both encouraged and subsidized by the U.S. Government. Until 1973, protectionism ruled the roost in agriculture: the home market was guaranteed against fluctuations in world market prices. But when the latter

Table I.1
World Trade in Grain, 1974 (millions of metric tons)

Exports		*Imports*	
North America	91	Asia	43
Australia	6	Eastern Europe and U.S.S.R.	27
New Zealand		Western Europe	19
		Africa	5
		Latin America	3
Total	97		97

took off, under the combined impetus of massive purchases by the U.S.S.R. (26 million tons) and the increased demand brought about by the inadequacy of Third World production, it was liberalization which soon became the order of the day. This change from protectionism one day to liberalism and the conquest of foreign markets the next is contradictory only in appearance. It represents the two sides of a strategy whose principal purpose is to defend and promote a key sector of the American economy.

Concentration and Integration

The volume of U.S. agricultural production has grown by about 50% over the last twenty years, during which time the manpower employed has been halved. The area under cereals in fact fell by about 50 million acres between 1950 and 1970. In March 1972 the National Farmers Union announced that 2,000 farms were going out of business every week. The replacement of men by increasingly powerful machines was only possible on the basis of a complete reorganization of the structure of U.S. agriculture.

Table I.2 shows the changes in various production factors which made the increase in agricultural production possible.

Only 2.9% of farms had a sales figure of over $40,000 in 1960. By 1971 this percentage had risen to 8.8% and corresponded to 5.5% of total farming revenue. This evolution is the result of a low price level for agricultural products and of a deliberate Washington policy. Until 1964, prices tended to remain stable or to fall, whilst costs climbed steadily. Since then prices and costs have moved more or less at the same rate. Agriculture, having become a serious matter involving a high level of capital investment, was no longer a field for small-scale enterprise. Only the big farms were capable of meeting costs, and still making a profit through an enormous increase in productivity. This industrialization was largely accomplished with the help of capital brought in from outside the agricultural sector. The farmers tended to lose their independence as they integrated themselves into the capitalist system – either by signing production contracts with supermarkets, food industries and

Table I.2
Indices and Factors of the Volume of Agricultural Production (1950 = 100)

	1955	*1960*	*1965*	*1971*
Agricultural production	112	123	133	149
Livestock production	112	116	127	141
Crop production	108	121	129	146
Crop production per acre	107	128	145	159
Land under cultivation	100	95	89	92
Workforce	85	67	55	47
Agricultural assets	102	98	104	107
Mechanical energy and agricultural machinery	115	115	122	130
Fertilisers and lime	141	169	250	368
Other means of production	113	129	145	171
Production per man hour	134	191	260	346
Production per unit of means of production	109	126	133	138

Source: USDA, *Handbook of Agricultural Charts,* 1971.

Table I.3
Integration of Agricultural Production into Capitalist Industrial Production and Distribution

	Percentage of Supply Produced under Contract	*Percentage of Supply Directly Integrated into Vertical Linkages*
Chickens	90	7
Turkeys	42	12
Eggs	20	20
Fatstock	18	4
Pigs	1	1
Fresh vegetables	21	30
Vegetables for processing	85	10
Potatoes	45	25
Citrus fruits	65	30

sometimes even with fertilizer manufacturers, or by integrating themselves at one end of the agro-industrial linkage. This phenomenon was not uniform for all types of products. In 1970, the situation was as outlined in Table I.3.

A real agro-industrial complex has thus come into being: at one end of the linkage are the agricultural industries which manufacture the machines, the fertilizers and the means of processing the products. At the other end are the food industries (milling, preserving, sugar, meat, biscuits) and the distribution sector. Taken as a whole, it has become the most important sector of the American economy – hence the administration's attitude. A handful of firms, all giant corporations or multinationals, have established a firm grip on this sector. These companies have instituted the widespread use of an elaborate technology drawn from the discoveries of biological and agronomic science. They have done so both within the U.S. and abroad, thereby making the development of certain kinds of production completely dependent on American agriculture. For instance the quantity of foodstuffs needed to produce a kilo of meat has fallen by half since 1945. The animal feed which has made this possible is protein concentrate, mainly soya bean cake. The U.S. accounts for 70% of the world supply of this product and handles about 95% of the world trade in it. In 1973 Europe found out what this dependency meant, a dependency produced by a technological change engineered through the low-prices policy. The U.S. suspended its soya exports. Whole sections of European agriculture would have collapsed if this measure had been maintained. The dependency of the whole world will be even greater if the big American firms manage to use the lasting disequilibrium in world food supplies to impose industrially produced vegetable proteins as an important source of food for human beings.

The tight grip of the American economic system over world food supplies is not based only on U.S. exports. The giant American corporations, closely linked with the big financial groups, have also established themselves in the importing countries themselves.

The U.S. dominates the world trade in basic agricultural products: soya (95% of world trade), maize (56.3%), wheat (28.5%) and rice (31.4%). The maintenance of this privileged position is one of the fundamental reasons underlying the American administration's efforts to assist agriculture and to eliminate everything which might stand in the way of its development. The Department of Agriculture's credit budget rose from $6,300 million per year in 1961-63 to $10,400 million per year in 1971-73. These subsidies helped stabilize supply and hold up prices, whilst at the same time encouraging the modernization of equipment in line with technical progress. Naturally the larger enterprises received far more subsidies than the small-scale ones (see Table I.4).

For a long time now, the American authorities have thought that highly technological agriculture had many important advantages and was one of the main areas on which the country could rely to increase its export revenue. Furthermore, the important reserves of 'frozen' land provided considerable manoeuvring space, by allowing for a rapid adaptation of supply to any increase in demand.

In early 1973, once the price of cereals had already taken off thanks to the massive orders from the U.S.S.R., the Nixon administration could, without running any risks, launch its new agricultural policy, encouraging the bringing back into cultivation of all arable land and moving towards the

Table I.4
Sales and Subsidies Granted under the Agricultural Programmes, 1969 (by size of enterprise)

Sales	*Percentage of Total Sales*	*Percentage of Subsidies under Agricultural Programmes*	*Percentage of Enterprises*
$40,000 and upwards	51.3	40.3	7.1 (8.8 in 1971)
$20-40,000	21.3	22.5	12.0
$10-20,000	16.0	19.4	17.0
$2,500-5,000	6.3	8.8	13.1
Less than $2,500	2.7	5.3	41.2
Total	100.0	100.0	100.0

Source: Charles L. Schultze, *The Distribution of Farm Subsidies: who gets the benefit?* (Washington, 1969).

Table I.5
Movement of Export Prices of Principal Foodstuffs, 1971-74 (dollars per metric ton)

Product	*1971*	*1972*	*1973*	*1974 (Jan)*	*1974 (Mar)*	*1974 (Aug)*
Wheat (U.S. No.2)	62	70	139	214	191	170
Rice (Thai)	129	151	368	538	603	520
Maize (Yellow No.2)	58	56	98	122	126	115
Soya	126	140	290	261	265	236

Source: O.E.C.D.

abolition of all the subsidies which had been granted to farmers in order to prevent a drop in prices. Most agricultural experts already agreed that it would be practically impossible to achieve a worldwide equilibrium in food supplies during the next decade. Speculators happily complied with the President's unspoken wishes and gave a considerable boost to the rising trend in agricultural product prices.

The 'rescue of the dollar' was thus well under way. In 1973 agricultural export prices rose by 56% and the volume of exports went up by 20.5%. The combination of these two factors produced an agricultural trade surplus of $8,500 million, thereby contributing considerably to re-establishing a positive balance of trade in 1973 (+$626 million), after two years in deficit (–$6,986 million in 1972).

This success was nonetheless tinged with bitterness, perhaps even with a deep resentment. It would have been far more resounding were it not for the E.E.C. agricultural policy, which has been the bugbear of the American administration for the last few years. In 1971 Senator Humphrey called the Common Agricultural Policy (C.A.P.) 'a significant source of tension in world agricultural markets'. The Americans estimated that the Common Market was losing them $200 to $300 million a year, and, according to *Forbes* magazine, they 'fumed' at the idea of losing a further $500 million as E.E.C. membership expanded to include Britain, Ireland and Denmark. Congressman Al Ullman, who in 1972 presided over a Congress mission in Europe, did not mince words either: 'The Common Agricultural Policy must disappear and will disappear.' And Peter Peterson wrote in his 1973 report that 'when some of the Market's other partners can produce and sell agricultural goods much more efficiently . . . there can be no real justification for a system which forces other nations to bear the expense of adjustment and which interferes with national production and exchange.' The Americans considered the E.E.C. as a key area to which they could export agricultural products and hence re-establish their balance of payments. They were therefore particularly critical of the Community levy system in terms of which trade between E.E.C. members is effectively encouraged and E.E.C. exports are subsidized and can therefore compete 'unfairly' with U.S. products in markets which the U.S. once dominated. In his official report, Flanigan, Nixon's adviser for international economic affairs, was just as categoric as Ullman: he concluded that the only solution to the agricultural problem was the total liberalization of world agricultural trade by 1980. Flanigan outlined the efforts which could be made to bring about an eventual abolition of the C.A.P. and envisaged the possibility of sanctions if the E.E.C. did not co-operate: the U.S. could withdraw from the General Agreement on Trade and Tariff (GATT) and impose very heavy import duties. The threat was quite explicit. Recent political and economic upheavals have only put off what remains an essential feature of the American strategy to reinforce 'the structures of peace'. The basic goal of the U.S. is quite unchanged.

Effects on the Third World

The American agricultural policy has already had disastrous effects on the Third World. The experts estimate that the dramatic situation faced by the many countries whose ability to meet their balance of payments deficit is nearing its limit can be attributed equally to the rise in oil prices and to the rise in the price of manufactured and agricultural products.[3] One should add that the price rise originating in the developed countries, especially the U.S., came first. Cereal imports cost the Third World countries $3,000 million a year from 1970 to 1972 and their total import bill for foodstuffs came to more than $9,000 million. The World Bank estimates that the *supplementary cost* of cereal imports, under the combined influence of increases both in price and in volume imported, amounted to $5,200 million in 1973 and $8,400 million in 1974. In 1973 the growth in the Third World deficit was almost entirely due to the increased prices of Western manufactured products. Table I.6 shows the importance of these costs as compared to total imports and gross national product.

Table I.6
Estimated Supplementary Cost of Cereal Imports for Certain Developing Countries, 1973-74 (relative to 1970-72 average)

		1973			*1974*	
Country	*Cost ($millions)*	*% of Total imports 1970-72*	*% of 1971 G.N.P.*	*Cost ($millions)*	*% of Total imports 1970-72*	*% c 19 G.I*
Developing countries	+ 5,176	8	—	+ 8,376	13	—
Bangladesh	+ 337	—	7	+ 413	—	8
Sri Lanka	+ 85	21	7	+ 111	27	9
India	+ 255	11	0	+ 667	28	1
Pakistan	+ 105	13	1	+ 303	36	4
Egypt	+ 369	44	5	+ 603	73	8
Philippines	+ 84	7	1	+ 167	13	2
Senegal	+ 79	32	8	+ 70	28	7
S. Korea	+ 430	19	5	+ 564	25	6
Brazil	+ 221	6	1	+ 125	3	0
Mexico	+ 179	7	1	+ 283	11	1
Chile	+ 142	15	2	+ 323	33	4

Source: World Bank and O.E.C.D. Secretariat.

The expense involved grew considerably over the following years. Until the beginning of the '70s, up to 45% of the payment burden for imported food was alleviated by deliveries which came under food aid. In 1973 this aid was cut dramatically. In terms of cereal volume the cuts were even more striking (see Table I.7). The underlying reasons were essentially the rise in prices and the drop in cereal surpluses within the O.E.C.D. countries. In other words, it is safe to say that the United States, the world's biggest producer, had until then treated aid mainly as a way of absorbing its surplus production. One particularly significant aspect is the changing role of the various O.E.C.D. donor countries over time. The 'disinterestedness' of U.S. aid programmes shines forth with a pure and untarnished light: as a percentage of total O.E.C.D. aid it fell from 96% in 1963 to 77% in 1969 and 1972; in 1973, the year prices really took off, it was down to 55%.

As long as America had a surplus, it promoted exports through the programme of government aid to developing countries which was launched in

Table I.7
Cereals Distributed under O.E.C.D. Aid Programmes (millions of metric tons)

	1964	*1966*	*1969*	*1972*	*1973*
Volume of cereals distributed	16	14	13	11	6

1954 (the Agricultural Trade Development and Assistance Act). The sale of agricultural products for local currency was the most important aspect of the Act. Once the surplus had been absorbed and prices became firmer, the conditions attached to the aid became much more draconian; payment in strong currencies became the rule. The 'assisted' countries first became customers just like any other, and then, as prices really took off, second-class customers.

Food aid has always been and continues to be in the interests of the donor countries. In the November 1974 issue of its publication, *Co-operation for Development,* the O.E.C.D. admits that 'an important part of traditional donors' aid in agricultural sectors has concentrated on the development of tropical produce for export rather than on the development of basic food supplies for the local population. In the last few years, however, this tendency has been somewhat less marked.'

The same applies to aid channelled into livestock rearing. The O.E.C.D. report goes on to say that: 'During the 1960s most aid channelled into the rearing of livestock has been used to promote the development of beef and sheep herds in temperate or semi-temperate regions, with the aim of providing meat for export – hence the stress laid on stockrearing projects in Latin America.' In other words, Third World aid, like investment, is seen in terms of the advantages it confers on international companies and consumers in rich countries. But the consequences of domination may take more subtle forms. In an article published in the October 1974 issue of *Le Monde Diplomatique,* Erich H. Jacoby, a Swedish professor, analyses the devastating effects of technological transfer to Third World countries. He shows how the multinationals destroy rural societies and take over the use of lands and skills in order to produce crops destined for the rich countries, to the detriment of the production of food destined for local consumption. 'Their intervention in agriculture has a definite bearing on the likelihood of famine.'

In much more cautious terms the O.E.C.D. has sketched the outline of a critique which tallies with Professor Jacoby's analysis: 'Finally, it is quite clear that donor countries and organizations should set out to increase productivity through the introduction of modern production methods, through pilot projects and show farms. *However* alongside such projects, which artificially recreate the optimal conditions for growth, they should also promote projects which operate in a normal environment, that is to say in the existing rural environment, in order to transform it gradually.'

Having organized the pillage of the Third World, the United States has emerged as the granary of the whole planet, 'controlling a larger part of the world trade in cereals than the Middle East does in oil,' as Lester Brown puts it in his *The Next Crisis: Food, Foreign Policy*. The O.E.C.D., noting an F.A.O. forecast according to which total Third World food production could run up a deficit of nearly 85 million metric tons by 1985 (as against 22 million in 1972), concludes that, 'The risk of excessive dependence on North America and Australia has not been averted.' The American companies can expect to rake in the profits for some time yet! Under such conditions, agriculture can become a more dangerous political weapon than oil, playing on the hunger of people rather than on the hunger of machines. The threat of an American embargo on agricultural exports has already been brandished several times. At the beginning of 1974, when the oil embargo was (marginally) affecting the U.S., an official at the Department of Agriculture issued a warning to the Arab oil producing countries. President Ford and his Secretary of State, Henry Kissinger, reiterated the threat in order to 'convince' the oil producers to lower their prices. In short, there may come a day when U.S. soya or wheat will be reserved for co-operative and sympathetic countries. American agriculture is already an integral part of the arsenal of U.S. domination.

3. American Imperialism's Crack Troops: The 'Multinationals'

Concluding a report on the likelihood of a code of good conduct being adopted by O.E.C.D. multinationals, William Casey, ex-Secretary of State and now President of the Eximbank, had this to say: 'The multinationals are the most important mechanism whereby the U.S. inserts itself into the world market.' It would be hard to find a more apt description of the role of these corporations, which we shall continue to call multinationals, although the term is inaccurate. In reality, 'multinationals' have the nationality of their top management, even when they conduct their activities in several nation states. In the developed countries this insertion into the world economy is effected in order to conquer new markets; in the Third World it provides access to raw materials, cheap labour and the outlets that certain developing countries afford. These firms' motive, whatever their nationality, is rationally to exploit all existing inequalities, including human ones, purely and simply for their own gain.

The more liberalization there is, the more these companies will grow. A world without customs barriers and without any restriction on investment is the ideal setting for attempts to internationalize production and to establish an international division of labour. It is therefore quite understandable that the multinationals faithfully support American Government policy. And, correspondingly, these firms are the best propagandists for a certain conception of the world, the 'new world order' demanded by the U.S. administration. This order obviously has nothing in common with the one demanded by President Boumedienne when, speaking for all the countries of the Third World, he addressed the General Assembly of the United Nations in March 1974.

Japanese and European companies, whose interests would also be served by a world without trade barriers, prove themselves faithful allies of the U.S. firms and the American Government. They are all participants in a capitalist system which must be international if it is to flourish. In this context, 'international' means under American leadership, it means the propagation of American culture and ideology. And why not? There can be no room for nationalism when profits are at stake. Accordingly, there is no point in drawing a sharp distinction between U.S. multinationals and those based in other countries, especially as U.S. companies will continue to be the main 'heavy-weights' in this 'multinational' world for some time yet.

To counteract the possibility that any country might allow some play to nationalist reflexes, the U.S. Government preaches an interconnection of interests: to demonstrate its good faith and its belief in the system it sponsors, the U.S. administration makes it clear that all are welcome to invest in the U.S. In any case, any putative defensive reactions on the part of Western companies and governments fade into thin air when they are faced with the question of how to spread the risks involved in ventures aimed at the Third World: pillaging others' resources can quite easily be organized as a collective enterprise! Nonetheless, the power of the multinationals, and their potential for growth, does arouse some worries. States and trade unions feel impotent when faced with these monsters whose operations span the entire planet. During the last few years, people have become aware of the problem. Several books and reports by international (U.N.O., O.E.C.D.) and national organizations have tried to pinpoint the various issues brought out by the existence of these companies: why do they grow faster than other companies? At whose expense? What world are they shaping for us? Are they politically neutral? Is their growth compatible with the national interest? Who has ultimate control over the actions of their subsidiaries? Is national independence still possible? All sorts of people are trying to find the answers, with varying degrees of sincerity.

An important event on the international scene recently highlighted the crucial importance of these questions: the fall of Chilean President Salvador Allende. His assassination and the overthrow of democracy in that country were the result of the conjoined actions of I.T.T. and other U.S. firms in Chile, the C.I.A. and the State Department. There is ample evidence of an organized campaign to cause economic chaos. Yesterday's headlines may be today's litter, but one should remember that the events in Chile join a long list which includes the overthrow of Mossadeq in Iran, the boycott of Iraq following the 1961 nationalizations, several *coups* in Central and South America, etc. – not to speak of the less obvious day-to-day pressures these companies can exercise on governments, the financial manipulations, attacks on local currencies, avoidance of fiscal laws, etc.

Some Facts on the Power of the Multinationals

In 1971, responding to worries expressed by the American people and their trade unions about the loss of Stateside jobs supposedly implied in the foreign expansion of the multinationals, Senator Russell Long (Democrat, Louisiana), Chairman of the Senate Finance Committee, called for a report on 'the implications of multinational companies for world trade and finance, and for trade and employment in the U.S.' The Report was published on 12 February 1973 by Senator Abraham A. Ribicoff, Chaiman of the Foreign Trade Subcommittee; it is now known as the Ribicoff Report, and remains the most detailed study of the American multinationals.

Of course the Report's conclusions demolished the trade union argument : American multinationals, it argued, have a very positive influence on foreign trade and generate many new jobs in the U.S. itself. On the other hand, they play a key role in the monetary crisis and can sidestep all the economic and financial measures taken by national governments.

The Report concentrates on the 298 most important firms. These companies accounted for 26% of world trade in 1971 ($78,000 million out of $300,000 million). They accounted for 75% of total international foreign investments. Again in 1971, they employed 12% of the industrial workforce in the seven countries (Canada, Britain, Belgium, Germany, France, Brazil and Mexico) which attract three-quarters of their investments. This does not mean that these companies do not play a role at home, of course. In 1970 they accounted for 62% of U.S. industrial exports, but only for 34% of equivalent imports. Thanks to their technological lead they almost all contribute to a net inflow of $2,000 million a year from royalties, patents and licences. According to U.S. sources, by 1972 their direct investments abroad had risen to $90,000 million in accountable assets. These figures rose sharply in 1973 after the 'crisis'. In fact the O.E.C.D. estimates that direct investments in the Third World rose by 50% that same year. An interesting aspect of the power of these corporations is brought out by a comparison of their annual turnover with the Gross Industrial Product (G.I.P.) of some of the richest countries (not to mention the farcical comparison between, say, General Motors and Haiti, Lesotho or Togo).

The Growth of the Multinationals

The figures below give some indication of the sheer scale of the U.S. multinational phenomenon, at one particular moment. But the story is not over yet, and the problem continues to grow. The average growth rate of the multinationals is about twice that of the economies in which they operate. These companies' share of the world economy can thus only increase as long as there are no important changes in political regimes, impositions of tariff barriers or significant resurgences of protectionism. Furthermore, these companies' characteristics make them very adaptable: they have had no problems in doing business with Eastern Bloc countries and they know how to deal with any upsurge of nationalism. Nationalizations and host nation demands for participation have been coped with quite easily, as long as they were not part of an overall strategy aimed at seizing real control of the national economy. The differences in growth rate are largely due to the economies of scale these companies can institute, their ability to capitalize upon worldwide differences in the production costs of various components of production, their financial power, their penetration of rapid growth industrial sectors and their capacity for innovation. Except in fiction, there have been no examples of a multinational collapsing or even regressing significantly. They are the only ones to profit from the crisis they were largely

Table I.8
Comparison of G.I.P.s of O.E.C.D. Countries with Annual Turnover of Various Companies, 1973 ($000 millions)

G.I.P./O.E.C.D.		*Multinational Turnover*	
U.S.	1,178		
Japan	294		
Germany	258		
France	196		
U.K.	154		
Italy	118		
Canada	106		
Australia	47		
Netherlands	46		
Spain	45		
Sweden	41		
Belgium	36		
Switzerland	30	General Motors	30
Denmark	21	Exxon	20
Austria	20	Ford	20
Turkey	17	General Electric	10
Norway	15	Chrysler	10
Finland	13	I.B.M.	10
Greece	12	Mobil	9
Portugal	8	Texaco	9
Ireland	6	I.T.T.	9
Luxembourg	1.35		
Iceland	0.76		

Table I.9
Multinationals' Production Abroad ($000 millions)

	1968	*1978*	*1988*	*1999*
G.N.P. of non-socialist world	1,800	2,900	4,800	8,000
U.S. firms' production abroad	200	450	950	2,000
Foreign firms' production in the U.S.	90	200	425	900
Other production	130	300	600	1,300
Total production abroad	420	950	1,975	4,200
Production abroad as % of G.N.P. of non-socialist world	23%	33%	41%	53%

Source: J. Polk, *Internationalization of Production.*

responsible for provoking: in 1973 their profits were the highest ever and their investments in the Third World rose by 46%; these trends continued in 1974.

The internationalization of production is accelerating. The 'decline' of America will, if it continues, be handsomely compensated for by an American boom abroad. This internationalization will generally benefit international capitalism, the rules of which will be laid down by the dominant part of the system.

Had pre-crisis growth rates continued, tomorrow's world economy might have looked like Table I.9.

Deployment of the Economic Troops: Criteria and Finance

The deployment of American investments throughout the world is no mere coincidence. Based at first on the control of raw materials, it then followed the development of the big markets. The appropriation of raw materials, notably oil, was originally geared to supplying internal markets. It was only after the Second World War that the first barrel of oil was imported into the U.S.

The great departure point for U.S. companies came after 1945. The American market no longer offered prospects of unlimited growth, and the Department of Justice was at the time very strictly enforcing anti-trust laws. The big companies began their geographical diversification quite cautiously; for a long time the two American continents remained their main area of operation. In 1950, 69% of their foreign investments were in Latin America (38.8%) and in Canada (30.2%). Whilst Canada's share remained relatively stable over the decades that followed, Latin America's was cut by half and Europe's doubled. Europe became a veritable magnet as it recovered from the War, as its rate of economic growth accelerated, and as it re-emerged as the second largest market in the world. The creation of the Common Market in 1957 induced American capitalists to stake their claims from within. American demands to eliminate customs barriers are only a recent development – protectionism is now useless and even harmful for the American economy. The developing countries have always been low on the multinationals' list of priorities. They only interested investors inasmuch as they were rich in raw materials or had attractive growth prospects.

Developing countries have only received 29% of all American direct investments, half of which went into oil and mining. This geographical 'distribution' accentuates existing distortions: Africa (not including South Africa), Asia and Oceania (excluding Australia) received only 10.6% of all direct American investments, although these countries are the home of two-thirds of the world's population.

The multinationals' penetration of manufacturing industry is very sector-variable. The greater the prospect of profits, the greater the penetration. Such prospects can be linked to very different factors: weak development of technology in the host country, bad organization, scattered national industries, etc. Penetration, measured globally in terms of industry as a whole, only presents half the picture. For instance in France, multinationals only account for 16.1% (of which 7.4% is American) of pre-tax sales, although they are very strongly established in key sectors of the economy.

Table I.10
Main Sectors Penetrated in France (%)

	Employees	*Sales*	*Investments*
Agricultural machinery	37.6	52.2	44.4
Oil	42.8	51.0	42.8
Electrical and electronics	26.2	32.5	50.2
Non-ferrous minerals and semi-finished goods	27.5	27.6	22.3
Fats and starches	28.0	25.8	16.7
Chemicals	20.4	24.0	28.2

Source: *D.I.S.*, November 1973

The multinationals' role is also very variable within particular sectors, such as, for example, the electrical and electronics industry which produces an enormous variety of goods, from small motors and coffee grinders to steam turbines and nuclear reactors. Westinghouse gets all the orders for nuclear reactors, I.B.M. and Honeywell-Bull completely dominate cybernetics.

Even within a region like Europe, U.S. investments are very unequally distributed. American firms have pumped far more money into Germany than France. The reasons underlying such a choice are difficult to pinpoint. Van den Bulcke's study of 842 firms set up in Belgium brings out the following factors, in decreasing order of importance: the situation in the labour market; the infrastructure; the fiscal system; state aid. It must be underlined that governments are constantly bidding against each other to attract the big foreign firms, competing to offer significant inducements and aid, all of which affects the U.S. companies' investment stake in a particular country.

The attitude of the investors to the political situation in a country also plays an important role, especially in Third World countries. It is referred to as evaluation of the 'investment climate'. Managers have paid great attention to the recent wave of nationalizations (not just in the oil industry, but also in phosphates, aluminium, etc.) and to the way in which countries have indemnified the former owners. They keep a careful watch on the increasingly general tendency to demand national participation in multinational-owned enterprises. But one can easily make too much of the relevance of this factor. Shortly after the Shah of Iran's 1973 take-over of the oil consortiums, the Vice-President of Mobil was heard to say that 'One should not overestimate the importance of ownership. The agreement reached with the Shah is a very good one.' What really matters to the big companies is the proportion of a country's output of crude oil which will go to them.

Generally speaking, a country's take-over of companies operating there is usually an illusion as long as the companies retain control of management, technology and marketing. Since the companies are integrated into a vast whole they can always, at worst, fix things so that some other link in the chain produces their profits. Above all, multinationals fear the instability of regulations. In order to take long-term decisions, they need a stable situation. In the above-mentioned 1974 Report, the O.E.C.D. concludes that 'to the extent that the new, stricter regulations established by many of the host countries are likely to remain in effect for considerable periods, they can actually contribute to ameliorating the investment climate and host country participation in one form or another.'

The idea of direct investment conveys a picture of a flow of money from the multinationals to the host countries which is quite inaccurate. Most investments in such cases come from the mobilization in one form or another of local financial resources. Globally speaking, the growth of U.S. subsidiaries abroad is financed by tapping local, not U.S., finance. The accumulation of American capital is facilitated by a rate of profit which, especially in the Third World, is incomparably greater than that achieved by any firms in the U.S. itself, and by a very rapid recovery of initial investment outlays (to avoid 'surprises' great efforts are made to recover investment as quickly as possible). The result of this pillage is that the investment revenue officially repatriated each year represents more than twice the flow of fresh money to the developing country in question. In the developed countries this drain is far less significant and is sometimes even reversed, since the balance of forces is much more even. But when American firms first established themselves in Europe, they behaved as if the pillage of the Third World (especially Latin America) could be extended to this newly invaded realm. Although somewhat out of date, Table I.11 gives some idea of the sources of finance drawn upon by U.S. subsidiaries abroad. Imported capital provided by the parent company represents on average less than 20% of funds invested.

Why Is It So Easy for Multinationals to Penetrate an Economy?

The attitude of host countries to the multinationals presents a striking paradox, with the developing countries and certain industrialized countries both denouncing the multinationals and at the same time attempting to woo them with investment facilities, various forms of state aid, tax exemptions, loopholes in currency regulations, etc. Why the inconsistency, why the hypocrisy? What advantages does the implantation of a multinational have to offer?

In March 1974 an O.E.C.D. report[4] pointed out that 'All the members agree that, fundamentally, international enterprises have a positive role to play, and that there are powerful economic arguments which explain their development.' International experts have listed the potential advantages

Table I.11
Sources of Capital for U.S. Subsidiaries Abroad, 1972 (%)

	Imported U.S. Capital	*Local Loans*	*Reinvested Profits*	*Amortiz-ation*	*Various*	*Total*
Worldwide	12	30	18	35	5	100
Oil industry	18	33	9	34	6	100
Manufacturing	7	23	25	39	6	100
Canada	6	19	30	38	7	100
Latin America	26	33	2	36	3	100
Europe	9	30	18	39	4	100
Other developed countries	13	27	23	30	7	100
Other developing countries	12	39	15	26	8	100

Source: *Survey of Current Business.*

presented by such firms. As far as the industrial structure of a country is concerned, they make for a better utilization of the host countries' resources and promote the reorganization and structural adaptation of the various sectors. This argument tallies with the logic of international capitalism recognized by the O.E.C.D. The multinationals can therefore install themselves in western France, for instance, where they make good use of an existing underpaid labour force. A more than 'moderate' political environment and the relative absence of militant trade unionism are added bonuses. One of the reasons underlying Motorola's refusal to set up in Laval was the fact that the local council was at the time headed by Robert Buron, a dangerous socialist!

The multinationals do indeed promote structural adaptation. But what sort of adaptation? The arrival of a multinational usually takes the form of either buying up existing companies or taking a share in them. Soon afterwards, to meet the demands of profitability, factories shut down and workers are made redundant. Then the smaller competitors find it difficult to cope with the changed situation and are in turn gradually drawn in by the blandishments of the foreign capitalist.

Other factors regarded as advantages of having multinationals include the introduction of new products and the general impact on prices and competition. But the two main arguments which are generally taken to present the strongest case for penetration by foreign firms are the qualitative and quantitative development of employment and the diffusion of new technical knowledge. However, even the O.E.C.D. Report does indicate that there are 'potential risks' in both these areas, 'risks associated both with the international enterprises' reluctance to observe the rules of the labour market, which causes difficulties notably for the trade unions, and with the problems created by the sudden arrival or departure of foreign firms. Concerning technology, the potential risk stems from the concentration of research and development activities in some country other than the host country, and the consequent reduction in this type of activity within the subsidiary itself.'

These are not just potential dangers. They are frequent occurrences stemming from the internal logic of the growth of a multinational. The search for optimum profits on a world scale implies the manipulation of qualitative and quantitative differences in human resources. The attempts by trade unionists to join up on an international level to counterbalance this power have not had much success to date. The adaptability of the various companies' system of production enables them to resist pressures from governments and trade unions alike: the threat of closing down factories is an efficient and persuasive weapon which the companies do not hesitate to use (Ford in the U.K., Chrysler in France).

For a transfer of technology to have a *positive* impact on the host country's economy, two preconditions have to be met. Firstly, the technologies in question must apply to durable products. Secondly, mastery of the technology must lead to research and development programmes, failing which the acquisition of new technology is relevant only in terms of performance. These two preconditions are in fact not met. The multinationals introduce new products very fast. Given that it takes them far less time to perfect these products than their competitors (essentially for financial reasons), they can dominate the markets they have created. This propensity to innovate, and the corresponding accumulation of capital, is one of the causes of the ever-increasing size of these companies. Machines rapidly become obsolete and are replaced by other more advanced machines, which produce more sophisticated products, products which will, in turn, soon be obsolete.

This is one of the vicious circles of the unequal development characteristic of high technology sectors even in the developed countries. Through sheer size, the multinationals are in a position to dominate the whole innovatory process – hence they can constantly launch new products and conquer new markets, hence their profits increase, hence they grow even bigger . . . (For example, the I.B.M. 360 computer will have cost $5,000 million to perfect.) This situation also implies that a great deal of money must be invested in publicity and advertising to create needs corresponding to the new markets.

Table I.12 shows the differences in the research and development expenditures and advertising budgets of the various types of firms in the U.S. The importance of the multinationals' research and development expenditure is mainly due to the fact that most of the innovatory process is localized in America itself. The foreign subsidiaries make use of these innovations by buying the resulting technological advances from the holding company.

In the key sectors (nuclear, chemical, aeronautics, computer and automobile industries) it would now seem that bridging the gap between American firms and those of other countries is no longer feasible. The American companies have too great a lead, a lead which keeps growing, propelled as it is by the dynamic of increasing size and accelerated innovation. Furthermore this

Table I.12
Research and Development, and Advertising Expenditure of 3 Types of Companies ($millions)

Expenditure/Average Company	*National Enterprises*	*Transnational Enterprises*	*Multinationals*
R and D expenditure	14	40	119
Total scientists and engineers employed	130	360	910
Scientists and engineers employed in R and D	30	100	310
Scientists and engineers employed in sales	8	36	96
Scientists and engineers employed in production	50	120	270
Total advertising expenditure	56	41	170
Advertising expenditure on magazines and newspapers, T.V. and radio	25	3	22

Source: *Harvard International Business Project*.

Table I.13
Balance of Technological Transfer

Country	*Year*	*Exports ($millions)*	*Imports ($millions)*	*Balance ($millions)*	*Exports/ Imports (%)*
France	1971	155	286	–131	54%
Germany	1971	169	458	–289	37%
U.K.	1970	356	287	+ 69	124%
Japan	1971	60	483	–424	12%
U.S.	1970	2,480	230	+ 2,250	1,080%

dynamic is not fuelled solely by U.S. business enterprises; since 1945 the American Government has itself been spending very considerable sums on research and development programmes.

Table I.13, which shows the comparative balance of technological transfer, is a good indication of the world's economic dependence on the U.S. It also confirms that the flow of technological transfer between a parent company and its subsidiaries is only a one-way process. It should also be noted that the sales value of these transfers contributes more than $2,000 million to U.S. income – one of the strong points of the U.S. balance of payments. Of this positive balance, 90% is attributable to the multinationals, especially to the ones operating in high technology sectors. And it is these very companies which invest most abroad.

The Multinationals as Propagators of Inflation

The Ribicoff Report is quite unambiguous about the multinationals' determining role in the breakdown of the international monetary system. These companies control a large proportion of the world's floating capital (the liquid assets available to the Central Banks are far smaller), and they have poured this capital into those countries with strong currencies. They are thus in a position to counteract any decisions which governments of individual states can take.

The Report explains all the techniques these firms can use to forestall any currency problems, notably their extensive manipulation of 'leads and lags' in order to accelerate payments from countries with weak currencies to countries with strong currencies and to slow down transfers in the opposite direction. They borrow on the low bank rate money markets and lend on high bank rate markets. The big firms have perfected a computerized system for the administration of all their subsidiaries' financial resources. This speculation on a world scale not only increases their profits, it also contributes to the instability of the monetary system. But such monetary manipulations are not the only way the multinationals further the propagation of inflation. Their power and their dominant position in several markets enables them to play around with prices. Having announced in a blaze of publicity that 'cheap energy is a thing of the past' and that $1,000 billion would be needed for the development of energy sources up to 1985, the oil majors approved and even contributed to rises in oil prices which, in fact, served their ends perfectly, in that U.S. and other Western oil reserves were thereby increased in value. The oil majors' 1973 and 1974 profit levels broke all records.

In order to maintain their power and their domination, the multinationals are 'condemned' to a constant forward propulsion bringing rising prices in its trail. It is in their interest to maintain inflation as a safety valve, especially as economic conditions in the U.S. are quite difficult.

As Charles Levinson put it in the October 1973 issue of *Enterprise,* 'These companies push prices up as much as they can, so as to optimize the cash flow which their long-term strategy and their investment programmes depend on. Investment requirements reach astronomical proportions . . . In fact all this money comes from playing around with price rises: 99% of these investments are "self financed" by the cash flow.'

A New World Order

> It was a time when the wealthy countries, bloated as they were with industries and chain-stores, had at last discovered a new law, a new project worthy of the arduous efforts enjoined upon man during all those

> millenia: to turn the whole world into a single enormous business enterprise.
>
> R.V. Pilhes, *L'Imprecateur*

'Recent examples provide striking illustrations of the extent to which this notion of "public service" can introduce muddle-headedness and confusion into areas to which competition brings rigour and clarity.' In saying this, Andre Benard, a French member of the Shell directorate, expressed naively and in good faith the conviction held by the managers of multinationals that their participation in the construction of tomorrow's world is for the good of all humankind.

Once freed from the constraints imposed by the existence of groups with conflicting interests, the multinationals would be able to take on no less a task than the pursuit of human happiness itself. Their directors do not confine their thinking to mere products, but, in the phrase coined by the futurologist, A.C. Decoufle, they also aspire to 'societal goals'. To achieve these, they want to take over 'functions which have traditionally devolved upon public authorities', as Fred J. Borch, President of General Electric, puts it. These firms intend to control whole systems: energy, transport, information, food – in short, they want to solve every problem there is. Jacques G. Maisonrouge, President of I.B.M. World Trade, considers this as his firm's 'mission': 'Our business isn't building computers: it's contributing to the solution of every administrative, scientific and even human problem. Such efforts necessarily involve a greater unification of the world.' His words are echoed by the directors of the big multinationals, who all speak of the need for a truly internationalized economy.

How similar all this is to the old utopia of the ideologues and the dreamers; the abolition of frontiers and the setting up of a world government is the leitmotiv of all the giant corporations. They often add that this new world would be ideologically neutral. If the trade unions and the workers are not careful, they will find themselves in the world described by Stephen Hymer, 'a world built in the image of a multinational corporation. An international division of labour will be established in accordance with an internal allocation of tasks. All the important decisions will be taken in a few big towns in the industrialized countries; the rest of the world will be stuck with a secondary role and a lower income.' Such a world would be swamped by the ideologies and institutions of advanced industrial capitalism; in other words, it would be dominated by American ideas. A 'free' world under the multinationals would be a world of incontestible unequal development in which giant corporations would remorselessly expand. Profit would reign supreme, fixing the world in an order which, while golden for some, would be bleak for others.

It has been said that during the last ten years the multinationals have lost much of their political power. In many Third World countries they have been nationalized and Chilean-style *coups* tend to be the exception. Direct intervention in the affairs of nation states is too easily unmasked, too blatantly unacceptable, and is thus becoming increasingly rare. But still the fact remains that the growth of the multinationals in an 'internationalized' world does imply a certain degeneration of nation states and a concomitant take-over of some of their attributes by the multinationals. The attraction of 'internationalization' is indubitable. Many heads of state, including Valery Giscard d'Estaing, find positive features in the idea, and apparently do not grasp its real economic, and eventually political, implications in concrete terms. Several liberal economists preach the setting up of such a world. Octave Gelinier, a C.E.G.O.S. director, hopes for a symbiosis between 'the nation state, which administers a given territory, and the commercial company, which makes the most of economic opportunities, furthers progress and fights against waste.' Indeed, Gelinier holds that the multinationals have a major role to play 'in creativity, in the transfer of technology and *in the diffusion of culture.*' Howard Perlmutter, another advocate for the multinationals, has depicted this marvellous world of tomorrow, and its inexorable advance, in glowing terms:

> The forces moving towards the spread of an industrial and commercial world free of ideological ties seem irresistible . . . some multinational companies will deliberately seek and eventually obtain institutional status in the world economy. I mean that a situation will arise in which it will become apparent: a) that the multinationals are technically capable of creating wealth and helping to distribute it on a world scale, whilst remaining profitable for the country of origin or for the host country, whether it be a developed or a developing country and whatever its political system (East or West); b) that the resulting social policies are legitimate and to everybody's advantage (consumers and producers) both individually and collectively. It is no accident that some directors of multinationals are already trying to set up international institutions through which the multinationals can emerge as a new sort of social structure which is particularly well suited to the last decades of the twentieth century.

Perlmutter nonetheless recognises that this 'internationalist' spirit will come up against many obstacles. He outlines the means to overcome them, many of which are already being used: organizing language courses; forming international conference teams; establishing a head office operating on a world scale; drawing up systematic plans for international careers; extending the advantages conferred by the firm to non-nationals; encouraging the directors of the subsidiaries to participate in the pursuit of world-scale aims; improving the international communications system; finding ways of harmonizing conflicting tendencies. These brainwashing techniques for poor misguided souls still befuddled by nationalist irrelevancies are supposed to bring about a new understanding and the creation of a new breed of human being.
Dr. Max Gloor, director of the Swiss company, Nestle Foods, has given us a definition of this new phenomenon: 'We cannot be considered as either completely Swiss or as completely multinational, completely integrated into the world as a whole, inasmuch as such a thing is at all possible. We probably

fall somewhere between the two, forming a breed apart. In short, we have a special nationality, the Nestle nationality.'

All these new 'nationalities' are not organically federated, but, since they pursue the same aims and use the same means to achieve them, they are effectively the limbs of a single body: American-dominated international capitalism. The multinationals tend to impose a specific international culture complete with its own values: the liberalization of the world and the abolition of all frontiers which, with the help of a flood of advertising, should lead to the homogenization of all habits of thought and consumption. The ensuing increase in the size of the market will then enable the multinationals to grow even more. In the light of all this, it is hardly surprising that protectionism in any form should be the multinationals' main bugbear, nor that its main opponent should be the U.S. The U.S.'s desire to divide Europe is no accident. The aim is to eliminate all impediments to the expansion of U.S. economic power on a world scale. As Perlmutter says, 'The directors of the multinationals see economic and political nationalism as one of the main outside forces hampering the firms' efforts to survive, thrive and prosper. It is thus hardly surprising that they welcome the possibility of a decline in the influence of the nation state.'

The freedom demanded by the multinationals is the freedom to act without constraints in order to submerge everybody in a flood of new products and to impose a 'happiness' which serves the interests of a privileged few. In this line of thinking the dream of every citizen should be to belong to 'private transnational groups'. The bait is easily taken.

The developed countries often believe themselves to be safe from the devastating effects of multinational imperialism. And yet . . .! To take just one example, let us quote from a report submitted to Pierre Trudeau by Herbert Gray, Canada's Chancellor of the Exchequer. It is a perfect description of the way the country's wealth is drained to the greater benefit of 'American happiness'. One should remember that Canada is not India or some South American republic:

> The considerable and growing extent to which Canada's economic activity is foreign- and especially U.S.-dominated has led to the emergence in the country of an industrial structure which reflects mainly the growth priorities of foreign firms. Many of these firms have invested in Canada in order to extend the market for their manufactured products. As a result Canada finds itself imprisoned in a system of technological development and innovation which is remote-controlled from abroad. Other enterprises have invested in Canada in order to extract natural resources which will be consumed in the firms' country of origin. In both cases, to the extent that these enterprises are influenced by their home environment, their investment decisions reflect the priorities of foreign economic systems or governments. In turn, this evolution has contributed to the integration of Canada into the world economy in a way which may make it difficult for the country to achieve its own growth and employment targets.
>
> Another aspect of this foreign domination is the apparition of *truncated*

enterprises, many of whose most important functions are carried out abroad, in the parent company, with the result that fewer such functions are being carried out in Canada and the country's ability to carry them out has been reduced. All these phenomena have made it more difficult for the Government to keep control of the national environment; they have also affected the social, cultural and political atmosphere of Canada.

The ever-growing internationalization of many important sectors of industry and the expansion of multinational companies – the institutional consequences of the scale of direct foreign investment – contribute further to the complex of factors which limit the Government's ability to control the national economic environment. For instance, although many U.S. companies began their international operations in Canada, they now have subsidiaries in several other countries. The control they exercise over productive enterprises situated in various countries augments the power and flexibility they can call upon in their dealings with the Canadian Government. Furthermore, this aggravates the problems posed by the truncation of Canadian firms, in that it reduces the likelihood that the multinationals will localize more of their functions in Canada; foreign Governments do not hesitate to intervene directly to control enterprises belonging to non-residents established on their territory. The agreements reached by other governments with the multinationals may well have harmful consequences for Canada, especially if this country has not negotiation mechanism available or chooses not to use it.

4. The Pillage of the Third World

Merchants have no country. They do not care where they are. All that concerns them is the profits they make.

Salvador Allende
at the U.N.
4 December 1972

Serving people and nations everywhere.

I.T.T.

Statistics cannot convey the extent of the pillage perpetrated upon the Third World. Very high growth rates and high production levels do not necessarily mean that the local population benefits from this apparent wealth. The dominant cultures have imposed their way of thought as well as their language. In fact, the national accounts of Third World countries draw no distinction between extra-territorial production and national production. If one takes overall statistics as one's criteria, a country can appear to be prospering whilst it is really being drained of its wealth and the majority of its population is getting poorer. This is happening to two-thirds of the human race.

Following the success achieved by the oil producing countries, other Third World countries thought that perhaps the end of the tunnel was in sight. They all dreamt of carrying out an OPEC-style *coup* with their own raw materials. Unfortunately, it is unlikely that the new world order they hope for will be imposed on this basis, for, contrary to popular belief, the Third World, as compared to the developed countries, does not enjoy a dominant position in the supply of many raw materials. It cannot exert much pressure, a weakness which the multinationals and the developed countries are all too ready to exploit. The West did not accept the North-South dialogue without certain reservations, foremost amongst which is the West's intention to reduce the scope of any such dialogue, by playing as much as possible on economic and political contradictions between the Third World countries themselves.

Aid: The Illusion of Development

The U.S. has been, and still is, the main supplier of capital to the developing countries; this aid will increasingly be conditional upon the political attitudes of governments *vis-a-vis* the U.S. In the last few years, the multinationals have taken over the role played by government organizations. Official aid by governments, expressed in dollars, has remained constant. While it represented 58% of all O.E.C.D. aid in 1962, this fell to only 32% in 1973. On the other hand, direct American investment rose by 46% from 1972 to 1973. But this rise should not mislead us : The U.S.'s investments in the Third World represent only a third of its investments abroad; half of this input goes to the exploitation of raw material resources; less than a third goes into manufacturing industry. Furthermore, only certain Third World countries attract U.S. capital. (What the members of this privileged group have in common is a rapid growth rate and a 'respectable' regime, as in Brazil, Ecuador, the Dominican Republic, Turkey, South Korea, Zaire and some South-East Asian countries. They form an important outlet for the multinationals' products.) And finally one should never forget that the profits officially repatriated by the multinationals are more than double the inflow of new investment.

But this pillage is not the exclusive prerogative of American capitalism. Although competition between American and European or even Japanese multinationals is certainly a feature in manufacturing industry, it usually ceases to be so in the mining industries. International capitalism keeps tight ranks when it sets about extracting sub-soil wealth. The basis for this attitude is a desire to share the risks involved. Not that this means that 'rights' acquired in the past are put into question.

We have seen the consequences for Third World agriculture of the multinationals' policy : concentration on the production of export crops leads to the breakdown of old agricultural structures and to a decline in the production of essential foods. More generally, the multinationals' goals do not tally with the development needs of Third World countries. The companies install themselves in order to produce previously imported goods. Because of the lack of industrial infrastructure these new firms go in for import substitution. Importation of consumer goods is replaced by importation of capital goods or of parts which are then put together in the companies' local assembly plants. This type of enterprise has no lead-on effect on the local economy; it amounts to little more than the establishment of a captive market for the parent company. Samir Amin argues that, 'in fact, the ["lead-on"] effects are transferred abroad, back to the supplying countries; the various sectors of the underdeveloped economy figure as mere extensions of the dominant developed economy.' The apparent growth of certain Third World countries is only a myth. It 'aggravates the fundamental disintegration of the economy, the main characteristics of underdevelopment; it actually develops underdevelopment,' as A.G. Frank[5] puts it. The U.N. Economic Commission on Latin America confirms the theoreticians' judgement. 'Concerning the effects of constant import substitution, it would generally be fair to say that they tend to slow down the rate of economic growth.' Partial or complete nationalizations have partly – but only partly – limited this phenomenon.

Pierre Jalee[6] gives a useful analysis of how 'take-overs' in the mining sector are often quite illusory: 'The monopolies have nearly always given in graciously to such demands [for the Third World state concerned to hold 51% of shares in the subsidiary] because, as long as the monopolies remain in charge of the overall conception, the organization, the sources of supply and the marketing methods pertaining to their subsidiaries, their control is in no way impaired by being only minority shareholders. A local majority shareholding and a majority of local nationals on the board are mere formalities compared to the above, formalities which do nothing to change the company's essential status as a remote controlled instrument of the foreign monopolies whose interests it continues to serve.' Pierre Jalee also describes the deceptiveness of associations between local private or public capital and foreign capital. 'It makes no difference who holds the biggest stake in such associations; given the inequalities in technical potential and economic power between the parties involved, the enterprises will always be controlled by the foreign capitalists. By associating with the big international companies and tagging along behind them, national capital "denationalizes" itself.'

Good examples of these illusions are provided by the various South-East Asian countries which have welcomed the inrush of the multinationals. In Hong Kong there were 114 American, 59 Japanese and 21 English firms operating in the electronics and textiles sectors at the end of 1972. In Singapore there were 86 important foreign projects by mid-1973, 48 of which were American. In Formosa, more than $1,000 million had been invested by 1973. Indonesia has the highest volume of investment in the whole area. Malaysia, Sri Lanka and the Philippines are also jumping on the multinational bandwagon.

All these countries strive to outbid each other in order to attract the companies. As a result, the states concerned draw very little benefit from the multinationals' arrival, apart from the salaries paid by the companies. And of course the latter are very low, since the availability of cheap high-quality labour is the main reason the companies choose to set up such export-oriented factories in the first place.

Of all the areas in the Third World, it is Latin America which has 'benefited' most from the American 'manna': it is also the most economically and politically dominated area. Ricardo French Davis, a Chilean economist, has calculated that, in order to increase the gross *domestic* product of Latin America as a whole by 1%, the input of capital needed would be about two and a half times the amount represented by foreign investments from 1966 to 1969. He concludes that 'foreign capital cannot, never has and indeed should not play a decisive role in the development of Latin America.'

For all their aid programmes and talk about development, the governments of the industrialized nations have either actually contributed to broadening the gap between the rich countries and the proletarian countries, or, in particular countries, have merely promoted an economic take-off geared to the needs of the industrialized world rather than to those of the country in question. So, despite all their proclamations, the multinationals have had no positive and decisive effect on Third World development. Some privileged countries figure as exceptions to this rule, notably those which find themselves in the position of 'objective allies' of the multinationals in their effort to raise raw material prices, or those whose political system guarantees stability and submissiveness. The two tables below give some idea of the way the rich country/poor country relationship has evolved recently. Despite price rises in base products, the terms of trade have worsened for all the developing countries apart from the oil producing nations (see Table I.14); the Third World's purchasing power has thus effectively diminished.

Table I.14
Terms of Trade for Developing Countries, 1960, 1969-74

Year	*Main Oil Exporting Nations*	*Non-Oil Producing Nations*
1960	100	90
1969	100	100
1970	98	99
1971	114	93
1972	117	94
1973	137	100
1974	300	96

Source: O.E.C.D.

The Third World's weak growth rate was achieved at the expense of a considerable increase in its indebtedness *vis-a-vis* the industrialized countries (see Table I.15). In 1972 capital repayments and interest charges on their external debt amounted to $9,000 million, as compared to a total inflow of $19,900 million.

The Rise in Raw Material Prices: A Redistribution of Wealth?

At first it seemed that the rise in all prices of basic products, which began in 1972 for agricultural products and in 1973 for industrial materials, was going to bring about a major reshuffle, to the advantage of the Third World. But by Autumn 1974 the hopes of all non-oil-exporting Third World countries had been dashed. Furthermore, even in 1973, the increase in prices for basic products proved to be more advantageous to the industrialized countries, notably the U.S., than to the Third World ($29,000 million, as against $11,000 million). The $11,000 million in question was in any case soon eaten up by the price rises affecting manufactured products

Table I.15
Level of Indebtedness (Including Undrawn Credits) of 86 Developing Countries, 1965-72 ($000 millions)

End of	*Total*	*Oil Producing Nations*	*Others(according to revenue levels) High*	*Medium*	*Low*
1965	38.1	5.9	14.6	6.4	11.1
1966	43.4	6.5	16.2	7.6	13.1
1967	50.3	7.3	20.1	8.7	14.2
1968	56.9	8.4	22.7	9.8	15.9
1969	63.5	10.0	25.0	11.2	17.2
1970	72.9	12.1	29.0	12.6	19.2
1971	85.1	15.0	34.5	14.5	21.1
1972	99.4	17.7	41.9	16.7	23.1

(+ $4,500 million) and food products (+ $5,000 million). Nonetheless, it did seem as if the reserves available to Third World countries would enable them to resist Western capitalism's efforts to lay down the law. At the very least, there were hopes that the UNCTAD resolution might be invoked in order to 'ensure stable, equitable and remunerative prices for raw materials, with a view to increasing the currency earnings of the developing countries.' But such a goal, which is after all simply a matter of elementary equity and justice, is still far from being achieved. Of the global population 70% still receive only 20% of the world's income and produce only 7% of its industrial output. According to the F.A.O., 400 million people suffer from hunger. The equilibrium can obviously only be re-established by some relative reduction in the industrialized countries' share. In fact, exactly the opposite has happened: the U.N. had decided that 1963-73 was to be the decade of development. The ten years in question were indeed marked by an unprecedented prosperity – in the Western industrialized countries. Their G.N.P. increased by about two-thirds in real terms and between them they accounted for 70% of world trade. And during the same period the crumbs from the banquet got smaller and smaller: the volume of aid per inhabitant of the Third World fell by 30%. And by the beginning of 1975 the UNCTAD index of the average price for raw materials was back at the 1973 level, which was itself 40% below the 1950 level of correlation with the O.E.C.D. retail price index.

Why is it that the Third World has proved incapable of imposing a new international economic order? One cannot avoid the fact that, despite the many resolutions passed by the U.N., by the Group of 77 and by other international organizations, the developing countries have not managed to maintain high prices for any raw materials – except oil.

Several OPEC-style organizations have been set up, but to little avail. They include CIPEC, which represents the copper exporting countries (Chile, Peru, Zaire, Zambia), the bauxite exporters association and the mercury producers organization. The case of CIPEC is quite illuminating in this respect: copper is

Table I.16
Index of World Prices: Raw Materials (1970 = 100)

	1971	*1972*	*1973*	*1974* 1st Semester	*1974* October
Total	90	109	164	207	204
Agricultural Products	95	120	173	219	262
Total industrial materials	85	96	153	192	133
Fibres	98	134	235	237	172
Metals	78	77	113	170	109

Source: O.E.C.D.

still subject to price fluctuations. The price of copper, having reached 140 cents a pound in April 1974, was hovering around only 57 cents a pound a year later, barely above its average price during 1971. Two 10% cut-backs in production had hardly any effect on the market. More generally it seems unlikely that any other cartel could be as successful as OPEC, which is very much a special case, for its member countries account for 56% of world oil production, 85% of world oil exports and more than 60% of world reserves. No other raw material is so closely controlled by the developing countries. The Third World is not as important a reservoir of raw materials as is generally thought, and substitutes can be produced for many materials, although, not, in the short term at least, for oil.

For instance, the Third World produces only 30% of the world's output of minerals, as against the market economies' 45% and the socialist countries' 25%. On the other hand, the industrialized countries consume much more than they produce and must therefore draw on outside sources to bridge the gap (which represents 20% of world consumption and 37% of these countries' own needs). Tables I.17 and I.18 bring out the various strengths and weaknesses of the developing countries. Whilst the Third World clearly dominates tin and bauxite production, the same cannot be said for the production of copper, phosphate and iron. And the Third World as a whole is dependent on the developed countries for supplies of nickel, lead, zinc and fertilizers. As for agricultural commodities, the Third World's situation is catastrophic since, as we have seen, it does not produce enough even to satisfy its own needs.

The Third World thus faces the following paradox: although raw materials account for 70% of the value of its exports, it does not dominate the market for most of these materials since it does not control production, and big multinational companies dominate the transport, processing and distribution of the product. Furthermore, the volume of production and/or exports is too low for the Third World to be able to take advantage of the developed world's dependence in order to dominate prices.

Even more seriously, many developing countries' foreign trade in raw materials results in a net deficit so that a price increase would benefit only a

Table I.17
Relative Shares of the Value of World Exports, 1970 (%)

	Energy Products	*Minerals and Metals*	*Agricultural Raw Materials*	*Other Exports*	*All Products*
Developing countries	67.0	33.2	32.8	7.3	17
Market economies	24.2	62.5	61.4	81.4	73
Planned economies	8.8	4.3	5.8	11.3	10

Source: *Annales des mines*, January 1975.

Table I.18
World Exports of the Main Minerals and Metals

	Third World	*Market Economies*	*Socialist Cou*
Aluminium			
bauxite	88	12	11
metal	5	84	–
Chrome			
mineral	22	37	41
Copper			
mineral	42	58	–
metal	44	54	2
Tin			
mineral	64	36	–
metal	77	58	–
Iron			
mineral	42	23	–
Manganese			
mineral	51	34	15
Nickel			
mineral	24	76	–
metal	7	93	–
Lead			
mineral	12	88	–
metal	11	84	8
Zinc			
mineral	14	86	–
metal	12	74	14
Crude Fertilizer	43	22	35
Total	33.7	61.8	4.5
minerals	(40.7)	(54.5)	(4.9)
metals	(30.6)	(65.0)	(4.4)

Source: Doc.A.9544/Add.I., 3 April 1974, established by the U.N. secretariat for the 6th extraordinary session.

very small minority of the world population, and impose considerable suffering on the majority. In 1970 the U.N. conducted a study of 28 countries, whose 1,177 million inhabitants represented 67% of the Third World's total population. Three-quarters of the population in this sample have a foreign trade deficit in mineral raw materials, and 59% have a trade deficit in raw materials as a whole.

The discovery that the 1973-4 raw materials price boom was much more to the advantage of the developed producing countries than to the Third World helps us understand the mechanisms of the present crisis. The United States is by far the biggest producer of basic products. On the surface it would appear that the U.S. has certain interests in common with Third World producers yet the rise in prices does not affect the U.S. in anything like the way it affects Japan (which depends on the Third World for 90% of its supplies of raw materials) or Europe (which is poor in several essential substances).

Table I.19
The U.S. as the World's Largest Producer of Raw Materials (%)

Raw Materials	*U.S. Ranking*	*% of World Production*	*Year*
Oil	1	18	1973
Copper	1	27	n.a.
Lead	1	17	1972
Zinc	1	17	1972
Iron	2	11	1970
Steel	1	20	1970
Aluminium	1	37	1970
Wheat	2	12.5	1972
Cotton	1	23	1972
Maize	1	45	1974

We have seen how American agricultural prices took off in 1972, to the greater benefit of the U.S. balance of payments, but at the expense of greater suffering in the Third World. All liberal economists agree that the starting point for the rise in prices for raw materials was 'monetary instability', in other words the August 1972 devaluation of the dollar and the declaration of inconvertibility issued the year before. The fall of the dollar (and the equivalent decline in sterling), combined with the ensuing acceleration of inflation, incited speculators to unload dollars and buy raw materials. This speculation was not infrequently initiated by big firms who were quite content to build up their stocks. All this was based on Nixon's decisions and fits into the context of an overall strategy aimed at reasserting U.S. domination.

In *Petrole : la troisieme guerre mondiale,* Pierre Pean explains how the American oil majors together with Washington 'permitted' the increase in oil prices, and the various reasons underlying this choice, namely : that it ensured the long-term security of the U.S. by decreasing its dependence on 'unstable' producers; that it increased the value of the U.S.'s unexploited reserves; that it increased company profits, which in turn made a gigantic research effort possible; that it penalized the Japanese and European economies by making energy dearer; that it helped to re-establish the U.S.'s leadership over the industrialized world; and finally, that it contributed to solving the problem of the Middle East.

Without wishing to deny OPEC's power, it must be said that the conditions which made the price rise possible were generated by the oil majors and by the American Government. Oil prices only took off after those of agricultural goods and other basic products. We believe that the rise in raw materials prices was also a direct consequence of the U.S. multinationals' speculative strategies. Mechanisms identical to those observed during the 'oil crisis' recur throughout the process. From 1970 onwards, American and indeed world public opinion was fed with the idea that there was only a limited supply of raw materials and that the world was therefore heading for major shortages. It was not the first time that Americans had heard talk of shortages. There hav been six panics about oil shortages since 1926, and in the 1950s people were particularly worried about tin and copper supplies. The high point of this new wave of concern was reached in 1972 with the Club of Rome's publication of *Limits of Growth.* America had already used up its best (least expensive) minerals. All the official studies laid great stress on the consequences of the dependence entailed by such a situation : the long-term security of the U.S. was at stake.

When the experts talk of reserves they refer to known reserves which are worth exploiting under the prevailing economic conditions or, to be more accurate, worth exploiting given the prevailing market price and the level reached by the technology of prospecting. The implication is, of course, that any alteration in these conditions means a change in the volume of reserves. Shortage is thus an essentially *economic* notion, and does not necessarily indicate any physical limitation on reserves (for the foreseeable future, at least).

In 1970 the U.S. Bureau of Mines issued a serious warning based on an investigation into the matter : 'The rate of discovery and development of reserves is declining for many minerals.' America, which had been a net exporter until the Second World War, had become a net importer. There was only one way out for the world's largest producer of raw materials: to increas prices. An article in the October 1972 issue of *Fortune,* the well known U.S. economic monthly, explains that 'even without any new discoveries, reserves of several metals would increase geometrically if prices rose by 50%, because many small-scale deposits could then be exploited. At the moment, for variou reasons, including the high cost of prospecting and taxes, the mining compani have little reason to "chase" or even to disclose reserves which exceed their needs for the next two decades or more.' Apart from its impact on the availability of reserves – notably U.S. reserves – a price rise allows the companies both to raise important sums for their future development and to cope with the wilder fluctuations of demand.

The low price level for raw materials was dealt with quite adequately by speculation and manipulation of the dollar – there was no need for the producing nations to step in as the oil nations had done. All that remained, as far as the companies were concerned, was to stabilize prices: frantic speculation produced its own antidotes, and the price of many minerals collapsed during the second semester of 1974, after which they settled at a level higher than the one which had prevailed at the beginning of 1973. The crisis, and the low level of demand, had led to an excess in supply.

It is difficult to establish any proof as to the real identity of the speculators, but one may note various declarations of intent as to the necessity of increasing prices to cope with capital requirements. As the Vice-President of Kennecott Copper put it, 'The possibility of avoiding shortages will depend on the response of the industry and the government to the new realities.'

Wall Street continued to treat mining company shares as good long-term investments. In June 1973, George Cleaver, a spokesman for the research outfit 'Alliance One', told *Business Week* that 'during a period of strong demand and high prices, profits can be immense, especially for low cost producers. A 2 cents per pound increase in the price of copper means 40 cents profit per share in a company like Phelps Dodge.' In the effort to strengthen their case for a price rise and to obtain government support, the directors of both the mining companies and the oil majors constantly invoked 'national security'. 'American dependence on foreign sources of minerals is reaching an unacceptable level,' declared the President of Anaconda.

The producer countries did indeed benefit from this American desire to raise the price for raw materials, but the well integrated companies did even better. The growth or falling back of Third World countries is still very much dependent on decisions taken by the multinationals. The euphoria is now over; production prices have dropped, but consumption prices have not.

5. The Reinforcement of American Hegemony

The 1970s will be remembered as a decade marked by a worldwide re-shuffle. The U.S. has redefined its foreign strategy, beginning by making the dollar inconvertible. Yet continuing American imperialist ambitions have not prevented a certain deterioration of the American economy. Will the U.S.'s long-term strategy to reconquer the world fail because the American system is cracking at the seams? Will the successes of imperialism be sufficient both to compensate for its internal problems and to maintain American hegemony abroad?

History alone can provide answers to these questions. We will make do with outlining the reasons for believing that, without radical changes in the world's political system, notably in Europe, the U.S. will emerge victorious from any new Yalta which is called in response to the U.S.-initiated economic warfare. Such is the complexity of the economic system, however, that mastery of the relevant mechanisms is by no means assured even to the world's number one power. The crisis may well work itself out to the advantage of the U.S., but there is also the possibility that the Americans, by playing sorcerer's apprentice, will bring the whole capitalist system falling around their ears.

U.S. imperialism's 'reassertion' policy undeniably carries a certain risk, since the economic structures on which it needs to rely are crumbling. At the end of 1975 two aspects stand out:

1. Growth has slowed dramatically to the extent that the economy has actually regressed in 1975; for example, the index of industrial production has fallen by 3.9%.

2. Unemployment has reached a very high level, more than 8% of the active population.

The U.S. has not managed to break out of the 'dilemma of underconsumption/overproduction'. On the other hand, it is better able to bear the greatly increased cost of oil. The U.S. had a positive balance of trade in 1975 and had turned the tables (in terms of growth) on the rest of the developed countries, especially Britain, France, Italy and Japan. U.S. firms established abroad considerably increased their share of international 'cash flow' (the system's real capacity to ensure its own development) throughout the operation. In other words, the multinationals benefited from the 'crisis' outside the U.S.

and took over from national units. Internally generated U.S. cash flow has increased by 84% since 1970, as compared to the 380% increase achieved abroad by the multinationals. The share of the total cash flow which is realized abroad has now reached significant proportions: over 9%. The oil companies' flexibility, their integration, and their oligopolistic control over world oil markets make it possible for them to adapt to the complete nationalization of their drilling concessions, especially as they retain their privileged positions *vis-a-vis* the OPEC countries, and as their 'superprofits' enable them to maintain control over significant reserves outside the OPEC zone, in 'stable' areas. But there is more to the victory achieved through 'operation oil'. After a few 'hiccups' in Autumn 1973, a new brand of Western solidarity has emerged. The idea of a 'new Atlantic Charter', launched by Kissinger in April 1973, is still around.

During February 1974 in Washington, Kissinger got all his Western partners, except France, to accept the idea of a united front of consumers, and this led to the setting up of the International Energy Agency in November 1974. The Secretary of State repeatedly outlined the reasons for this new solidarity. On 3 February 1975, before the National Press Club in Washington, he stated that the resolution of the energy crisis should lead to a reinforcement of solidarity in every field, since 'the whole of the industrialized world faces a serious crisis which affects not only its economy but also its political institutions and its sense of morality.'

He added that 'this moral crisis underlies all our difficulties.' As far as Kissinger was concerned, the only way to cope with this crisis, and to avoid the political disturbances involved, was to close ranks. Kissinger's leitmotiv became the need to save the Western democracies by a co-ordination of their economic and energy policies. In an interview published in the January 1975 issue of *Business News,* he claimed that America's friends and allies had accepted this idea: 'There has thus been a complete U-turn in the space of one year.'

The Secretary of State did indeed have good reason to be satisfied with his allies' 'attitudes'. Apart from France they all accepted an emergency plan, worked out within the framework of the International Energy Agency, to cope with any new oil embargo. To all appearances, this plan gives *carte blanche* to American policy-making, since it provides for an immediate reply to any eventual action by the producers (action which would, in all likelihood, have been triggered off by some American military or diplomatic initiative in the Middle East). Financial solidarity has also been achieved: if the recycling of petro-dollars takes place as envisaged, the U.S. will control the flow, thereby gaining an important means of pressurizing the other industrialized countries. The Arab-European dialogue, which so frightened the State Department, has remained a pipe-dream. All the countries grouped under the aegis of the International Energy Agency have now adopted a common stance in relation to OPEC.

In fact, the industrialised countries have reached a certain level of political consensus on the need to protect investments in the development of energy resources with the hope of diminishing their dependence on OPEC: a price floor is to be adopted. The U.S.'s main fear is an eventual drop in oil prices during the coming years, a drop which would jeopardize the profitability of the very high level of investments which have nearly all gone into developing resources within the U.S. itself (and which have mainly been provided by U.S. trusts). Kissinger has stated that 'the uncontrolled consumption of cheap oil is the main cause of the industrialized countries' present vulnerability.'

Nonetheless, the expression of this new solidarity has not been as total as the State Department might have wished. While this partial failure of American diplomacy is partly due to the fundamental divergence between U.S. economic interests, on the one hand, and those of Europe and Japan, on the other, it has also resulted from the various contradictions in U.S. energy policy which have emerged since Autumn 1973.

The elaboration of this policy has in fact catalysed all the existing tensions in U.S. society – national capitalism versus international capitalism, Democrats versus Republicans, Congress versus the Executive, the Zionist lobby versus the pro-Arab lobby, interventionists versus liberals, protectionists versus free-traders, hawks versus doves, Texan producers versus oil majors . . .

That national security was at stake was the only point on which all these factions agreed. Everybody was very aware of the nation's vulnerability during the embargo, even if the actual effects were quite minimal. It was clearly absurd for the world's greatest power to have to put up with being largely dependent on decisions taken abroad. Apart from this general level of consensus, however, controversy was rife.

Until November 1974, the official thesis, or at least the one which emerged from the various government statements, constantly invoked the need to bring the price of oil down considerably. Threats of intervention and various blackmail moves against the producer countries were made alongside apocalyptic descriptions of a world turned upside down by OPEC's 'irresponsible' policy. It was nonetheless quite clear that the U.S. had largely encouraged, if not provoked, the sudden increase in prices. Most of America's Western allies were convinced that the U.S. wanted the price of oil to go up, but were not sure by how much. The prevailing impression, however, was that, by the end of 1973, control of the situation had partly slipped out of the hands of the sorcerer's apprentices in Washington, especially as the U.S. Executive was sinking deeper and deeper into the Watergate mire.

In late Spring and Summer 1974, Washington was paralysed. The projected energy goal of 'independence by 1980' was temporarily forgotten. But the oil companies did not stop their operations, the experts and their computers kept on working . . .

Right up until the end of 1973, the U.S. oil companies judged that the prevailing economic conditions were not good enough to justify any major efforts geared to enhancing the value of new resources. All the more so, since as far as the most important companies were concerned there were far better profits to be made abroad. They claimed that authorized selling prices were not high enough to cover prospecting and extraction costs. When restrictions on the price of 'newly discovered' oil were lifted in November 1973 things got moving again. By the end of the first semester of 1974 the number of exploratory drillings had already increased by 21% compared to the previous year: the trend continued in the following semester. The price for 'new' oil settled at $10.50 a barrel (at drill-head), the same price as for Gulf and Iranian oil. The American oil industry's total investments reached $21,000 million in 1974, as against $15,300 million the previous year. A percentage figure gives some idea of the scale of the American effort: 46.7% of the world's oil prospecting teams were working in the U.S.! The fact that oil prices had quadrupled paved the way for renewed research, leading to a reversal of the declining trend in production which had begun in 1970.

Analysis of the Federal Energy Agency's (F.E.A.) report, published in November 1974, which served as the basis for President Ford's energy policies, gives one some idea of Kissinger's difficulties *vis-a-vis* his Western partners on the OPEC issue. There was clearly a blatant contradiction between the economic interests of the world's number one oil producing nation and its role as the saviour of the Western democracies : the new price levels for oil seemed to be the best way to ensure America's invulnerability, but, on the other hand, such a price level threatened the unity of the Western camp, in that it was likely to cause serious problems for governments friendly to the U.S. However, the U.S. was also aware that too low a price would give a considerable advantage to its European and Japanese commercial rivals and would prevent Washington from achieving one of its fundamental goals, namely the reassertion of its economic hegemony, which had been shaky ever since 1965. In short, the U.S. had to square the circle .

As the F.E.A. put it, 'the world price for oil largely determines American energy prices and will affect both potential U.S. production and the energy growth rate.' The F.E.A. experts assumed that the future evolution of world oil prices was unpredictable and might fall to $7 a barrel or even lower. American vulnerability to future perturbations therefore depended on world prices. If these fell to $7 a barrel, and given that no political measures were taken at home, imports would reach 12.3 million barrels a day by 1985 (610 million metric tons a year), of which 6.2 million barrels might be subject to embargo – in other words the situation might be far more dramatic than in 1973. But if the price settled at $11, imports would only amount to 3.3 million barrels a day, of which 1.2 million would be 'vulnerable'. A price of $11 dollars a barrel would have a more detrimental effect on the trade balance than one of $7 a barrel – but only until 1980, when the opposite would be true.

The oil majors, the big energy companies, and the U.S. Government were therefore afraid of a drop in prices. Mastery over new forms of energy is only achievable if the reference price for energy is kept high. The U.S. aims to secure a monopoly over the new technologies. Europe has already given in to this manoeuver by agreeing to build its nuclear power stations under American licence, even though the technology involved will soon be out of date.

The technological gap between the U.S. and the other industrialized countries is already huge and continues to grow under the combined efforts of the American Government and American big business. In 1974 the federal research and development budget reached the impressive sum of $1,000 million. This effort is geared to every possible source of energy, whereas in other countries there is a drift away from solar and geothermal energy research. American research investment grew by 49% in 1974. In 1975 a further growth of 81% is projected. Most of this goes on nuclear research (63% in 1974) but the sums devoted to solar and geothermal energy have also increased remarkably (by 400% in 1974). In these sectors, as in coal mining, U.S. research and development expenditure is the same if not more than that devoted to research by all the other O.E.C.D. countries put together. In 1974 and 1975 the big American oil companies continued their diversification into coal and uranium mining, in addition to gaining access to new sources of oil.

But a tightening up of the Western alliance and favourable conditions for independence in energy are not all that the U.S. has gained. The increased financial resources of the oil producers reinforces the common front between the U.S. and the Gulf States (Iran, Saudi Arabia, United Arab Emirates), thereby putting Europe at Washington's mercy. Translated into financial terms, the oil crisis involves a flow of currency towards the U.S. The strength of its banking system, its economic power and its political regime attract most of the weakly populated oil producing nations, who are in effect already U.S. vassals. The U.S. is the only efficient source of protection for the feudal regimes in these countries – all the more reason for them to maintain the 'Pax Americana' in the Persian Gulf. This united front will struggle against the rise of every progressive force in the world. Thanks to its dollars and its oil it can support every kind of reactionary tendency.

For instance, Saudi Arabia intends to use its oil wealth to prevent certain countries moving towards socialism. Sheikh Yamani, the Saudi Oil Minister, who is regarded as an American agent even in his own country, spoke out quite plainly on the subject, when he indicated that Saudi investments will go to 'safe' countries; in other words to countries having a capitalist regime; the only exception will be those countries where inputs of Saudi money may prevent the crisis leading to socialism. The death of King Faisal has in no way changed Saudi Arabia's pro-American policy. On the contrary, it is Prince Fahd, the architect of the important June 1974 co-operation agreement between the two countries, who has increasingly emerged as the 'strong man' in the Saudi Government.

Furthermore, the deployment and reinforcement of the U.S. multinationals have not provoked any reactions amounting to a counter-attack. Although Europe regularly expresses its concern about the issue, this is never translated into concrete action. This is to be expected. Europe is the victim of its decision to pursue the same aim as its U.S. adversary, namely the international division of labour. 'The Commission is convinced that the correct response to the competition which E.E.C. industry faces from within its own territory does not lie in restrictive practices but rather in a reinforcement of the structure and dynamism of European business.' Jean Charbonnel, the then French Minister for Industry, put the same thing slightly differently: 'We must draw the consequences of a choice dictated to us by the general internationalization of industry, the choice of balanced interdependence. Total control of national industry is no longer a goal we can realistically set ourselves. A strategy based on an association between national and foreign interests must become an integral part of French and E.E.C. industrial policy.'

The condition for such a policy is to leave the U.S. as sole master of certain key areas of the new international division of labour, areas such as aeronautics, cybernetics and nuclear energy, which have become exclusively U.S. preserves. During his May 1975 visit to Europe, President Ford left no doubt as to his intentions. His first interview was with the Belgian Prime Minister, who was still hesitating as to the choice of a new fighter plane. The American President did away with all his doubts, as well as with any illusions the French Government might have held as to French participation in the famous 'sale of the century'.

Despite the burden of evidence to the contrary, the European states still insist that they will be able to repel U.S. imperialism by developing their own multinationals. Although a few victories over their U.S. competitors have been won, the European multinationals still have no chance of closing the gap and catching up, as their growth rate has not overtaken that of the U.S. companies. Since European governments and the main European companies expecting to participate in the 'big game' still entertain hopes of catching up, they accept rules of the game which perfectly suit the multinationals and give them everything they need to be able to defy state authority. The basic goal of these companies is the maximization of profit on a world scale, and so they continue to make a mockery of fiscal and labour laws, and, more generally, of the economic goals of the host states.

In the long term this economic 'internationalization' can only reinforce American imperialism, with the active collaboration of the rest of the world's capitalist companies – not to mention the blessing of the present Western governments, who seem quite willing to accept the division of labour imposed by the United States. One would have thought that the experiences they have undergone on the financial and monetary level would have made them more cautious. Despite various alarms and bouts of bad temper, the structure of the world monetary system has remained by and large unchanged since the end of the Second World War. Dollar imperialism has been the key factor which has enabled the U.S. to use all its other means of domination to preserve the American hold over the rest of the world. The analysis of the dollar's role in Part II of this book should help us to a better understanding of this domination.

References to Part I

1. Speech by Thomas Enders, Kissinger's assistant, delivered at Yale University.
2. As an example, we could look at Guinean aluminium. The state has a 49% holding and the remaining 51% is held by the Halco Consortium, subdivided as follows:

Harvey Aluminium (U.S.A.)	51%
Alcoa (U.S.A.)	17.5%
Alcan (Canada)	17.5%
Pechiney Ugine Kulhman (France)	6%
Vereinifte Aluminium Werke (G.F.R.)	5%
Montecatini (Italy)	3%

Zairean copper is another case in point:

State of Zaire	20%
Charter Consolidated	28%
Amoco (U.S.A.)	28%
Mitsui (Japan)	14%
B.R.G.M. – Paribas (France)	7%
Tempelsman (U.S.A.)	3%

3. The current payments deficit of non-oil-producing developing countries grew from $9,400 million to $45,000 million in 1975.
4. *Interim Report* of the Industrial Committee on National Enterprises.
5. A.G. Frank, *Le Developpement du sous-developpement,* (Maspero, 1962).
6. P. Jalee, *Le Pillage du tiers monde,* (Maspero, 1973).

Appendix to Part I

Economic Report/Administration Trade Strategy Taking Shape to Strengthen U.S. Bargaining Position*

The U.S. government is refining a controversial strategy for international trade negotiations this fall that would link the outcome of the talks to separate agreements on defense, monetary and energy issues.

The aim is to strengthen the U.S. hand in the trade talks in the hope of opening new markets to American producers and erasing the U.S. balance-of-payments deficit. The linkage strategy recognizes the weakness in the U.S. bargaining position on trade, and seeks to offset it by tying the talks to other issues, where U.S. negotiating leverage is greater . . .

The essence of the Peterson plan has been favourably received by the President's foreign policy adviser, Henry A. Kissinger . . .

[Despite European reluctance or objections] three factors weighed strongly in favour of the linkage strategy.

Both Kissinger and Peterson knew from earlier soundings that, public rhetoric notwithstanding, European and Japanese officials were not adamantly opposed to considering the trade question in a broader context. The possibility had been extensively discussed with officials of the individual European governments, the Common Market and Japan, and the reaction was generally encouraging. . . .

A second factor in favour of the strategy was the conviction, held by both Kissinger and Peterson, that it was not realistic to consider trade matters as though isolated from other concerns . . . It was therefore, not blackmail, as some Europeans might claim, but practical realism to consider them together.

The final, and perhaps decisive, argument . . . was that, on a less ambitious scale, it had been tested and found successful during trade negotiations with the Soviet Union in the summer of 1972.

In that instance, U.S. negotiators had been dispatched to Moscow under instructions from Kissinger to take the Soviets to the brink and then slam on the brakes. The object was to use the Soviet Union's eagerness for a trade deal to secure its quiescence on the Vietnam issue. Though the tradeoff never was stated explicitly, it did not have to be. The Soviets got the message; they adopted a close-mouthed attitude towards the war, and the trade agreement was consumated . . .

If the linkage strategy is followed, the trade delegation will be only one section in an orchestra of negotiators under the over-all direction of Henry Kissinger.

Kissinger's job would be to coordinate the play of all sections – including those on security, monetary reform and energy – to ensure that they complemented one another and that successes in one area were not achieved at the expense of another . . .

High on the U.S. shopping list when the Geneva talks get under way will be compensation for the adverse trade impact of the recent Common Market enlargement. Another important objective will be to obtain assurances that the emerging Common Industrial Policy will not be made at the uncompensated expense of U.S. exporters.

Although negotiation toward this end will be divided for the most part into consideration of a number of non-tariff barriers discussed below, the over-all objective will be to make certain that U.S. products such as computers and aircraft are not discriminated against.

One goal of the Common Industrial Policy is to stimulate European develop ment in these and other high technology areas – areas in which the United States currently enjoys comparative advantage and substantial exports.

A third area of major interest to U.S. negotiators will be the Common Market system of price supports, variable tariffs and export subsidies for agricultural products.

The variable levy, which rises as the world price falls, limits imports, the price supports cause overproduction and the export subsidies pump the surpluses into third markets which would otherwise be served by non-European exporters . . .

Although the CAP is buttressed by the considerable political influence of European farm constituencies, U.S. negotiators can nevertheless be expected to make agricultural concessions a primary objective . . .

A final hurdle is the fact that the United States is seeking to improve its trade position and thus by definition is asking for more than it is prepared to give up.

Though words like 'reciprocity' and 'balance' will be repeated in official rhetoric until they dissolve into nonsense syllables, they cannot obscure this fact . . .

Large U.S. balance-of-payments deficits have, in practical terms, been a greater problem for Europe than for the United States. The United States has compiled the bad books, but the Europeans have been left holding the bad money, money which has had several harmful effects on European economies.

The dollars Europe has been forced to accumulate have served as a medium for speculative attacks which, in several instances, have resulted in forced revaluations. They have fueled European inflation by swelling the money supply. In 1972, Germany experienced a 6.5 per cent rate of inflation as foreign exchange inflows increased its money supply by 13 per cent. And finally, in the process of accumulating the dollars, Europe has in effect financed the U.S. takeover of numerous European corporations.

The Europeans attach high priority to reforms which would insulate them from these effects in the future. The United States is not unwilling, but the two sides differ materially over the means . . .

Their predilection for more stable rates is explained in part by the fact that they fear the impact of frequent changes on trade, which for them is a far more important factor than for the United States. Whereas only about 5 per cent of the goods purchased and consumed in the United States are imported the figure for European countries ranges from 20 per cent to 50 per cent.

Exchange rate changes, therefore, have a substantially larger impact on employment levels and inflation rates in Europe than they do in the United States . . .

The irony of the monetary discussions is that the United States can have negotiating leverage because it is the source of much of the problem . . .

U.S. officials believe that favorable . . . balance-of-payments adjustments should be possible – either directly through larger foreign contributions to mutual defense or indirectly through trade adjustments designed to offset greater portions of the cost to the United States of maintaining troops abroad.

The security issue will afford the United States leverage in substantially differing degrees from country to country but it is an issue which, generally speaking, has increased in value as a bargaining chip.

Today, the U.S. balance-of-payments position is radically different, and the Nixon Administration's accommodations with the Soviet Union and the Chinese have created serious apprehension in Europe over the permanence of the U.S. military presence and over the dependability of the United States as a military ally. These fears are reinforced by growing congressional sentiment for unilateral reduction in U.S. troop commitments in Europe.

U.S. officials reckon that the confluence of these factors has substantially increased the likelihood that the United States will be able to secure larger balance-of-payments offsets either in the form of contributions to the defense effort or concessions in other areas, such as trade, in return for assurances that the U.S. military support will meet certain specifications for a prescribed period of time.

The security issue probably will afford the United States considerably more leverage in Europe than in Japan.

Although the European perception of external threat is diminishing, it remains large in relation to her ability to defend herself without assistance.

Moreover, the prospect of building a military capability which could stand without U.S. assistance suggests political problems both between and within the countries of Europe.

Progress toward European unity in the political and security areas has not kept pace with progress in the economic area. The buildup of nuclear capability to replace that of the United States is an option which the Europeans would like to preserve but one whose exercise would raise the thorny question of who would control it, a question which could awaken now dormant rivalries and animosities such as those between the French and the Germans . . .

Although the French are committed to a go-it-alone defense policy, U.S. officials believe other countries in Europe will be sufficiently interested in obtaining a continuing U.S. commitment to agree to some form of increased compensation.

Although the United States is increasingly worried about its reliance on foreign sources for oil supplies, the problem is much greater for Europe and Japan, a fact that may give U.S. negotiators a source of leverage in the upcoming trade talks.

Europe and Japan – relatively unendowed with indigenous sources – are currently far ahead of the United States in public awareness of the problem.

Both also are mindful that the emergence of the United States as a major oil importer will seriously affect them.

In 1970, Western Europe relied on oil for more than half of its energy but produced only 2 per cent of what it used. Japan, in the same year, relied on oil for more than 70 per cent of her energy but produced a statistically insignificant amount.

This record was in marked contrast with that of the United States, which imported only 21 per cent of its oil consumption. By 1980, however, the United States expects to import between 45 per cent and 60 per cent of its oil requirements.

Energy deficit nations could be pitted against each other in bidding to lock up available supply through long-term contracts.

A second danger is that the projected flow of oil payments from the deficit nations to the Arab world will far exceed the probable capacity of those countries to import. The result will be large balance-of-payments deficits for any energy deficit nation which is unable to attract its pro-rata share of Arab oil receipts in the form of capital or portfolio investment . . .

What worries government officials both in the United States and abroad is that pressure to maintain payments balance in the face of these energy deficits will lead the importing countries into destructive competition, competition bot for exports to the Arab countries and for the investment reflow . . .

While the supply and balance-of-payments problems are common to all the oil deficit nations, the United States occupies a relatively advantageous positior for the following reasons:

* It supplies, and will continue to supply, a far greater percentage of the oil it consumes than either Japan or Europe.
* It has the largest capital market in the world, a market which would serve as a magnet for Arab investment while permitting its absorption in large amounts without having U.S. firms fall under Arab control.
* Notwithstanding its balance-of-payments problems, the United States would be a formidable competitor in the event of an out-and-out bidding contest for energy supplies.
* Finally, all but a few of the major integrated oil companies are U.S.-owned,

and other countries might reasonably expect these companies to favor the U.S. market were the energy problem to reach critical proportions.

For these reasons, Europe and Japan see great advantage in joint approaches and cooperative policies which assure them that the United States will not exercise its greater leverage.

U.S. negotiators coincidentally see such energy agreements as potentially useful makeweights in the bargaining over trade.

Frank V. Fowlkes

* Extracts from an article by Frank Fowlkes, the aide to Peter Peterson, Secretary of State for Trade, *National Journal,* Washington, 7 July 1973.

PART II

The Reign of the Dollar: Hegemony and Decline

by Alexandre Faire

6. Introduction

After a period of expansion which lasted twenty years, imperialism is now going through a structural crisis comparable to the one which shook it to its foundations between the two world wars. Inflation, foreign deficits, production and unemployment are reaching levels unheard of since the 1930s. Apparently Western public opinion only became aware of this crisis in the Autumn of 1973, with the sudden quadrupling of oil prices. Memories are short. It is worth remembering that before its appearance in the guise of a possible raw materials shortage, the crisis had been gradually manifesting itself on the monetary level ever since 15 August 1971.

But it is not just because memories are short that this significant aspect of the problem has been so quickly forgotten. We must also take into account the fact that, for bourgeois imagery, monetary phenomena are features of a mysterious world unintelligible to the general public, a world of financiers and speculators, full of baffling formulae and incomprehensible exchanges of bits of paper. The monetary experts drown us in a sea of details and present a picture so confused that the essential features are camouflaged. Nonetheless, the abstract appearance of monetary phenomena does not prevent them from eventually being incorporated in human life; although their role is not a determining one, they do make up one of the essential mechanisms of imperialist domination.

Shorn of verbiage, the essential aspects of monetary mechanisms can be summarized quite briefly. The expansion and intensification of imperialism are synonymous with the expansion of the capitalist world market, of capital, and, to a lesser extent, of the labour force, in the context of a capitalist international division of labour. The existence of currency is as essential to this new form of expansion and intensification as it was to the growth of the various national capitalisms: there has to be an instrument which is at one and the same time a numerator, a means of payment and a way of establishing credits and debits, in other words an instrument for constituting reserves.[1] In its turn the existence of currency implies institutions to create it, manage it, and distribute the credits which are essential to the development of the world market.

Even in national capitalism's expansionist phase, the creation and regulation of monetary mechanisms was always determined *socially* (i.e. in a way which concerned the ruling classes as a whole) rather than *privately*. This explains why, at the national level, the creation and regulation of currency rapidly became monopolized by the apparatuses of the state, since only the latter could define and defend the overall interests of the ruling class or class alliance. Of course, this process was sometimes carried out in a manner detrimental to one of the fractions of the ruling alliance, and was sometimes (temporarily) even detrimental to the immediate interests of the ruling alliance as a whole. On the national level, both the contingent and structural aspects of monetary policy are, and always have been, determined by the nature of the problems facing the ruling class alliance.

Mutatis mutandis, the same applies on the international level. The structure of the international monetary system refers back to the structure of imperialism as a whole; international monetary policy refers back to this structure's needs and institutions. For instance, in the period which concerns us here, the dollar's dominant role in the international monetary system reflects the hegemony of American imperialism in general, and the gradual undermining of this role reflects struggles against this hegemony. In other words, changes in the structure of the international monetary system reflect more fundamental changes in the structure of imperialism: in the last analysis, the latter determine the former and not vice versa.

But although this thesis is fundamentally correct, it is far from the whole story. Perhaps an analogy would help: juridical relations confirm social relations but in the process they also have some impact upon them, inasmuch as the evolution of social relations is not usually immediately expressed in a corresponding evolution of the juridical relations. On the contrary, established juridical relations often serve as a means to stop or slow down the evolution of social relations. Furthermore, the evolution of the juridical relations is often the outcome of some clash or conflict, and serves to ratify or confirm the evolution undergone by the social relations. The same applies to the international monetary system. The Bretton Woods Agreement, drawn up following the Second World War, ratified a new structure for imperialism, a structure characterized by U.S. hegemony in the capitalist world. Just as newly established juridical relations further the generalization of the social relations they express – and this is why they are the focus of conflicts of interests – so the Bretton Woods international monetary system furthered the consolidation of this American hegemony.

During the 1960s concrete changes in the structure of imperialism raised, as one would expect, the problem of the suitability of this international monetary system to cope with the new situation created by these changes. The crisis in the international monetary system should therefore be seen both as a challenge to out-of-date superstructures corresponding to a crumbling U.S. hegemony, and as an attempt to maintain this hegemony by using advantages conferred on the U.S. by this superstructure. The stable dollar was both a sign of this hegemony, and also one of the means through which it was established and perpetuated. An unstable dollar indicated that this hegemony was declining, but itself could be one of the means used to struggle against this decline.

This double character of the dollar's role, in both ascendant and declining phases, explains the schematic and confused character of non-dialectical analyses of the subject.[2] The point of this essay is to grasp this double character, which reflects the contradictions inherent in the development of imperialism under U.S. hegemony. Such a grasp is indispensable if we are to understand the stakes involved and the possible outcomes of contemporary clashes. The above comments should have convinced our readers that the only way to achieve this is to retrace two parallel histories, that of the international monetary system and that of the development of imperialism, which interlock in three distinct moments: a phase of uncontested U.S. hegemony, a phase in which this hegemony was challenged, and the eventual crisis of U.S. hegemony and of the hegemony of imperialism as a whole.

Which challenge to U.S. hegemony are we talking about? Not that presented by an ambitious West European bourgeoisie anxious to seize its historical opportunity, for this bourgeoisie has, on the contrary, only participated in the recent historical movement by giving ground and by accepting American demands – as we shall see when we examine monetary developments. No, the real challenge stems from the facts themselves, as a product of imperialism's internal contradictions, the very contradictions which have enabled it to develop over the last twenty years. Facts such as Japanese and European reconstruction, which sets limits to U.S. hegemony quite independently of any conscious intentions; facts such as the domestic class struggle, which constrains the rulers of these countries; facts such as the struggle of the peoples of the Third World, both before and after the 'decolonization' movement.

We are taking the recent history of the international monetary system as an aspect and an index of the history of imperialism. This index is of course imperfect, since it is influenced only indirectly by the struggles of the working class at home and of Third World peoples, that is, through the inter-imperialist conflicts they engender.[3] The index can thus not avoid misrepresenting the importance of these events, and thus the relevance of all events, even if it does allow us to stress the privileged position of Europe and Japan in the structure of imperialism under U.S. hegemony. This inaccuracy will have to be taken into account.[4]

We avoid the congenital distortions of narrowly monetarist analyses, such as the idea that the crisis of imperialism is essentially a monetary crisis, or that its solution lies in the choice of one of the now innumerable proposals for a new international monetary system. Such proposals are only variations on a compromise between the American, Japanese and European bourgeoisies, with their dominated classes and the peoples of the Third World bearing the cost. Such proposals, such compromises are no longer relevant. The parties involved are prisoners. Other forces have come into play, and would have to be eliminated before compromises of this sort could be achieved. But unfortunately for the rulers of this world, there is no way to eliminate the rising forces of history, not even by pretending they do not exist.

7. Uncontested Hegemony: From Bretton Woods to the Gold Pool, 1945-60

The end of the nineteenth century was the era of British hegemony. During this period, marked as it was by direct colonialism and the consequent partition of the world between the various colonial powers, the world market played a far less important role than it does today. The development of the capitalist world market following the First World War led to the setting up of the first real international monetary system. It was based on gold and, above all, on the pound sterling. The crisis in the 1930s was forcible confirmation of the marked decline of British hegemony since 1918. The international monetary system changed, quite naturally, into a more symmetrical system based mainly on gold and reflecting the relative positions of the great capitalist powers.

In fact, uncontested British hegemony was being replaced by a British hegemony under attack.[5] Gold became the key standard during the 1930s because the pound could no longer fill the part, and the dollar could not yet do so in its place; because no imperialist power could lay down the law to all the others.

The Second World War accomplished what the First had failed to: American hegemony replaced British hegemony. This American hegemony, which was triumphant during the 1950s, and then challenged during the 1960s, is now precarious, and the international monetary system faces problems analogous to the ones it lived through forty years ago.

The formation of American monetary hegemony warrants detailed examination. Describing its mechanisms is one thing; showing that the monetary crisis it led to resulted not from some technical monetary error but from an overall crisis of imperialism under American hegemony is quite another.

As we have said, the post-war international monetary system confirmed a new balance of forces, a new structure of imperialism. The Bretton Woods Agreements were signed and drawn up under threat, in the middle of the War (in 1944) at a time when part of Europe was still occupied by the Nazis. There were two conflicting views within the Allied camp: Keynes's British standpoint and White's American one. Keynes's proposals for the post-war period included an international monetary institution (the International Monetary Fund) empowered to create a specific international currency (the 'bancor') which would eventually become the main reserve currency. The war loans owed by countries such as Britain would thus have been payable in bancors, in other words, in a currency over which they would have at least some control, rather than in a national currency such as the dollar, over which they would have no control.

The U.S. imposed the second solution (White's) by threatening not to grant any further credits to the Allies' war effort: Keynes had to give in.[6]

The I.M.F., the central institution of the Bretton Woods monetary system, became a body which could only lend money it had itself borrowed elsewhere. And who could lend to the I.M.F. at the time? Only the United States, which thus ensured its own control over the creation of international credits.

Furthermore, the U.S. imposed its right to veto I.M.F. decisions and insisted that only those countries whose adherence to the principles and practices of free trade was guaranteed by participation in G.A.T.T. (the General Agreement on Tariffs and Trade) and the World Bank could borrow from the I.M.F. In fact, thanks to its preponderant role within the I.M.F., the U.S. was in a position to formulate the guidelines of a general political economy to which all would-be borrowers from the Fund would have to conform.

What was at stake in this first post-war monetary confrontation, which at the time went unnoticed in the face of more pressing preoccupations but which was to have momentous consequences? As far as Britain was concerned, the goal was to ensure a continued possibility of drawing on credits in order to rebuild its economy, to re-establish and maintain its empire, and not to be forced into austerity by its creditors, especially the U.S.

The U.S., for its part, was convinced that Europe had to be reconstructed in order to stem the Communist 'menace' and to provide expanding markets for the American economy: the Americans had drawn the lesson from the catastrophes caused by German indebtedness between the Wars. But it was also important to the U.S. that such reconstruction should only be possible with its consent and under the conditions it laid down: in particular it was essential that too rapid growth or the re-assertion of old-style empire should not enable Europe to become once again the rival it had been during the inter-war years. Accordingly, Europe's debt had to be made payable in dollars, so that the U.S. could constantly demand repayment and so that new loans would have to be agreed to by the U.S., under the conditions it laid down. And so it was.

From 1945 to 1960, West European indebtedness to the U.S. was a sword of Damocles constantly held over the heads of Europe's rulers, who had to give in on a whole list of points in order to obtain the credits necessary for the reconstruction of their economies – or, in other words, in order to stay in power. The list, which included the eviction of the Communists from European governments at the end of the 1940s, the unequal G.A.T.T. treaties and membership of NATO, is too long for us to go through here. It is enough to point out that there were some cases in which no amount of concessions could convince the Americans to help: loans which would have enabled the Europeans to maintain their colonial sphere of influence or to transform it into a neo-colonial one were always out of the question. On the contrary, during the 1950s the U.S. by and large supported anti-colonial national fronts, especially the national bourgeoisies within such movements, in all geographical areas still dominated by European imperialism – in India, in South-East Asia, in the Middle East and in Africa. Once the colonial powers had been expelled, during which process the national bourgeoisies nearly always triumphed over their allies within the nationalist movements, the U.S. stepped in and once again the mechanisms of indebtedness ensured that these bourgeoisies stayed docile and that markets were kept open for American goods and capital – in short, that these bourgeoisies were turned into *comprador* bourgeoisies. But whilst the Third World countries incorporated into the world market never managed to regain lost ground, Europe and Japan succeeded in turning the tables; by the beginning of the 1960s the U.S. was in debt to them. How was this possible? The answer lies in the effects of the law of unequal development, which operates differently in countries dominated by imperialism and in countries which, for all their partial subordination to American hegemony, have nonetheless themselves remained secondary imperialisms benefiting from the structures of unequal exchange set up by the U.S.[7] This is a point to which we shall return.

First, however, we must stress the role of gold in the Bretton Woods system. It has been described as a system in which the dollar was 'as good as gold'. And indeed, by the end of the Second World War the U.S. held the overwhelming majority of world gold stocks (59% in 1945, 72% in 1948). At that stage the description was accurate, and it was possible to maintain strict parity between gold and the dollar: there was strict convertibility between the two international reserve instruments, and, secondarily, with the pound sterling.[8] This description of the Bretton Woods system holds true up to 1958, at which time American gold stocks were still high despite the Korean War and its inflationary consequences. But, bit by bit, during the 1960s the dollar became less and less 'as good as gold' and at the same time its role in the I.M.F. increasingly came under fire.

Is one then to say that the U.S. made a mistake at Bretton Woods by giving gold such an important role in the I.M.F.? Could it have avoided these eventual attacks on the dollar if it had been more brutal in 1944 and imposed a system based exclusively on the dollar? We do not think so. On the one hand, despite the unfavourable balance of forces, the U.S.'s allies, and especially the British, would probably not have accepted this kind of monetary system. Appearances to the contrary, the British, and the Europeans in general, did not have to give in to all American demands, since the reconstruction of the economies destroyed by the War was as essential to the U.S. as it was to Europe, and since the U.S. needed this reconstruction to take place in the context of an extension of free trade.

Furthermore, had the U.S. imposed an international monetary system based exclusively on the dollar, the monetary crisis and the challenges to the dollar's hegemony would probably have taken some other form, probably that of earlier and more intense world-wide inflation.

In other words, the specific forms taken by the international monetary system are less important than the balance of forces they express. We can learn much from the history of these relations. At the moment the proposals for reform of the international monetary system are evolving towards some Special Drawing Rights hybrid halfway between Keynes's bancor and a system based exclusively on the dollar, which the more cynical American experts have every intention of promoting. This, too, is a point to which we shall return.

8. Hegemony Contested, 1960-68

The main currencies of the capitalist world once again became convertible – into both gold and dollars – in 1958. This measure was indispensable for free trade and the development of the world market in goods and capital: it also marked the end of the period of Japanese and European economic reconstruction.

In 1958 the U.S. registered its first balance of payments deficit since the Second World War. Far from being an aberration, this deficit was to persist and to worsen steadily right up until the present day, with the exception of a few odd years characterized by a slowing down of economic activity in the U.S., or by measures which invariably proved to have a merely temporary effect. Even in the 1960s the most alert observers realized that this chronic deficit in the American balance of payments indicated an imminent crisis of imperialism under U.S. hegemony. The origins of this deficit warrant further examination, in that they demonstrate yet again that the present crisis cannot be reduced to some mismanagement of the American economy by the U.S. Government or to some disorder in the Bretton Woods monetary system resulting from disagreements between the members of the I.M.F. On the contrary, we will show that both the U.S. and a freely consenting Europe have done everything they could to preserve the essential characteristic of the Bretton Woods system, namely the dollar's hegemonic role. It was only because such a role for the dollar had become absolutely untenable that it was finally dropped on 15 August 1971. There were and still are several different causes of the American balance of payments deficit; the articulation of these causes reveals the structure of the specific form of imperialism established during the 1950s.

The first point is that, by the late 1950s, the U.S.'s trade surplus with what (as a useful shorthand) we may call the 'Second World' – Europe and Japan – had started to dwindle steadily due to the reconstruction of the latter's economy. A whole range of goods which the 'Second World' had had to import from the U.S. after the war (intermediary goods, consumer durables, everyday capital goods) were gradually coming to be produced on the spot, and at lower prices thanks to cheaper labour. At the same time, a whole range of goods which the Third World had been importing from the U.S. was gradually replaced by goods imported from the 'Second World'.

The creation of the Common Market also contributed to this evolution, even if only marginally. The tariff barriers the Market erected around itself were not particularly rigorous, especially when compared to American tariff barriers affecting industrial products. The U.S. therefore encouraged the setting up of this very modestly protectionist market which suited the scale of American business operations rather nicely and, most important, which constituted a firm guarantee against any eventual return to all-out protectionism. It was only later, when the E.E.C.'s very effective protectionist Common Agricultural Policy was established, and when attempts were made to enlarge the Community to include certain Mediterranean countries, that the E.E.C. really clashed with American interests. When this happened, the Americans had no hesitation either about informing the Europeans of their dissatisfaction or about acting on it. Negotiations between the E.E.C. and the Mediterranean countries are still blocked, and the U.S. makes no bones either about the fact that, with British help, it has succeeded in putting some serious dents in E.E.C. agricultural policy, nor about its intentions to complete the job during the current G.A.T.T. negotiations.[9]

Secondly, the task of maintaining the world capitalist order was more and more falling exclusively on the shoulders of the United States, inasmuch as the old colonial powers had withdrawn, or were in the process of doing so, to make way for American dominated neo-colonialism. Of course, military or para-military aid and economic aid were compensated for by the substantial profits the U.S. was drawing in from the Third World. But these were not really enough, even before the Vietnam War reached significant proportions.

Thirdly, the structures of unequal exchange set up by the U.S. following the Second World War were no longer serving the interests of their creators. Since 1945 the United States had been the world's largest producer and consumer of raw materials. Furthermore, as American reserves fell behind the rate of consumption, the U.S. naturally sought to gain access to other sources, and at the lowest possible price.

The deterioration in the Third World countries' terms of trade during the 1960s has been extensively analysed. One thing emerges quite clearly: it was certainly not a question of the operation of any hypothetical 'market laws'. The United States quite definitely imposed the change. But how? Firstly, by pitting atomized producer countries against big companies which totally controlled the transformation and marketing of raw materials, and which often acted in concert. Secondly, by locking the producer countries into the 'debt trap'.[10]

The local bourgeoisies' expenditure on luxury imports, military hardware or sometimes even on badly organized attempts at industrialization soon led to a very high level of indebtedness. The resulting need for foreign currency forced them to sell off their raw materials in a competitive market, and of course the problem was compounded by the fact that all prospecting activities were financed by the U.S. mining companies' super-profits. The vicious circle of underdevelopment as an active process closed around them. The I.M.F. also played its part, by imposing draconian conditions for the renewal or extension of credits. When such measures were not enough and some regime or other stubbornly insisted on attempting to accumulate national capital or to use nationalization as a means to repay debts incurred by a previous regime, the C.I.A. was called in,

It was these structures of unequal exchange which eventually turned to the U.S.'s disadvantage. Instead of exploiting 'expensive' deposits at home, the U.S. preferred to import raw materials for which it had imposed a low price. Instead of importing raw materials from the U.S., the West European countries returned to the old pattern of drawing on Third World supplies, thereby also profiting from the structures of unequal exchange set up by the U.S.[11] This joint pillage of the Third World, which excluded any possibility of 'development', fitted quite naturally into the logic of minimizing production costs and of inter-imperialist competition. But its effect was a significant deterioration in the U.S. balance of trade.

Nonetheless, despite this deterioration, which continued throughout the 1960s, it was only in 1971 that the U.S. registered a net trade deficit. But the roots of the problem were visible at the beginning of the 1960s: the U.S. trade surplus and the profits drawn from investments abroad (in the Third World and in the extraction sector) were no longer enough to compensate for the growing cost of maintaining the American Empire and for the high level of U.S. company investment in the 'Second World' and its immediate periphery.

Choices for the 1960s

At the beginning of the 1960s, the American ruling class was thus faced with an important decision. How was it to eliminate the U.S. balance of payments deficit? Several methods were available, but they all threatened American imperialism's strategy of expansion.

The U.S. could have cut back on the ever expanding military expenditure involved in administering its empire and maintaining military bases, troops stationed abroad and aid to regimes dependent on Washington. At a time when U.S.-Soviet *detente* was still very tentative, and given that U.S. neo-colonialism had not yet consolidated its hold over the newly independent Third World, such a programme would have been suicidal and was not even envisaged. There was no way that the America of the 1960s could give the impression that it was falling back upon itself and leaving its 'allies' in the Third World to face popular 'subversion' on their own.[12] Similarly, there could be no question of dropping the Third World aid programmes, which were in fact a gigantic system of export subsidies for U.S. agriculture and industry.[13] Nevertheless, throughout the 1960s, the U.S. sought to minimise its military spending abroad, by pursuing the dialogue with the Soviet Union and by forcing Europe to partake in the cost of U.S. military bases both on the Continent and in the Third World. The attempt failed, however, notably because of the Vietnamese people's resistance.

Another possibility was unilaterally to slow down domestic economic activity, thereby cutting down on imports and building up a foreign exchange surplus, making sure that the growth rate in internal production stayed higher than that in internal consumption. This alternative was also rejected. It should be remembered that in 1960 the American economy had just gone through a severe recession, spread over several years. The rate of unemployment was almost 7%. Let us also recall that the growth rate of the American economy had been rather poor during the 1950s, apart from the boom provoked by the Korean War. Finally, let us remember the explicit challenge to the American economy thrown down by Khrushchev and the implicit challenge posed by the economic miracles of the 'Second World' (Europe and Japan). Everything, from the need to maintain political stability at home to the need to preserve economic superiority abroad, made U.S. economic growth essential. The American rulers might well have taken a leaf out of Keynes's book and repeated the declarations he made at the end of the Second World War: 'We are decided to allow the value of the pound abroad to be determined by its value at home, which will in turn be determined by our domestic policy rather than the other way around . . . The responsibility of maintaining the equilibrium of the balance of payments will thus rest largely upon the creditor nations.' This expressed the U.S.'s own intentions quite exactly.[14]

There was one other possibility; to build up a trade surplus by devaluing the dollar. But such a devaluation would have implied a very different strategy from the one the American rulers did adopt – and it would have been far less advantageous for them. In fact, one can accuse the U.S. rulers of the time of just about everything except of having made mistakes and of having adopted a strategy contrary to their own short and middle term interests.

Studies carried out in the U.S. at the end of the 1950s estimated – quite correctly – that the American trade surplus would eventually disappear due to the mechanisms we have outlined above, especially the increased competition from the 'Second World'. A sharp devaluation of the dollar might have cancelled out this tendency but it would also have carried serious disadvantages. Firstly, a weaker dollar would have made it more difficult for the American 'multinationals' to expand. True, this expansion has in practice been mainly financed by monies drawn from local financial markets by the U.S. companies, but dollar exports were nonetheless a key element in the process, especially in the early 1960s. The same studies showed that the only way to stabilize the U.S. balance of payments in the long term was to promote the most rapid possible expansion of the multinationals and to rely on the profits which these firms would eventually transfer back to the U.S., rather than on an inevitably diminishing trade surplus. The annual profits of the previous generation of multinational subsidiaries implanted in the Third World – most notably in Latin America – already exceeded by far the new investments which could profitably be made there. The studies suggested that the same mechanism could well be set up in Europe. And in fact U.S. firms found that because of the low cost of European labour, it was far more efficient and profitable to compete with European firms on their home ground – in Europe itself – than by exporting from the U.S., even given a devalued dollar.[15]

They therefore had to choose between a foreign investment strategy based on a strong dollar, the effects of which have, as it turned out, been very marked, and an export strategy based on a weak dollar. The choice made was also, more fundamentally, an attempt to maintain and intensify the international division of labour, allowing the U.S. to preserve its monopoly over the fields in which it was gradually specializing, namely the production of goods with a high technological content, and leaving the 'Second' and Third World economies to share out between themselves the production of 'ordinary' goods in an increasingly competitive market. The alternative would have meant the United States losing its technological quasi-monopoly, making it possible for a new international division of labour to be set up, in which the 'Second World' would have been both the equal and the rival of the U.S.[16] A strong dollar guaranteed that wages in the States would continue to be significantly higher than in other countries and thus that the U.S. would remain a 'pilot' market, in which technological innovation would be more encouraged than elsewhere. Conversely, the quasi-monopoly over high technology goods made it possible to set the international price levels for such goods arbitrarily high, thereby ensuring better wages in the U.S. It would seem that, fundamentally, the choice in question was imposed by the specific nature of class alliances in the U.S. and was quite in keeping with the responses of imperialism as described by Lenin.

Above all, a devaluation of the dollar would have reopened the whole issue of a reform of the international monetary system ten years before it was necessary. Understandably, America's rulers would not even hear of such a thing. After all, it was precisely the myth of the 'good as gold' dollar which gave them the option to take the course they did at the beginning of the 1960s. The European rulers were well aware of the fact, and it must have chafed, especially when they were forced to impose austerity programmes which could have cost them their power; when, during the 1950s, they repeatedly had to devalue their currencies; or when they had to cut back on military expenditure and give up on wars which were no more, if no less, lost in advance than the one in Vietnam. Unlike their colleagues across the Atlantic, they had no choice but to stabilize their balance of payments; the alternative was to sink into debt and to fall into the tender mercies of the U.S. Thanks to the Bretton Woods Agreements, the U.S. rulers faced no such obligations and could carry on as before. On the contrary, without renouncing any of its aims, the U.S. set out to get the rest of the world to tolerate and accept the existence of a U.S. balance of payments deficit. The strategy was doubtless correct, since the rest of the world did, in fact, put up with it.

Willing Victims of the Swindle

More specifically, it was because the U.S. had no intention of modifying a balance of payments deficit which fitted in with its strategy of international expansion that it imposed the setting up of the Gold Pool. The Gold Pool's function was to ensure that the gold parity of the dollar would be supported by the central banks, the European ones mainly, who would thus have to sell their gold on the market as the occasion demanded. As a result the European central banks' stocks of gold dwindled. The price of gold was kept artificially low at a time when the overall price of goods was rising. The dollar thus stayed as good as gold and the U.S. was freed from the threat of having to support the gold parity of the dollar all by itself, or of seeing gold overtake the dollar as an international reserve instrument, which remained a theoretical possibility in the framework of the Bretton Woods Agreements. The U.S. spared no efforts in its campaign to impose and maintain the Gold Pool, thereby effectively ensuring that it could continue to operate its chronic balance of payments deficit whilst retaining the role of international reserve instrument for the dollar. From threats and deceptions to sleight of hand and pseudo-theoretical arguments, the Americans made use of any and every means available to pull off what must surely be one of the most astounding con-tricks of our time.

First, the threats: The U.S. made it quite clear to its 'allies' in the 'Group of Twenty' that any attempts to exchange the surplus of dollars, which was beginning to accumulate in the various central banks, for gold held in U.S. federal reserves would be taken as an expression of hostility towards the United States.[17] There was no shortage of ways of bringing pressure to bear on the relevant parties, especially Britain and West Germany. Only Gaullist France opposed the Americans, by buying gold and quitting the Gold Pool in 1967. Despite appearances, French opposition was actually quite timid and remained fairly limited, in monetary matters as in other areas. It is true that French foreign policy had some 'positive aspects', but its inconsistency becomes obvious the moment, for instance, one examines its attitudes concerning raw materials. Even then, it was clear that increasing dependence on Third World supplies meant that the French economy was also increasingly dependent on the United States, the only country which could ensure the security of these supplies. Furthermore, if Gaullism had really been a coherent and positive programme, it would have had to draw on a much higher level of popular support than its class nature allowed it to, given the internal consequences which would have ensued. It is not by chance that the beginning of the end for Gaullist foreign policy was the Paris Uprising of May 1968.

Pseudo-theoretical arguments next: The American experts worked hard to justify the thesis that the rapid growth of world trade and investment – which was directly linked to the 'universally beneficial' development of free trade – made the creation of substantial reserves of international liquidities essential, since world gold stocks could not meet the demands of the role.[18] The argument went that, although a return to the gold standard, as recommended by Rueff and taken up by de Gaulle in his famous denunciation of the U.S. balance of payments deficit, would probably have been fairer, it would also have been dangerous for everybody, in that it would probably have triggered off a world recession. Gold was thus no longer to be taken as a reference point and the U.S. would continue to put up with its balance of payments deficit despite the disadvantages which it incurred as a result. The U.S. balance of payments deficit had supposedly become essential to the general well-being.

The American arguments did seem to carry some weight, on the surface at least. In the world of imperialism it is quite true that the creation of international liquidities is essential to the expansion of world trade and international investment. But there is nothing to show that during the 1960s existing liquidities were inadequate. Indeed, the very opposite is indicated by the prevalence of worldwide inflation and phenomenal levels of indebtedness during the period, resulting in a situation which makes a crash of 1929 proportions quite plausible.

Even if these liquidities had proved insufficient, why not revalue gold? True, this might have conferred some unfair advantage on the U.S.S.R. and South Africa, but ways of coping with such minor problems could easily have been devised. The real issue was that such a solution would have implied a decline in American hegemony, which neither the U.S. nor even Europe and Japan were really prepared to countenance.

American propaganda continued to denounce gold as a 'barbarous relic'. But the real target was the principle of economic symmetry, of equal rights and duties concerning the balance of payments, which was an inherent feature of the gold standard,[19] and which is still the bugbear of the Americans today.

Sleight of hand: The American Government made some pretence of intending to limit the U.S. balance of payments deficit, in order to stem speculative pressures on the dollar and the pound, to relieve German fears and to undermine French arguments in favour of a return to the gold standard. The Government adopted a series of measures aimed at limiting the flow of American foreign investment; the U.S. administration began by appealing for self-discipline by U.S. firms, then imposed more specific constraints on the flow of U.S. capital going abroad. What more could one ask? In fact, the programme of 'voluntary restrictions' was full of carefully implanted loopholes, and had little or no effect. As for the imposed restrictions, they were only applied after the Euro-dollar market had been set up, so that American firms could still pursue their foreign expansion programmes whilst cutting back on the transfer of dollars from the U.S.[20]

This Euro-dollar market underwent fantastic expansion in the late 1960s. The subject warrants closer examination: it has played a fundamental role in both the workings of the international monetary system and its malfunction.

The European central banks held growing dollar surpluses which the United States had forbidden them to convert into gold. If that was the case, why not use these 'good as gold' dollars as a monetary base, and lend them out? This is precisely what the U.S. Government persuaded the banks to do; it had no difficulty at all in convincing the British, who were in any case looking for a way of giving a boost to the City, where operations in sterling were running down. Thanks to their size and financial capacities, American firms in Europe gained privileged access to this market, and drew upon it considerably.

However the most important factor was that the growth of this market led the European banks to accept increases in their dollar holdings; they had finally found a use for all those dollars. The U.S. balance of payments deficit might be growing, the central banks' dollar reserves might be quite excessive, but the profits being made on the Euro-dollar market by European financial circles were a powerful anaesthetic.

It was this anaesthetic which enabled the United States to get the European countries to accept the loss of control over their own monetary policy which the growth of the Euro-dollar market implied. A government could put a squeeze on credit but it could not prevent the bigger firms and banks drawing on the Euro-dollar market. National money suppliers were thus quite absurdly augmented by the accumulated deficit of the American balance of payments; any increase in the U.S. deficit had direct inflationary effects in Europe. Any national policy aiming to control the interest rate had great holes knocked in it by a Euro-dollar market whose interest rate was determined by the increase in the American deficit and by the level of interest prevailing in the U.S.

In the end, thanks to the growth of this market, the U.S. managed, from 1965 onwards, to get the Europeans and Japanese to accept a massive increase in its indebtedness (see Figures II.1 and II.2).[21] It was thus because of the sheer volume of the American debt that the European states came to oppose, or at least to share in the disadvantages of, any devaluation of the dollar, which had by then become a devaluation of their credit with the United States. It was through this mechanism that the U.S. turned the weakness of the dollar into an asset which it did not hesitate to use.

And finally, a bit of trickery: Another pseudo-theoretical argument 'observed' that the U.S. was playing the role of international savings bank in the world economy.[22] The fact that the European banks had agreed to keep their dollars and loan them out rather than convert them into their own local currencies apparently meant that they were willing to lend these dollars to the U.S. on a short-term basis. The U.S. then transformed these short-term credits into long-term loans to the European countries, through the American companies' foreign investment schemes. The U.S. could therefore claim to be performing the conversion of short-term into long-term loans just like a bank. Since a bank is not considered to be in deficit when it borrows short and lends long – on the contrary, this is its normal way of proceeding – the United States should not be considered to be in deficit either. Of course, this bizarre argument only made any sort of sense because of the ban on converting central bank dollar holdings into gold. But it was nonetheless on the basis of such arguments that the U.S. Government could decree that the traditional measure of a balance of payments deficit, namely the net liquidity balance, was an inadequate yardstick given the special role played by the United States in the world economy. Such arguments also enabled the U.S. administration to substitute for the traditional yardstick a 'balance of official transactions', which took no account of any increases in dollar holdings abroad apart from those of the central banks. The Euro-dollar market could thus create more and more money without in any way affecting the American balance of payments. This particular bit of humbug gave rise to endless meaningless debate, whose only role was to camouflage the real issues at stake.[23]

Figure II.1 The Fantastic Growth of the U.S. Debt[21]

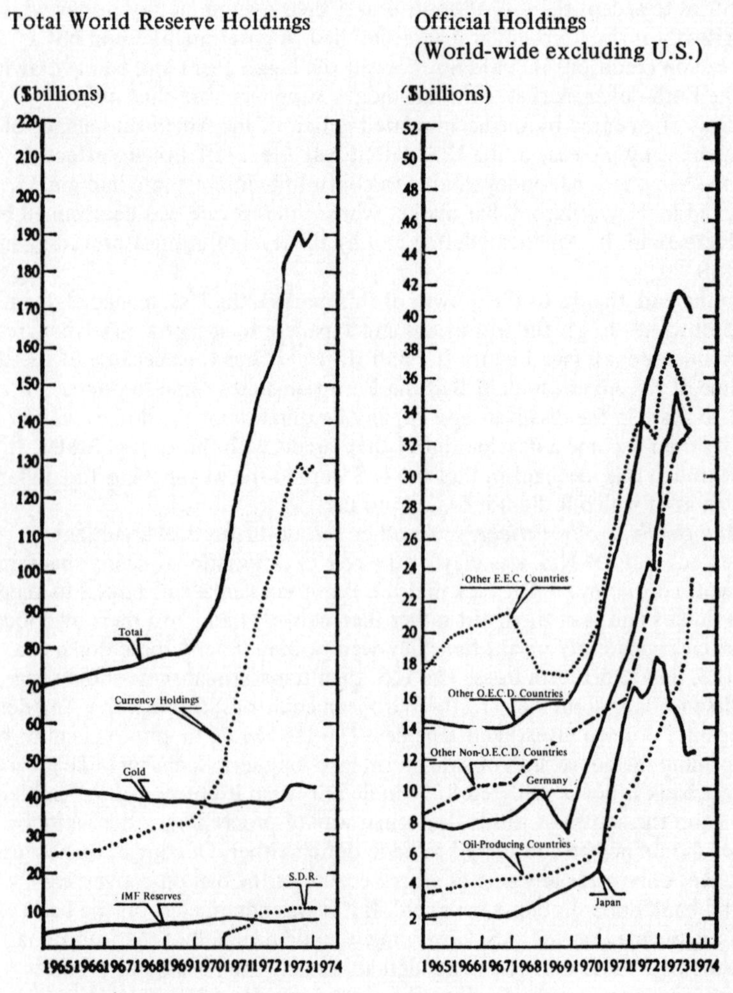

Source: O.E.C.D.

Figure II.2 The Development of the Euro-Dollar Market
Foreign Currency Commitments of the Banks of the 8 European Countries reporting to the Bank for International Settlements.

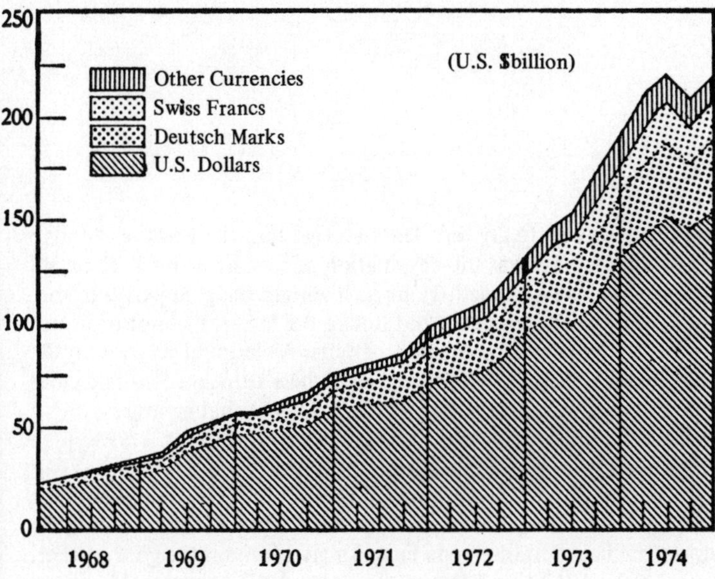

Source: Bank for International Settlements

9. The Second U.S. Line of Defence 1971-75

What had to happen eventually did. The first sign that the Bretton Woods system was on its last legs was the devaluation of sterling in 1967. Poor old Britain had been exhausting itself trying to maintain the gold parity of the pound during the last fifteen years, but unlike the U.S. it had not been allowed to run up balance of payments deficits. A victim of its own myths of imperial greatness, Britain fell prey to an endless stop-go economic cycle. In the hope of hanging on to the last few remnants of that greatness, the country's leaders clung desperately to America's apron strings, a costly policy which eventually proved disastrous.[24]

Since the pound was no longer 'as good as gold', it seemed unlikely that the dollar would remain so. Speculation hit the dollar violently, forcing the European central banks to intervene increasingly often on the gold market, in keeping with the 1961 Good Pool agreements. As European gold reserves melted away, the central banks became increasingly impatient, especially given that a particularly lax monetary policy was being applied in the U.S., due to the Vietnam War and the imminent 1968 elections. France discreetly pulled out of the Gold Pool in 1967. In March 1968, at a meeting in Washington, the governors of the central banks decided to do away with it altogether.[25]

One might have expected that the Europeans, exasperated as they were by U.S. monetary policy, would eventually have clamped down by imposing some degree of financial rigour on the U.S. or by initiating a reform of the international monetary system in order to limit the exorbitant privileges granted to the U.S. in 1944. They did nothing of the sort. The Gold Pool was merely replaced by a split gold market; all dealings in gold between central banks were to be conducted at the ridiculously low fixed price of $35 an ounce and there was to be no interconnection between such dealings and the state of the free market for gold. Since, as a result, speculation was temporarily diverted into the free market, the European central banks were persuaded not to turn their dollars into gold and the U.S. was allowed to pursue a policy leading to a systematic deficit in its balance of payments.[26]

In 1969, the recession in America stabilized this deficit. But as the 1972 presidential elections approached, the need for some sort of economic boost became pressing. The real meaning of the devaluation of the pound and the setting up of a split market in gold emerged and the Bretton Woods system finally collapsed when, on 15 August 1971, Nixon announced, amongst other things, that the dollar was no longer to be convertible into gold.

It matters little whether the measure in question was taken as a response to the first trade deficit registered by the U.S. since 1893, or whether it was necessary because of the massive speculation in dollars resulting from the movements of floating capital, which could find better interest rates in a Europe committed to fighting inflation than in a U.S. busily bolstering up its economy for the election, or whether it was provoked by the German central bank's decision to float the mark rather than see its reserves being frittered away in the effort to maintain the dollar/mark parity.[27]

The most important thing about this date (15 August 1971) is that it can be considered as the starting point for a second phase in a worsening crisis of imperialism, whose origins go back to the early 1960s.[28] The fundamental difference between the 1960-71 period and this second phase was that in the latter the U.S. could no longer control growing contradictions. Whereas, before, the U.S. could fall back on the letter of the *status quo* in order to defend the advantages it had obtained, after 1971 it had no choice but to go on the offensive in an open and brutal attempt to conserve these advantages. Obviously the dollar could not play one and the same role during two such different periods. During the first period, the idea was to preserve the dollar's gold parity for as long as possible, without giving up the aim of expanding U.S. imperialism economically; in other words the U.S. hoped to maintain the key features of the Bretton Woods system, even if this meant gradually distorting it.

During the second phase, once it had become clear that this was no longer possible, the objective was to promote a new international monetary system which would confer the same type of advantages on the U.S. as the old one.[29] But how could this be done, given the evolution of the balance of forces in the world scene? After all, if one compares the state of this balance of forces in 1944 and in 1971 or 1975, it immediately becomes apparent that American hegemony has declined. The difference was that, unlike the 1960s, American imperialism, in real danger for once, was prepared to play its highest cards. And as it turned out, the European bourgeoisie, undermined as it was by its own internal quarrels, proved incapable of seeking independence.

The American Counter-Offensive

As we have seen, the contradictions of imperialism which manifested themselves during the 1960s finally crystallized into open crisis during the 1970s. Without going into details, let us stress that one should not overestimate the role played by inter-imperialist conflicts in this evolution. Such conflicts only develop within a context framed by the class struggle and the liberation struggles of the dominated peoples. The eventually victorious resistance of the Vietnamese and the rising wave of class struggle in the imperialist centres, epitomised by May 1968, were crucial turning points in the history of imperialism in crisis. Clearly, similar turning points will also determine the final outcome.

Let us recall the main lines of the American counter-offensive. The starting point was the initiation of an economic and political understanding with the Soviet Union, allowing the U.S. to take various initiatives – in Europe, in Asia, in the Middle East – without running the risk of the other super-power taking advantage of such moves.

The second element in this strategy was to impose various economic and political conditions upon the Europeans and Japanese, in order to ensure that the U.S. would re-establish a trade surplus: conditions such as the lowering of tariff barriers, especially in agriculture; taking a share in American military expenses; pressure on European countries to buy U.S. goods, etc.

The third element in this strategy was based on demands for the increase in oil prices that the oil producing countries had been unsuccessfully pressing for since the early 1960s. The U.S. had a manifest vested interest in the matter. Given that 'on tap' American oil and gas reserves were running out, it seemed possible that by the end of the 1970s, the U.S. would become the world's largest importer of oil; on the other hand, should the price of oil go up to about $8 a barrel, many more U.S. reserves would become commercially viable. Had oil prices remained at the 1970 level, the dollar would have been undermined by the mounting payments deficit resulting from increased oil imports. High oil prices, by contrast, would eventually enable the U.S. to re-establish its independence in energy.[30]

The increase in oil prices led to a gigantic transfer of the payments surpluses corresponding to the U.S. deficit. Nearly all the European countries and Japan went into deficit as the surpluses shifted to the OPEC nations.[31] The U.S., thanks to its diplomatic and military might, could hope that its new creditors would prove less recalcitrant than the Europeans and Japanese had eventually become.

It is also worth mentioning a fourth element in the strategy, which has a bearing in the longer term, namely the fixing of new poles of industrial development which might eventually become important markets for the U.S., and significant rivals to Europe and Japan. In this scenario, Brazil, Iran, Spain, perhaps even the Soviet Union, will at some point stage a massive investment offensive in the wealth-producing sectors on which European and Japanese capitalism depends, thereby preventing it from accumulating sufficiently to penetrate the key sectors of the future successfully. One should always bear in mind that, in the long term, the whole American strategy is based on preserving a monopoly over these key sectors. What the U.S. is really aiming at is the setting up of an international monetary system which will ensure that the parity of the dollar remains high enough to enable certain specific U.S. objectives to be realized. These objectives include continued American investment abroad and the elimination or toleration of an American payments deficit, which might otherwise necessitate a cut-back in economic activity at home or in expenditure abroad.

The dollar is thus one of the main features of the American counter-offensive and can in no way be considered a secondary aspect of this strategy. Every one of American imperialism's mechanisms for expansion is based on a strong dollar, and in the long run the U.S. will do whatever it can to re-establish that strength. But the dollar is also one of the weapons in the U.S.'s armoury. It is only one weapon amongst others – in an arsenal which includes the economic importance of U.S. imports, 'Second' and Third World dependence on American cereal and soya bean production, the U.S. nuclear umbrella and the diplomatic and military guarantees it provides for 'Second' World investments and raw material supplies – but it is nonetheless an important one, as we shall see.

The dollar's role in the American counter-offensive is thus fairly complex. Given that the pretence of a 'good as gold' dollar can no longer be kept up, the U.S. will allow the dollar to devalue at appropriate times in order to re-establish its balance of payments and eliminate corresponding demands for thoroughgoing reform of the international monetary system. Will this devaluation threaten the dollar's role as an accounting and reserve instrument and as a means of payment? The U.S. will probably consent to the setting up of other such instruments and means of payment, but will do everything in its power to ensure that these modifications do not carry any obligations which would force it to alter its economic policy at home and abroad. The U.S. has not given up any of its objectives. It has simply allowed the dollar to devalue during this phase of its counter-offensive. And it has managed to change the Bretton Woods system into a very different international monetary system which allows U.S. plans to mature with a maximum of flexibility.

One would have thought that the Europeans and the Japanese would have welcomed the successive devaluations of the dollar. After all, during the 1960s, they had constantly claimed that the dollar was overvalued. In fact, their reaction was quite different. This was due partly to the sheer scale of America's dollar debt, and partly to the increasing competitiveness of U.S. products as the dollar devalued. Each devaluation of the dollar was preceded by European and Japanese concessions aimed at avoiding it – but the concessions proved useless. And, although the competitiveness of U.S. products has not as yet struck home, due to the high rate of inflation in the U.S., the American debt has been steadily devalued along with the dollar.[32]

Monetary history since 15 August 1971 has been quite turbulent, as Figure II.3 illustrates. But one recurrent theme does emerge: the setting up of the second line of monetary defence we have described above.

This theme can be followed through three movements: December 1971-Summer 1973; Autumn 1973-September 1974; September 1974-Autumn 1975.[33] It is also worth pointing out the weaknesses of this second line of monetary defence, some of which have already manifested themselves and others of which will soon do so. Cunning as it may be, the U.S.'s counter-offensive strategy cannot resolve contradictions beyond its ambit.

The first movement, from the December 1971 devaluation of the dollar to Summer 1973, began quietly. In order to keep the devaluation to a

Figure II.3 The Rate of Change of the Main Currencies
(%age Change in terms of October 1967 Dollars)

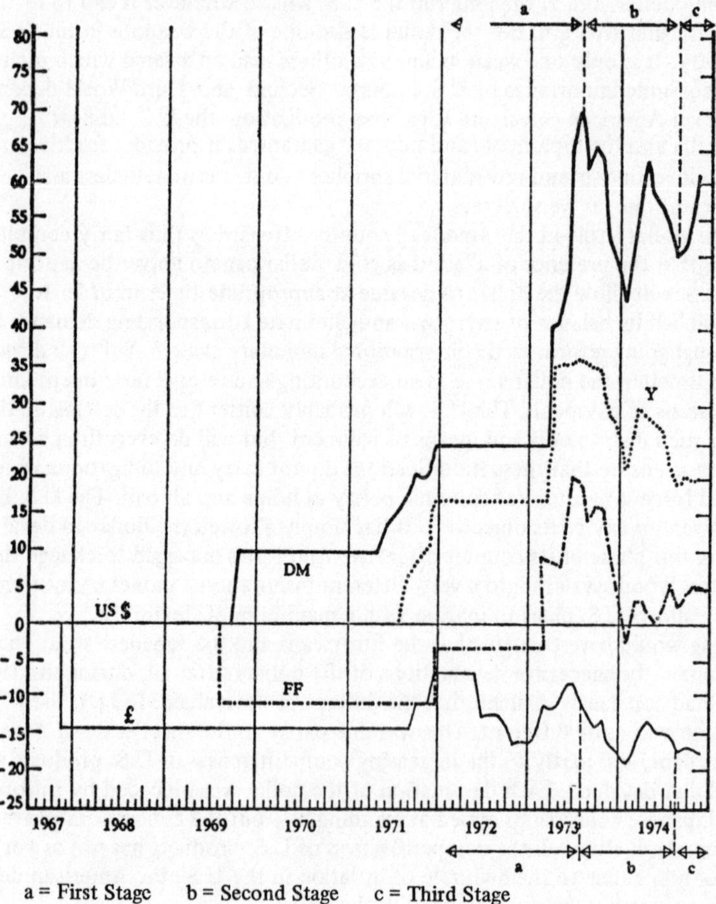

a = First Stage b = Second Stage c = Third Stage

Source: O.E.C.D.

minimum, the U.S. put heavy pressure on Germany and Japan to revalue their currencies,[34] which they did in December. The Smithsonian Institute Agreement then re-established new 'fixed but adjustable' parities; it held until March 1973.

Thanks to such readjustments, 1972 was a relatively peaceful year in which many negotiations took place. By now, everybody was convinced that reform of the international monetary system was inevitable; after a brief interlude in

Autumn 1971, parities had been fixed again, although the dollar had still not been declared convertible into gold. The formula was in any case a compromise: the French took it to imply fixed parities, the Americans took it to imply adjustable ones. The idea of a new monetary standard was discussed, and some progress made. Bit by bit, the Americans managed to calm things down and quieten suspicions. As for the Europeans, they decided to set margins of acceptable fluctuation around fixed parities as defined by the Washington agreement, in order to facilitate trade and E.E.C. agricultural policy.[35] The result was the European 'snake' which was supposed to evolve within limits set by the Smithsonian Institute Agreement. It was rightly seen as an outline for a new monetary zone, but the outline was not filled in, and nothing irreversible was set in motion.

The first signs of renewed tension came in Summer 1972. The pound, which was due to enter the European 'snake' on 1 January 1973, when Britain joined the Common Market, was still floating freely. The Europeans, and especially the E.E.C. agricultural policy, suffered in consequence, which was the desired effect. But above all, speculation hit the dollar again, as the inflationary effects of a U.S. domestic monetary policy geared to the forthcoming elections began to bite. In February 1973, the dollar was devalued by 10%. But speculation continued, reaching a peak in March 1973. As the U.S. showed no signs of intervening on the currency markets to defend the dollar, the Bundesbank had to pick up the tab.[36] On 2 March 1973 the Smithsonian Institute Agreement of December 1971 was cancelled. The situation then changed quite naturally into one where currencies were floated without any fixed parities and it was up to the various central banks to defend them. Market pressures and purely optional interventions by the central banks were allowed to determine exchange rates on a day to day basis. This system of floating exchange rates seemed quite attractive at first, since it relieved the central banks of the burdensome task of supporting fixed parities and made it unlikely that any one currency would have to bear the brunt of massive speculative pressure.

Floating Exchange Rates

The first disadvantage of a floating exchange rate system is, of course, that it interferes with the development of international trade. Under such a system, export or import commitments, especially long-term ones, carry exchange risks, which can be avoided but only at a price, as the experience of the last two years has shown.[37]

Naturally, the United States has nothing to gain in the long term from a slowing down of international trade and the growth of tariff barriers; American imperialism depends essentially on the development of free trade, as Washington is well aware. But, in the short term, floating exchange rates have the advantage of hindering those countries whose economies depend mainly on exports – Germany and Japan for instance – without carrying any corresponding risk that such countries will react against the principles of free trade.

The second disadvantage of floating exchange rates lies in the fact that countries whose currencies are *de facto* reserve currencies may run up significant deficits which will not register directly in the exchange market.[38] This obviously applies to the dollar, and is in fact one of the main reasons why the system suits the U.S. In other words, there is no longer a special *de jure* reserve currency, and the U.S. is thus relieved of its obligations, as world banker, to support the dollar. Of course, the *de facto* reserve currency continues to benefit to some extent from the special advantages of a reserve currency; it is not disposed of immediately according to market fluctuations, as happens with other currencies. Although apparently symmetrical, the system of floating exchange rates is in fact nothing of the sort.

The third disadvantage of this system lies in the absence of an international standard stable over time. Here again, international transactions and finance are disturbed as a result. The movements of the dollar and the 1973 U.S. inflation soon made it essential to define a new standard, and the argument over whether to re-adopt the gold standard or a system based on Special Drawing Rights (S.D.R.'s) once again became the key feature in monetary negotiation.[39]

Then came the October and December 1973 oil price increases. The second stage of the evolving U.S. monetary strategy had come to the fore; the key problem was now the recycling of petro-dollars.[40]

At first, the increase in oil prices had an extremely beneficial effect on the dollar; between September and December 1973, the latter gained a few points on the markets for the first time since 1971. The U.S. was less affected by the price increase than other countries and did not depend quite so heavily on imports for its energy supplies. The price increase also opened up the possibility of profitably exploiting untapped reserves in America itself, thereby allowing the U.S. to move towards an eventual independence in energy again. Under such conditions the only remaining problem would be how to strike the correct balance between the existing, dwindling but already exploited, reserves and the exploitation of the new reserves.

By contrast, Japan and all the European countries, except West Germany, suddenly found themselves operating at a deficit, and the European and Japanese currencies ceased to gain on the dollar. In short, as far as oil or other deficits were concerned, the whole O.E.C.D. was for the first time in the same boat (see Table II.1).

The new payments surpluses were abruptly transferred to the OPEC countries, or, more precisely, to those OPEC countries whose small population and high oil output made it impossible to use their surpluses to accelerate their development programmes and vastly increase their imports.

Throughout this second stage, the U.S. pushed for these surpluses to be placed either in the U.S. itself or on the Euro-dollar market, which amounted to the same thing from the point of view of the American balance of payments.[41] In this, they were successful for only a few months (see Table II.2). But they have not given up trying, for the stakes are high. Let us suppose

Table II.1
Changes in Oil Consumer Countries' Balance on Current Operations (in U.S. $ billions)

	1972	*1973*	*1974*
Canada	–0.62	–0.34	–1.25
United States	–8.55	3.04	–1.00
Japan	6.62	–0.14	–7.75
Australia	0.33	0.55	–1.75
France	0.29	–0.15	–6.20
Germany	1.04	4.73	7.00
Italy	2.04	–2.53	–8.75
U.K.	0.19	–3.71	–9.75
Belgium/Luxembourg	1.35	1.50	–0.10
Netherlands	1.05	1.79	0.85
Other E.E.C. countries	–0.21	–0.75	–1.35
Enlarged E.E.C.	5.50	1	–18.50

Source: O.E.C.D.

Table II.2
Petro-Dollar Placements in 1974 (in U.S. $ billions)

United States	
U.S. Treasury Bonds	6
Money market and bank deposits	4
Equities and securities	1
Total	11
Eurocurrency Market Placements	
London	13
Others	8
Total	21
Total U.S. and Eurocurrency	32
Britain	
Bank deposits and Treasury Bonds	6
Equities and securities	2
Total	8
Other Industrialized Countries	
Loans to private companies and shareholdings in Europe and Japan	9
Loans to public institutions in Europe, Canada and Japan	5
Others	2.5
Total	16.5
World Bank and I.M.F.	3.5
Total	60

for a moment that the petro-dollars were automatically placed in the U.S. The U.S. would then be saddled with a permanent and growing debt to the oil surplus countries. But although it would have to pay the interest on such a debt, it would be in a strong position to negotiate the value of the balance with the OPEC countries, and above all, it would never really be called upon to repay the debt in question.

What would happen to all the dollars circulating round the world under such conditions? The answer is that, having passed through Europe and Japan, and then through the OPEC countries, they would end up back in the U.S. And these dollars would only re-emerge from the American banks on America's terms and as a result of America's decisions.[42] The U.S. would then be in a position to put the finishing touches to a new international monetary system by resolving the only remaining problem posed by the floating exchange rate system, namely the definition of a monetary standard.[43]

In the long term, given that the bulk of petro-dollars were being recycled through U.S. or U.S.-controlled financial institutions, the dollar, having once again become a stable currency, could itself play the role of international monetary standard. Under such conditions and given normal growth, the Europeans and the Japanese would need to borrow from these institutions in order to balance their payments. This would probably enable the U.S. to extract important commercial concessions and thus to re-establish the American trading surplus. Also, in the long term, the U.S. could even become an oil exporter rather than an importer, as long as the floor price was guaranteed.

That petro-dollars should be recycled through the U.S. and that the floor price for oil should remain high were thus absolutely vital for U.S. imperialism These were the two main goals of Dr Kissinger's International Energy Agency.[4] Once achieved, the dollar could again become the only international reserve currency, with all the advantages that that implies. It might even regain its convertibility into gold. But such a return to a modified Bretton Woods system was quite impossible as long as the two above-mentioned conditions were not met. In the meantime, the most urgent task was to prevent the monetary instability inherent in the floating exchange rate system from having unfortunate consequences, such as leading to the definition of a new monetary standard which would gradually take over the role of international reserve currency and means of payment, the outcome of which would not be controlled by the U.S. If that happened, both the internal and the external growth of the American economy would be bound by the constraints of its balance of payments.

There was thus never any question of the U.S. accepting a return to the gold standard. None of the apparent concessions made under German or French pressure permitted such an irreversible and, as far as the U.S. was concerned, irrevocably damaging step to be taken. U.S. strategy has, on the contrary, been concentrated on promoting the use of Special Drawing Rights.

Special Drawing Rights

The Special Drawing Rights have a long history, which goes back to Keynes's proposals concerning the bancor and Triffin's suggestions in the early 1960s. The idea is quite simple. An international central bank, controlled by the main monetary powers, is empowered to create international liquidities. S.D.R.s are issued when the central body, in this case the I.M.F., votes to do so. In principle, the S.D.R.s thus granted are allocated proportionally to the quotas of gold the various countries involved contributed to the I.M.F. in 1945, when it was first set up. Any change in these allocations cannot be more than temporary and must be decided by a vote of the I.M.F.

The creation and attribution of S.D.R.s may seem fairly democratic – even if it does apply only to a small group of countries – but this impression is in fact belied by the preponderant importance of the U.S.'s contribution to the I.M.F.[45] Indeed, the U.S. was able to use S.D.R.s to grant itself loans in order to support the dollar between 1970 and 1974.[46] Each of these loans, each issue of S.D.R.s, was opposed by all the European countries – except Britain, which benefited considerably from special loans – but in the end all the loans were agreed to, under American pressure.

Until 1971, the S.D.R.s played only a subsidiary role in the international monetary system. Furthermore, their value was defined in gold, through the intermediary of the dollar.

The dollar's inconvertibility into gold thus raised the whole question of the value of the S.D.R.s, as well as the associated question of the monetary basis for S.D.R.s. There was no longer any guarantee that S.D.R.s would not be issued excessively; in which case many of the sanctions and inducements which encourage nations to reduce a payments deficit would no longer be applicable and world inflation would definitely accelerate.

This question, which is at the heart of the current debates concerning the international monetary system, was not resolved by the 30 June 1974 agreements, which defined the value of S.D.R.s in terms of a basket of 16 different national currencies.[47]

Defined as above, S.D.R.s could play the role of a monetary standard which would be more stable over time than the dollar, since their value would also be linked to that of the stronger currencies. In fact, for certain contractual agreements, they would be preferable to the dollar, in that such agreements would be partly protected against further devaluation of the dollar. The recent decision of the OPEC countries to set the price of oil in S.D.R.s illustrates the point.

S.D.R.s could thus take over the role of international reserve currency and means of payment for transactions between central banks, gradually replacing the dollar: this would of course depend on the central banks' ability to unload their existing dollar holdings.

But all this presupposes the elimination of the American balance of payments deficit. The new definition of S.D.R.s clearly indicates that the U.S. has no such intentions. As formulated, the S.D.R.s can in no way play the part of reserve currency or means of payment as far as private agents are concerned. Such agents will continue to use the dollar, and, to a lesser extent, the mark and the Swiss franc in their operations. The dollar thus remains *de facto* the main international reserve currency, and the U.S. has nothing to fear from the operation of the exchange market other than some devaluation of the dollar. Effectively, this has been made possible by the new definition of S.D.R.s.

Should it become desirable to avoid a devaluation of the dollar or to increase the dollar reserves of central banks overseas, these objectives could be achieved by increasing the issue of S.D.R.s. This is precisely what the U.S. is demanding; the U.S. would take a lion's share of such new issues – and the way the I.M.F. is set up makes such a scenario quite feasible.

There have been many monetary swindles but they have all had one thing in common – sheer scale. One only has to think of what the U.S. has obtained in the way of concessions from the Europeans since 1971, in exchange for a semblance of symmetry – the S.D.R.s are after all defined in terms of a basket of currencies rather than just in terms of the dollar – a semblance which is, in any case, belied by the importance of the dollar in the basket and by the U.S.'s right of veto over the I.M.F.! The I.M.F. has taken upon itself the role of a sovereign body and creates paper money based on nothing more than what confidence one may have in such a sacred pseudo-international institution.

True, the U.S. has had to concede that the dollar can no longer play the role allocated to it by the Bretton Woods system. But so what? The Federal Reserve Bank's total sovereignty over the creation of dollars is now no longer even limited by the linkage with gold. The U.S. also enjoys a new sovereignty – shared only slightly with other members of the I.M.F. – over the creation of S.D.R.s.

The swindle becomes manifest when one looks carefully at the inherent limits of the S.D.R.s as a monetary standard. An S.D.R. is only worth what the basket of currencies which go to make it up are worth, and that depends on the monetary policies of the Group of Twenty. In an international monetary system characterized by the absence of a standard stable over time, all international placements, notably those of the oil producing countries, melt away with inflation.

The situation would have been quite different had the S.D.R.s been defined in terms of gold. But the U.S. made it quite clear that that was out of the question. Things would also be different if the OPEC countries were to require payment in gold. But again, the U.S. has given everybody to understand that such a demand would constitute a *casus belli.* The indirect monetary imperialism of the post-war era has been replaced by direct political intervention within the I.M.F. and by monetary confrontation between members of the I.M.F. and other countries; this transition from implicit control to an attempt at explicit control is one more sign of the seriousness of the crisis.

Can all this go on? Clearly not, and the American rulers are well aware of the fact. But as far as the U.S. authorities are concerned, it is only a question of gaining enough time to resolve as advantageously as possible the problems posed by the trade balanace and the recycling of petro-dollars. The S.D.R. is the best temporary solution they could come up with.

American tactics would thus seem to have attained a certain coherence during 1974 and 1975. These two years were relatively quiet ones on the international monetary scene, for two main reasons: world inflation slowed down as a result of the deflationist measures taken by the industrialized countries, and the devaluation of the dollar was limited by the American recession and by the fact that the petro-dollars were transferred mainly to the U.S.

The dangers resulting from the rise of unemployment in the capitalist world, and the imminence of the U.S. elections [1976] will soon make some renewed expansion essential, and this will raise the key problems all over again, including world inflation, the price of oil, the recycling of petro-dollars, the devaluation of the dollar and the international monetary system. The confrontations among imperialist countries themselves and between imperialist countries and the raw material producing countries are far from over. And as the working classes tire of paying for a crisis for which they bear no responsibility, there is every chance that we will see a rising tide of radical struggle.

Postscript, August 1979

The European Monetary System and the Dollar's Second Line of Defence

In January 1976, following the Jamaica Agreements, Special Drawing Rights (S.D.R.s) became the main *de jure* international reserve instrument, but the dollar was allowed to remain the main *de facto* reserve currency. The floating exchange rate system was formalized and various measures taken to minimize the role of gold in the international monetary system. It was agreed that no country would fix its currency's gold parity, and the International Monetary Fund's stocks of gold were released on the free market.[48] These Agreements, which amounted to the first fundamental change in the rules of the international monetary system since Bretton Woods in 1944, effectively represented an almost total victory for the American approach, as outlined earlier in this book. Then came Watergate followed by Carter's weak presidency; three years of relatively expansionist U.S. domestic economic strategy, combined with a rather shaky foreign policy and the failure of all attempts to establish U.S. independence in energy matters. The dollar has continued to fall steadily against stronger currencies. Given all this, it may seem surprising to us today, in 1979, that the U.S.'s partners and competitors ever consented to the Jamaica Agreements.

But one should recall the situation as it was immediately after the 1973 oil price hike. The United States was (and despite its misadventures still is) far less dependent on the outside world for its energy requirements than either Europe or Japan. The oil price hike was supposedly going to make it feasible to begin the exploitation of abundant untapped energy reserves within the U.S. itself, thereby eventually ensuring American independence in energy matters. Furthermore, the struggle against inflation had produced results in the U.S. And there was no guarantee that Europe and Japan would be able to repair the damage done to their balance of payments. In short, West Germany and Japan expected the U.S. payments deficit to remain at a reasonable level and believed that the dollar would remain fairly stable against the mark and the yen. In this context, the Jamaica Agreements did have something to offer. They would increase international liquidity to the level required in order to pay for oil without choking the Western economies – in other words, the oil would be paid for in paper money. The main point, however, was that it was clear that only the U.S. was capable of directing the resistance to what was seen as a general Third World economic offensive, compounded by an upsurge of popular movements in Southern Europe. The Western bourgeoisie felt very strongly that this was no time to break ranks.

As it happened, things turned out rather differently. The rate at which existing 'on stream' U.S. energy resources were being exhausted was much higher than had been thought. The untapped reserves still proved too costly to exploit. Except in armaments, West Germany and Japan were far more successful than the U.S. in penetrating the OPEC markets. Solid German and Japanese surpluses were being counterbalanced by a record U.S. balance of payments deficit. Carter seemed incapable of 'setting his own house in order' On the contrary, his efforts at reducing the balance of payments deficit seemed to consist mainly of putting pressure on Germany and Japan to reduce their trade surpluses: 'self-limitation' trade agreements were imposed on Japan in 1976 and 1977, efforts were made to sabotage the sale of German nuclear reactors to Brazil, and the neutron bomb project was abandoned reminding Germany that it might one day find itself facing the U.S.S.R. alone, etc. The policy of 'benign neglect' *vis-a-vis* the dollar was continued, in keeping with this approach.

The German and Japanese leaders thus found themselves facing the following choices. They could either support the dollar through massive purchases or let their own currencies be revalued against the dollar or prevent such a revaluation by giving a boost to demand in their own economies.

The first of these policies had already shown itself to be ineffective. The countries concerned would merely find themselves accumulating rapidly depreciating dollars without in any way exercising pressure on the U.S. So in Summer 1977, the second policy was adopted, not without reservations since it tended to reduce the profit margins of export-based companies, even when salary increases were held down. Exports did in fact decline and there was reason to fear that they might fall dramatically. Even more worrying, especially in Europe and Japan, was the prospect that the continued depreciation of the dollar would trigger off a crisis of confidence, perhaps leading to the sort of international financial panic which had been so narrowly avoided in 1974 when the Herstatt bank folded.

The third policy was the one Carter tried to impose on West Germany and Japan. It, too, aroused anxieties outside the U.S. The German and Japanese leaders were well aware that an economic upturn in their countries – and hence throughout the world – would give new impetus to inflation and would cause the sort of increasing tension on the oil markets which only Washington would be able to control. Everyone realized that the stability and good behaviour of Iran and Saudi Arabia did not depend on Tokyo or Bonn.

The consensus of opinion was that Carter was trying to compensate for the shakiness of the U.S. economy by forcing West Germany and Japan to adopt policies which would not only put them at a disadvantage but might also threaten the relative stability in international relations which the capitalist world had managed to establish over the previous two years.

This is the context in which we must situate the creation in 1979 of a new European Monetary System (E.M.S.), an event which has been presented as a major change in the evolution of the international monetary system, and one which represents a significant shift in the relations between the U.S. and Europe.

The Acceptance of the German Approach in Europe

The intra-European economic and political aims of those who launched the new system are fairly clear.[49] For West Germany, the main point was to establish an economic zone in which German exports would no longer be threatened by the strength of the mark against currencies which tended to align themselves with the dollar.[50] This simple objective was worth paying for, especially since such payment would take the form of German credits to those countries whose currencies would come under attack, and that these credits would have strings attached, probably according to the usual I.M.F. pattern. In other words, through such credits, West Germany would not only protect its exports but would also gain the right to have a say in the domestic economic policies of its debtors.

Significantly, the setting up of the European Monetary System coincided with the dropping, for the time being at least, of the Brussels Commission's proposals for a concerted E.E.C. effort to boost the Community's economy. The setting up of the System was very much in keeping with the triumph in Europe of the German approach to economic policy during the present phase of the crisis. What is much less clear is what West Germany's partners had to gain, especially the French, who emerged as the System's co-sponsors.[5] Monetary devaluation, the traditional instrument used by France during the Fifties to maintain export competitiveness despite a relatively high rate of domestic inflation had become far less efficient and reliable under the floating exchange rate system.[52] But the fact remains that it is in no country's interest, not even West Germany's, as is clear from its support for the European Monetary System, to keep its currency overvalued. Furthermore, France's foreign debt is very small and she can in any case always draw on the Euro-dollar market for credit at a low rate of interest and with no strings attached. It would thus seem very unlikely that it was the promise of eventual German credits which motivated France to play a major role in setting up the European Monetary System.

For the French Government, and for the governments of the other European countries whose inflation rate is higher than Germany's and whose currencies are correspondingly weaker than the mark, participation in a European Monetary System, which means they must give a deflationary bias to their economic policy if they are to maintain their currency's parity against the mark, is essentially a political decision.[53] These governments act for a more divided ruling class and face a more aggressive working class than the German Government does. It is therefore in their interest to be able to suggest that their deflationist policies are attributable to an international monetary commitment – even better, a European commitment – rather than to their own desire to restore profits, even if it means rising unemployment. The French Government, for instance, can now find an external justification for the policies which it has been pursuing since 1976, policies it has been pushing much harder since the defeat of the left in the March 1978 elections.

Toward A Trilateral Capitalist World

All this should not, however, obscure the fact that West Germany's purposes in promoting the European Monetary System also have an extra-European dimension. Until recently, Germany has always been opposed to any developments which seemed to question the dollar's international role, as for instance in 1967, when France left the Gold Pool or in 1974-75, when France attempted to resist the institutionalization of floating exchange rates. Yet we now find Germany promoting a course of action which has been presented as a move towards a more symmetrical international monetary system.[54] It would appear that there has been a real change in the attitudes of the German leaders. They are now deeply worried about what they see as the irresponsibility and inadequacy of the U.S., not only in monetary matters but also in its capacity as leader of the Western world against the East (SALT talks, cancellation of the neutron bomb project, etc.) and against the Third World (U.S. non-intervention in Iran). So the question is what are the precise extra-European aims the German Government hopes to achieve by promoting the European Monetary System. Could it be that they intend to halt the depreciation of the dollar whether America wills it or not? At the moment, the effect the System can have on the dollar-mark parity is extremely limited. At best, speculation will tend to bear more heavily on the yen than on a German mark 'carried downwards' by weaker European currencies. Normally, only European currencies will figure in the central banks' E.M.S. interventions.

But this is not the main point. The only way the present System can affect the dollar-mark parity is through a policy of buying into dollars massively. Perhaps it would be more effective in this role than the Bundesbank by itself. But in the end it would still be Europe who met the bill; the U.S. naturally has no objection to seeing Europe bear the cost of stabilizing the dollar.

The real threat to the U.S. lies elsewhere. West Germany's interest in the present European Monetary System is mainly as a step towards a more general European monetary programme. Let us imagine a possible development. By 1982, there has been a substantial increase in the amount of European Currency Units (E.C.U.s) released, and they are playing a more significant economic role than that of simple counters. These E.C.U.s have been accumulated by the central banks of those countries with positive trade balances. The dollar is still depreciating. Why not negotiate guaranteed oil supplies in exchange for linking oil prices to the E.C.U.? Why not even offer to pay for oil in E.C.U.s? Why not start borrowing and lending in E.C.U.s? Everything would be set for the creation of a real rival to the dollar as the international reserve currency, a rival over the issue of which the U.S. would have absolutely no control. The competition between the dollar and the E.C.U. would force the U.S. to apply orthodox economic self-discipline, just as Britain was forced to by the dollar-sterling competition. The mere threat that Germany might promote such a development in the European Monetary System sets definite limits to the U.S.'s freedom of movement in monetary matters, and helps regain some of the ground that was lost at Jamaica.

Are the German leaders already aiming to set up this second stage of the European Monetary System? One should not underestimate their irritation with the present American leadership. However, it must also be said that, in the existing system, the German leaders have taken care to minimize any elements which might prefigure the development of such a second stage. During the negotiations to determine the definition of the System, they succeeded in restricting the range of possible interventions in dollars by the central banks. The E.C.U.'s role was reduced from that of a real reserve currency circulating between the European central banks, as the Brussels Commission had proposed, to that of a simple accounting unit. It was arranged that E.C.U. stocks would be held only for a given period of time and in limited quantities.

The care with which the German leaders have avoided anything which might lead to an irreversible break in their relations with the U.S. leads one to think that, far from seeking to establish an autonomous European currency which would rival the dollar, they merely hope that the European Monetary System will serve as a vague threat which will enable them to recoup some of the concessions made to the U.S. over monetary relations at Jamaica. The idea is to convince the U.S. to begin serious negotiations towards a practical trilateral administration of the world monetary system, and, more generally, of world capitalism. In fact, the present German position on monetary relations with the U.S. fits in with a long tradition in which German-American collusion has always been more important than any rivalry whenever matters became serious. This configuration will probably persist until West Germany is in a position to provide for its own defences through the E.E.C. and to carry out its own military interventions in the Third World.

The Crisis and the Future of the International Monetary System

On the basis of the preceding analysis we can speculate as to two possible future developments in the international monetary system, corresponding to possible changes in U.S.-German relations.

In the first possibility, the E.C.U. would gradually evolve into an important alternative reserve currency, along with the yen. 'Western' imperialism would then be divided into three relatively autonomous blocs, centred in the U.S., Europe and Japan, and relations amongst them would probably be fairly tense.[55]

But the fact that the capitalist world market has never been able to function without one principal, clearly dominant reserve currency would suggest that it is more likely that a second solution, based on a compromise between Germany and the U.S., will prevail. Such a solution might be defined by a policy based on the massive issue of Special Drawing Rights (S.D.R.s) which would ensure a pre-eminent role for the U.S. and Germany. But, in practice, this policy would run the risk of producing a dangerous increase in international liquidity. It would only work if the issue of S.D.R.s was a substitute for the issue of dollars, and not merely a supplement. The I.M.F. would then become a real world central bank. The U.S. would retain a pre-eminent influence on the international money system, but its power would be less than it is today. The U.S. might nonetheless be brought to accept such a compromise in coming years. This possibility was behind the Spring 1978 I.M.F. proposals concerning the purchase of dollars for S.D.R.s, which would have sterilized part of the American foreign debt.[56] But the proposals were rejected, since America refused to commit itself to restricting its money supply. Clearly the three main capitalist countries, the U.S., Japan and West Germany, have not yet achieved the level of agreement which the acceptance of such proposals – and their consequences – would imply. The September 1978 I.M.F. decision to boost liquidity by issuing 32 billion new S.D.R.s over three years (1 S.D.R. being worth about $1.25 as of mid 1979) is nonetheless an indication that progress in this direction is being made. In the longer term, this compromise over S.D.R.s can, in its turn, lead either to monetary fragmentation or to a reassertion of the dollar's hegemony.

However, such speculations are dangerous. They lay too much stress on purely monetary matters and tend to grant an excessive importance to inter-imperialist contradictions, especially U.S.-German contradictions. We should always remember that world inflation, the monetary instability, the oil shortage and the employment crisis can only be grasped in terms of understanding the overall crisis of U.S.-dominated world imperialism.

References to Part II

1. These were the functions of money described by Marx and the classical economists. The important thing to realize is that the double identity between numerator, means of payment and reserve instrument only holds for periods of relative stability within the imperialist system; in fact, experience indicates that it is a precondition for such stability. The monetary aspects of imperialist crises can be seen as the results of contradictions which break up the terms of this double identity.
2. This is not the place for a critique of the currently fashionable 'neo-Keynesian' or 'monetarist' monetary theories. We will only point out that their economism is increasingly being discredited by the facts. It would seem that the bourgeois discourse has degenerated to the point where only its politicians and historians still retain any contact with reality.
3. When we speak of 'the U.S.', or 'the Americans', we are of course,

referring to the U.S. Government, in its role as the representative of the alliance of dominant classes in American society. The term is convenient, but one should be aware of its limitations.

4. For a more complete analysis of the crisis, see S. Amin, A. Faire, M. Hussein, G. Massiah, *La crise de l'imperialisme* (Editions de Minuit, Paris, 1975).
5. For a more detailed analysis of the origins of inter-imperialist conflicts in general, see Lenin's *Imperialism, The Highest Stage of Capitalism*, various editions.
6. See M. Hudson, *Super Imperialism* (Holt, Rinehart and Winston, 1972).
7. See S. Amin, *Unequal Development* (Harvester Press, Sussex), A. Emmanuel, *Unequal Exchange*, (New Left Books, London).
8. The hopes that British rulers placed in their 'special relationship' with the U.S. led them to exhaust their economy in the attempt to maintain the pound's gold parity. Right up until 1967, when the pound was devalued, it played a very useful role for the Americans, as a buffer for speculative pressure which would otherwise have been brought to bear upon the dollar.
9. The first negotiations between the E.E.C. and the Mediterranean countries go back to the late 1960s. Eventually the U.S. gave its consent for the signature of the first special agreement, with . . . Israel.
10. See C. Payer, *The Debt Trap*, (Penguin, 1974).
11. The U.S. preferred to consume low cost imported raw materials rather than more expensive domestically extracted resources. This was particularly true in the case of energy resources, which the U.S. preferred to conserve for reasons of long-term strategy. In so doing, the U.S. and the free market economy forced less far-seeing European leaders to follow the same course, and the latter jumped at the opportunity to rid themselves of the coal miners. Once again, we see that the European ruling classes were indeed the victims of U.S. hegemony, but consenting victims, accomplices in the process.
12. There were at the time no signs of isolationism in the U.S. It was only at the end of the 1960s that this phenomenon began to re-emerge from its thirty years of slumber.
13. See T. Hayter, *Aid as Imperialism* (Penguin, 1971).
14. This declaration highlights the link between Keynesian reformism and imperialism, in that it can only be applied by a dominant imperialism. This is a clear indication of the limits which the so-called Keynesian 'revolution' in economics has come up against in reality; see J. Tobin, *The New Economics, One Decade Older* (Princeton University Press, 1974).
15. Would American capitalism have done better by concentrating on the development of exports rather than on investment abroad? Studies of the effects of U.S. investments abroad upon the U.S. balance of payments tend to show the opposite.
16. This highlights the limitations of all theories of international exchange based explicitly or implicitly on the idea of 'comparative advantages'. Comparative advantages are not 'natural', they are created and change with the evolution of the inter-imperialist balance of forces.
17. Furthermore, the Europeans and the Japanese were 'urged' to invest in

U.S. Treasury bonds specially created for the purpose by the then Secretary to the Treasury, R. Roosa.

18. Especially after the stabilization of gold prices following the setting up of the Gold Pool. For the main U.S. views on the matter, see *The International Monetary System*, edited by L.H. Officer and T.D. Willet (Prentice Hall, 1969).
19. In any case, the Gold Pool precluded any revaluation of gold and any development which might have made a return to an international monetary system based on gold at all likely. At the time, Triffin's proposals for an I.M.F.-issued 'paper gold' were considered sacrilegious by the Federal Reserve, in that they implied at least a semblance of symmetry. It was only ten years later that the U.S. was forced to fall back on the second line of defence for the dollar. See J. Tobin, *op. cit.*
20. Euro-dollars are dollars released through the U.S. balance of payments deficit and circulating freely in Europe, as opposed to being exchanged through the central banks by the private agents involved. See C. Goux and J.F. Landeau, *Le Peril Americain* (Calmann-Levy, 1971).
21. These two figures deal exclusively with the reserves of the central banks, dollars held by private agents are not represented. They do not take account of the revaluation of rèserves in gold decided by certain central banks, such as the Bank of France in 1975.
22. See E. Despres, C. Kindleberger and V. Salnot in L.H. Officer and T.D. Willet, eds., *op. cit.*
23. There were other such smokescreens, including double accounting of the U.S. I.M.F. gold quota. The Director of the I.M.F., P.P. Schweitzer, was quite simply fired when he tried to put an end to it in 1971. See M. Hudson, *op. cit.*
24. The close link between social democracy and imperialism has never been clearer. The inability of the ruling classes and the labour aristocracy to break a now out-dated pact is the other side of a British crisis which goes all the way back to the 1920s.
25. Many monetary experts have cast the increasing scale of speculative pressure on currency rates as the main cause of the collapse of the Bretton Woods system – the idea being that such pressures had become so intense that they could ensure a shift in parities and consequently ensure the success of speculation. In reality, of course, speculative movements are produced by a monetary instability which they merely amplify but in no way cause. The system of floating exchange rates, which was supposed to absorb such pressures, has proved just as unsatisfactory as the fixed parities system.
26. S.D.R.s also first appeared in 1968.
27. Even in the early 1960s, U.S. economic advisers to the President had attempted to modify the U.S. interest rate. The idea behind this 'Operation Twist' was to lower long-term rates and raise short-term rates, in an effort to prevent an outflow of floating capital. But the international transmission of interest rate structures through the Euro-dollar market resulted in equivalent effects in financial centres abroad and frustrated the project. Once again, the problem was not one of monetary technique. See J. Tobin, *op. cit.*
28. 1965 seems to have been the turning point. See A. Fahri in *Le Monde*

Diplomatique (November, 1974).

29. This does not mean that the U.S.'s long-term goal is not a return to the 1960s type of international monetary system, with a strong dollar and a significant U.S. trade surplus. But this goal is not immediately realizable. In the meantime the U.S. will use fluctuations in the dollar as a weapon, without allowing the use of this weapon to interfere with U.S. domestic economic policy. It is important to understand that the move from the Bretton Woods system to the S.D.R. floating exchange rates system is merely a matter of tactics for the U.S. Of course, reality may not conform to the plan.
30. American encouragement was manifest during the 1971 Tehran Oil Conference, which decided to raise oil prices for the first time since the end of the 1950s. But the unilateral price hikes decided upon by OPEC in 1973 should not be seen as the result of U.S. machinations. *On the contrary, in the context of the October War, the more militant OPEC countries managed to carry the whole assembly with them and go much further than the U.S. was prepared to accept, thereby creating serious difficulties for the U.S. strategy of transition to independence in the energy field.* This is why the U.S. led the opposition to the new very high oil prices, although it did recommend a $7 a barrel floor price. In 1975 the world recession tilted the balance of power in favour of the OPEC 'moderates' and the price of oil fell compared to that of industrial products. But the struggle is by no means over.
31. One should not be misled by the temporary and purely contingent recovery of the French balance of payments between Summer 1974 and Summer 1975. Government experts foresee no real lasting recovery of the French balance of payments before 1980, at best.
32. American commercial competitiveness may itself soon become a powerful means of blackmail if the dollar continues to fall.
33. Keeping to the rhythm of the U.S. electoral cycle which we will deal with at the end of the chapter.
34. Let us recall the 10% import surcharge, the threat of withdrawing U.S. troops from Europe and the thunderous outbursts of J. Connally, the then Secretary of Trade.
35. The operation of the C.A.P. becomes very difficult without a system of fixed parities within the E.E.C. The possibility of major fraud becomes quite real.
36. U.S. monetary experts were recommending a policy of 'benign neglect' *vis-a-vis* the dollar. According to some sources, Washington even encouraged speculation against the dollar by warning the U.S. 'multinationals' that it would not intervene on the exchange markets.
37. The practice is known as 'hedging' and involves the purchase or sale of currencies well in advance.
38. In a floating exchange rate system, no currency serves as *de jure* standard, or means of payment or reserve currency.
39. The floating exchange rate system could not ensure the promised disjunction between internal and external economic developments. Lax domestic monetary policy leads to a devaluation of the currency, which produces inflation as the price of imports rises. The only countries for whom the disjunction holds are those whose currencies are *de facto*

reserve currencies – and this has little to do with the parity system in question.

40. For an analysis of U.S. oil strategy, see P. Pean, *Petrole, la troisieme guerre mondiale* (Calmann-Levy, 1974).
41. One should not forget that, since the end of the 1960s, dollars held outside the U.S. by agents other than the central banks do not figure in the balance of official transactions.
42. Borrowers would in fact contribute to servicing the U.S. debt to the OPEC countries. It is thus hardly surprising that the U.S. brought political pressure to bear in order to ensure that the petro-dollars would be channelled in this way. European or Japanese competition in the matter would have caused a serious upheaval.
43. However, such a stabilization of the petro-dollar recycling process carries serious risks: saturation of the short-term Euro-dollar market, bank crashes and massive speculation against the dollar. The U.S. has taken steps to improve New York's position as a financial centre in order to counterbalance these dangerous tendencies.
44. As formulated during the March 1974 Washington Energy Conference.
45. These quotas are unchanged since Bretton Woods and give the U.S. veto powers over all I.M.F. decisions. However, the new Article 21 of the I.M.F. (28 July 1969) also allows Europe (including Britain) to veto the issue of S.D.R.s. The need to rely on British support somewhat invalidates the U.S. veto power. Recent negotiations over Article 21 have further watered down its importance.
46. S.D.R.s were first mooted in 1967, and first issued in 1970. See M. Hudson, *op. cit.*, for a description of their role up to 1972.
47. S.D.R.s are made up as follows: 1 S.D.R. = 0.40 U.S. dollars + 0.38 German marks + 0.045 pounds sterling + 0.44 French francs + 26 Japanese yen + 0.071 Canadian dollars + 47 Italian lira + 0.14 Dutch florins + 1.60 Belgian francs + 0.13 Swedish crowns + 0.012 Australian dollars + 0.11 Danish crowns + 0.099 Norwegian crowns + 1.10 Spanish pesos + 0.22 Austrian schillings + 0.0082 South African rands. These coefficients were reached in terms of the value of the various currencies, but because of its role in international exchange the U.S. dollar was given a particularly high weighting.
48. The United States sought a commitment from the central banks not to buy into the market during the I.M.F. gold sale, but did not get one. The effect was to carve up the gold market. Gold thus remains a last resort reserve even for the central banks, and its role in the international monetary system has not yet been completely eliminated.
49. See *The Economist,* 9 December 1978, for a description of the European monetary agreements.
50. Until 1978, the rise of the mark against the dollar and most European currencies restricted the growth of German exports in volume terms, but not in value terms. This was only achieved at the expense of a significant reduction in the profit margins of German export-oriented firms. These firms eventually played a very considerable part in West Germany's decision to promote the European Monetary System despite Bundesbank opposition to the programme.
51. The present European Monetary System is, in fact, fairly similar to

the old mini 'snake', but with France as a member. Italy sought, and obtained, wider margins for fluctuation than the other countries (6% instead of 2.25%) and has made it plain that if the lira was attacked in the currency markets, it would be devalued. Eire's membership was secured in exchange for substantial credits.

52. Less efficient, in that the considerably increased importance of oil in the import bill had reduced the average price elasticity of both exports and imports. Less reliable, in that the exchange markets can turn a moderate depreciation into a whirlpool which leaves a currency's exchange rate too low for too long.

53. Of course, these governments promise that eventually growth and employment will pick up again, when the economy has had time to 'recover'. As Mr. Schmidt puts it: 'Today's profits are tomorrow's investments and the day after tomorrow's jobs'. This approach betrays serious misapprehension of the role demand plays in investment. It also ignores the dangerous historical precedent of the deflationary spiral the European Gold Bloc ran into during the Thirties.

54. At least, this is the version which is currently being propagated amongst the 'pro-European leftists', who are sometimes tempted to see the European Monetary System as an instrument in the struggle against American imperialism. What is most astonishing about such an interpretation is not so much the absence of any real analysis, but more the fact that it treats the E.M.S.'s effects on Europe itself, and especially on the European class struggle, as less important than its effects on a hypothetical struggle between German imperialism and American imperialism.

55. See A. Faire in S. Amin, A. Faire, M. Hussein, G. Massiah, *La crise de l'imperialisme* (Editions de Minuit, Paris, 1975).

56. *International Herald Tribune*, 13 April 1978.

PART III

The Crisis and the Third World War

by Jean-Pierre Vigier

10. Introduction

Eventually, with hindsight, people will probably consider the series of events triggered off by the oil price rise organized in Autumn 1973 by Nixon and Kissinger as the starting point for a world crisis, surpassing that of 1929 in both depth and scope. The capitalist system has just gone through a long period of prosperity and expansion. Its experts and its political and economic leaders are ill-equipped to understand what is happening. They had put their faith in a Keynesian technocratic optimism, which argued that the capitalist system had 'changed its very nature', that it had 'dynamically transcended' its contradictions, and that Marx's analysis of the contradictory, and in the long term, fatal character of its economic foundations was out of date. The development of the crisis came as a brutal disproof of their theories. The analogy between what is happening today and the 1929 Crash is clear. For example, stock exchange crashes are following rather than preceding events; prices are rising instead of falling.

It is quite obvious by now that all this is not simply an 'energy crisis', a mere 'hiccup' in the system. Nixon, Kissinger and Ford are no longer in control. The crisis is steadily getting worse.[1] It is making a mockery of the promises held out by the European bourgeoisie and its left opposition, promises which were all based on constant economic progress. It signals the end of the capitalist system's 'second wind'. There has been a general reversal of trends, which may well last for years. At this stage, Marxists cannot content themselves with vague and empty phrases about the 'general crisis of capitalism'. We have to tackle the concrete mechanisms of this crisis, concentrating on their economic and political roots and on the evolving balance of forces between classes which has thus been set in motion.

The current crisis is developing in a context which has no economic, technical or political precedent in the history of capitalism. It can only be understood through a precise application of the economic analyses developed by Marx and his successors; the starting point must be the concrete conditions affecting inter-imperialist clashes and the development of class struggles in the world of 1975. Marxist theory must confront the development which capitalism has undergone since the Second World War, a period which has been mainly characterized by the brutal development of American imperialism.

At the end of the Great War, the October Revolution opened the first breach in capitalism's hegemony, a breach which was widened by the Chinese Revolution, following the Second World War. Whatever one may think of the eventual internal evolution of the socialist countries, it is clear that the consequent contractions of the world capitalist market upset the economic and political context in which the system was evolving. The revolutions aroused tremendous hopes for change in the Third World, hopes which crystallized in the exemplary struggle of the Vietnamese people first against the French, and then against the Americans.

However, contrary to the hopes and predictions of its opponents, the capitalist system survived these successive blows. From 1945 to 1965 it even went through one of its most brilliant periods of progress. There really was a case for talking of capitalism's 'second wind', and the underlying basis for this requires serious analysis.

With hindsight, it seems clear that the impact of the scientific and technical revolution accounts for much of the expansion of capitalism following the Second World War. The recent upsurge of technical progress has nothing in common with a revolution in the Marxist sense of the term. The analogy between the nineteenth-century 'industrial revolution' and the 'scientific and technical revolution' (S.T.R.) is somewhat stretched. But this scientific and technical revolution is nonetheless an essential infrastructural development, and it is important to assess its impact on the political superstructures. We need to look at the scientific revolution and imperialist domination simultaneously; this will seem paradoxical only to those who still believe that the development of knowledge can be independent of the social structure in which it takes place, and that scientific progress automatically leads to social progress. Our purpose here is not to expose the well-intentioned nineteenth-century bourgeois positivism underlying such a viewpoint: suffice it to point out that during the last decade we have witnessed humanity's first ventures into outer space, whilst back on Earth the material conditions of two-thirds of the world's people have deteriorated.

A closer look at contemporary American prosperity reveals that it is based on three main elements:

1. A temporary increase in the rate of profit (the ratio of surplus value over fixed capital and variable capital), as technical progress and the pillage of Third World raw materials increased the yield from variable capital.

2. The use of economic and financial methods made available by the growth of state capitalism and the imperialist reorganization of capitalism's structure on a world scale.

3. The extension of the home market and the conquest of new markets abroad.

Our aim in this study is not to provide a complete analysis of contemporary capitalism, but to concentrate on the most important infrastructural phenomenon of the period, namely the scientific and technical revolution, and to measure its impact on the contradictions which are tearing the system apart today.

Our analysis is thus set out in three parts: 1. This revolution and its repercussions on the process of capitalist production; 2. Contemporary capitalism and the roots of the crisis; 3. The 1973 crisis and the objective conditions affecting contemporary class confrontations.

11. The Scientific and Technical Revolution

Generally speaking, people are only just becoming aware of the key role scientific progress plays in economic growth. Even in the U.S., computers were available for several years before their importance was realized. In 1950, John Marchly, an important figure in the American computer industry, estimated that 'only four or five giant firms could usefully employ these machines.' In 1960, U.S. Government experts predicted that by 1965, 15,000 computers would be in use in U.S. industry as a whole. The actual figure turned out to be 25,000.

In Western Europe it is striking that the Treaty of Rome which set up the Common Market in 1958 considered scientific research only as an aspect of cultural policy. In other words, in 1958 Europe had still not grasped that scientific research was a means of economic growth.

If one takes the disparity between the use of technical progress in the U.S. and the U.S.S.R. as an index,[2] it would seem that the socialist countries were also unaware of the fact for quite a while. Indeed Marxists have hardly touched on the subject, although they, more than anyone, should have noticed it. This lack of analysis is yet another consequence of Stalinism. In fact, difficulties in integrating scientific progress into production are just as much an expression of Stalinism as the absence of literature. On top of this general backwardness in understanding the importance of the phenomenon, there has been a very strong tendency to deal with it on the basis of a purely empirical sociology.

The extent of the contemporary scientific and technical revolution emerges clearly when one considers that during the last twenty years:

1. Humanity has seized upon a source of energy which is several thousand times more powerful than those previously available, such as coal and oil. Qualitatively new ways of transmitting and controlling this energy have been developed (electronics).

2. The top speed of transportation machinery has gone from 700 to 30,000 km. an hour. Humanity is beginning to explore the solar system. In the long run, this exploration will have far more important consequences than the expeditions of Columbus, Cook or Magellan.

3. Progress in solid state physics has increased the reliability of electronic equipment tenfold – the transistor is a good example. The analysis of data

Table III.1
Computers in Operation throughout the World

Country	*1970*	*1974*	*1978*
U.S.	62,600	116,950	210-250,000
Japan	5,350	14,800	25-35,000
Germany	5,700	12,810	20-24,000
France	4,939	10,850	19-23,000
U.K.	4,800	8,490	16-21,000
U.S.S.R.	X	8,000	18-28,000
Italy	2,050	4,760	9-12,000
World Total	100,000	200,000	350-400,000

by binary logic is now measured in 1,000 millionths of a second rather than in milliseconds.

4. There has been an extraordinary development in the means of communication, both in terms of the availability of receivers (worldwide television etc.) and in terms of technology. The quantity of information which can be transmitted at one go has increased a thousandfold with the development of the laser. The Japanese physicist, Yukawa, has even compared the invention of television with Gutenberg's discovery of the printing press.

5. The number of scientists in the industrialized countries is increasing by 7% a year; in other words, it is doubling every ten years.[3]

6. The power of explosives has multiplied by ten million with the move from gunpowder to the H-bomb. For the first time in history, human beings can destroy the planet of their birth.

In short, scientific progress has been more marked in the last forty years than in the preceding forty centuries. The curve of technical progress over time is almost exponential: it moves along the horizontal for a very long time, then suddenly, in the middle of the twentieth century, it becomes practically vertical.

However, the picture we have painted above is a somewhat naive one. The key question is why we are talking about a scientific revolution at all. Has there really been a qualitative leap forwards? Let us see how all this compares with the industrial revolution during the nineteenth century.

The first striking thing is that that earlier revolution resulted from the application of a limited number of specific technical and scientific achievements: there was an 'age' of coal, an 'age' of electricity, then an 'age' of oil. In other words, there was a series of successive breakthroughs without any real continuity, although, of course, their effects were cumulative. Each 'age' was followed by a period of adaptation and relative stabilization in terms of technology. Nowadays the opposite is true. Scientific and technological breakthroughs in automation, chemistry and energy follow on one another's heels and react one upon the other. For instance, genetics is very much influenced by information theory. The delay in discovering how to apply new research is now very short; three years for integrated circuits (1958-61) as opposed to about fifty years, in the case of the telephone, during the previous century. Apart from this constant flow of discoveries, there is also the fact that for the first time human societies are beginning to master the process of scientific discovery itself, as they come to understand how its rhythm is determined by decisions concerning scientific, technical, intellectual and industrial investment. This in itself gives us some idea of the scale of the upheaval which has taken place in the technical and social division of labour.

The Mechanisms of Innovation

How does innovation come about? There are two different mechanisms and although they are not completely independent, it is important to distinguish between them, for their effects are dissimilar. Innovation can consist either in producing a new product with old methods of production (electronics or scientific instruments) or in producing an old product with new methods (motor cars, for example).[4]

In the first case, that of a new product, there will obviously be an increase in the unit value of the product which a company is making – otherwise the company would have stuck to its old lines. Increases in value will tend to be a function of novelty, which is itself the result of research carried out by the company, or by some other company if the product is being manufactured under licence. That part of the total value of the product due to the proportion of labour time spent actually making it diminishes, if we assume that the labour time spent producing the product, i.e. the duration of the work and the number of workers involved, remain constant. This type of innovation therefore implies an intensification of capital. If we treat innovation as an isolated event, as something fortuitous, it has to be admitted that Marxist concepts do not account for it. This is hardly serious, since in Marx's time such innovations occurred accidentally, quite independently of the system's evolution. If, on the contrary, we take up the notion of a scientific revolution, in the sense of a permanent utilization and institutionalization of scientific research, then clearly Marxist concepts can account for this increase in the intensity of capital, which is due to the increase of the share of dead labour in the unit value of the product.[5]

Given all this, there is no reason to be surprised that some companies at the forefront of innovation (the manufacturers of semi-conductors, for example) deliberately outdate their own products by launching new ones on the market. The public at large is well aware of how drug companies deluge doctors with publicity material. They may not be aware that the makers of semi-conductors and scientific instruments operate in a very similar manner. One only has to flick through a copy of *Electronics* or *Scientific American* to realize that most of the adverts presenting new products contain little information about the product's intrinsic qualities and concentrate more on building up 'consumer appeal'. Controlled prices, the long-standing dream of all managers, actually seem within reach.

We have emphasized this first type of innovation (producing a new product with old methods) because the picture of the effects of the scientific revolution on mass production is all too often one-sided, presenting only the effects of the second type of innovation, that is, the production of old products by new methods.

This second type entails a direct increase in the productivity of labour, and hence in the relative value of the labour time sold by the worker to the company. Once again the proportion of dead labour in the value of the finished product increases relative to living labour. There are too many examples to mention, since this second type of innovation, in fact, affects the whole apparatus of production, and even extends into the most traditional sectors. Agriculture is a classic case since, for a given market, it is the only branch of production in which demand cannot increase indefinitely.

These two types of innovation operate differently because they do not bring the same economic categories into play. Any attempt to trace their impact empirically must take two factors into account. Firstly, scientific and technological progress is a continous process. Secondly, the two types are inter-linked: a new product manufactured by old methods will often turn out to be part of the new equipment for producing an old product.

The most accurate estimates of the way the apparatus of production has been transformed by the scientific revolution usually stem from an examination of the relative rates of growth of the various branches of production in the U.S. During the period 1947-58, the value of electronic components rose by 82%, whereas that of chemicals rose by 31%, that of office services by 42% and that of communications by 33%. This evolution is all the more striking when one considers that over the same period the value of traditional mechanical components fell by 23%, that of iron-based raw materials by 27%, that of wood by 26%, and that of coal by 40%.

The Scientific and Technical Revolution and the Rate of Profit

It now becomes necessary to evaluate the impact of the scientific and technical revolution on the fluctuations in the rate of profit, and its consequences for the 'law of the tendency of the rate of profit to fall' which Marx presented as one of the key problems of the capitalist mode of production.

We shall start from Marx's definitions of the relations between surplus value, fixed capital and variable capital, as manifested in the reproduction of capital, and we shall then see what happens when we introduce the dynamic of continually accelerating progress. Marx's analyses were made at a time when progress was fairly slow. To put it mathematically, they were based on periods when progress was following a weak linear slope, and so they could legitimately ignore incidental movement along that slope.

To begin with, let us recall the classical definitions: the *organic composition of capital* (C/V), reflecting the ratio of constant capital C (investment in machines, tools, raw materials and energy) to variable capital V (wages); the *rate of profit,* expressed in the ratio S/(C + V) where S represents surplus value; finally, the *rate of increase in surplus value,* S/V.

Summarizing his general theory of profit in the *Grundrisse,* Marx writes: 'As it represents the general form of wealth – money – capital has a frenetic and endless tendency to go beyond its own limits. Every limitation is and must be a barrier to it, otherwise it would cease to be capital, that is to say, money which creates itself. If capital creates surplus value in determinate quantities, it is only because it cannot produce unlimited quantities of it all at once. But it is the movement of its constant increase.'

Marx adds that, 'The limitations that capital overcomes must thus appear as fortuitous. This emerges even in the most superficial analysis. When capital which started at 100 reaches 1,000, the fact that it has increased tenfold no longer counts for anything. The profit and interest themselves become capital. What appeared as surplus value has quite simply been absorbed by the capital itself.'[6]

Let us now return to the period following the Second World War, when the Scientific and Technical revolution began to make itself felt in the capitalist economy. In 1944-45 all the conditions were set for a great leap forward by the capitalist system. The massive destruction of plant, the demand to reconstruct and the necessity of meeting the needs of the masses all gave a tremendous impetus to production both in Department I (capital goods) and in Department II (consumer goods). The capitalist economy as a whole embarked on a new cycle of expansion.

The take-off of technical progress was partly due to the fact that any capitalist could exploit the situation to improve productivity by using new technology, thereby extracting a higher relative surplus value than less well-equipped competitors. From the moment that scientific and technical knowledge had reached a level at which it was possible to institutionalize scientific and technical progress, the nature of the capitalist system itself became the main motor of technical progress, as each capitalist strove to make the most of the situation. This explains both the acceleration of technical progress and its ideological by-products. The bourgeoisie eulogized progress while dreaming of profits to come.

There are five main points worth noting at this stage. The first is that the accelerated pace of technical progress introduced new contradictions in the capitalist system. In fact, it tended to shorten the time for which a capitalist could take advantage of a particular position within the market, since in principle every technical innovation could now be improved upon by somebody else. This acceleration posed enormous investment problems which, as we shall see later, became part of the underlying basis for the permanent inflation which was to plague the system from then on. Amplified as it was by the techniques of modern advertising, the resulting need for constant progress meant that investments had to be renewed faster and faster. Consequently, C/V had to increase, which meant that in the long term the rate of profit tended to fall; naturally this had to be compensated for, by ever larger and more frequent injections of investment capital. This explains why, after a sudden rise, from 5% in 1945 to 15 to 20% in the 1950s, the rate of profit gradually declined during the rest of the period, falling to 10% in 1965 and less than 5% in 1974. The law of the tendency of the rate of profit to fall, which was seemingly suspended for a while, thus re-asserted itself even more forcibly in the context of the scientific and technical revolution. In the end, it provided extra impetus to the forces pulling the system apart.

The second point is that, for the first time, and in more and more sectors of production, the capitalist system was straining against objective limits, set by the gradual exhaustion of certain raw materials, the constant development of 'nuisances' such as pollution, and the development of increasingly unbearable social constraints associated with the level of hierarchy, the type of organization and the division of labour called for by post-S.T.R. capitalism.

The third point is that this revolution accentuated the system's imperialist characteristics, in that it opened two main avenues as means to struggle against the falling rate of profit. One way of reducing C was to obtain cheap raw materials and energy, by pillaging the Third World. During the last twenty-five years the system's advances have depended on profits linked to sources of cheap energy. The 1973 fourfold increase in oil prices thus considerably accelerated the development of the crisis. The West's attempts to contain or reduce oil prices come down to a struggle to maintain the industrial rate of profit. The other avenue opened up by the scientific and technical revolution is constantly to develop new methods of production, using new raw materials which can be substituted for the traditional ones. The boom in petrochemicals, latex-based products and plastics, along with the substitution of fuel oil for coal, underlie the deepening contradictions between rich and poor countries, and the United States' recent adoption of the threatening diplomatic style typical of the English and the French in dealing with their colonies during the nineteenth century.

The fourth point to note is that the rate of surplus value has declined partly as a result of an increase in the services which go into realizing surplus value, an increase in V. This increase obviously cancels out some of the profits capitalism can draw from increases in the productivity of labour.

For the first time we can verify one of the predictions made by Rosa Luxemburg in her attempt to extend Marx's analyses to the stage of imperialist domination.[7] Her prediction was based on incorporating into Marx's schema technical progress and the rise in C/V described above. It can now be shown that 'the introduction of technical progress as a factor in the system of production produces a relative shortage of capital goods or investments and an excess of consumer goods.' And this leads directly to the development of a new contradiction within the system, a contradiction which has been developing in the U.S. since early 1974.

We can illustrate the argument with a simple numerical example.[8] Let C_1 and C_2 stand for the constant capital of Departments I and II, V_1 and V_2 for the variable capital, R_1 and R_2 for the part of surplus value which is consumed, Sc_1 and Sc_2 for the part of surplus value which is set aside to purchase new capital goods, Sv_1 and Sv_2 for the part of surplus value which is set aside to pay the wages of new workers.

During phase 1 we will have:

Supply of capital goods

$$C + V_1 + S_1 \quad = \quad 44 + 11 + 11 \quad = \quad 66$$

Supply of consumer goods

$$C_2 + V_2 + S_2 \quad = \quad 16 + 4 + 4 \quad = \quad 24$$

$$\text{GNP} \quad = \quad 90$$

Thus $C/V = 4$ and the rate of surplus value, $S/V = 100\%$.

Let us assume that in each department half the surplus value is set aside. This half of the surplus value, which will be used to buy new capital goods and to pay new workers, will thus also be divided into C and V according to the same ratio. *The assumption is thus that C/V is constant,* which is Marx's hypothesis in his reproduction schema.

We thus have:

$$S_1 \text{ set aside:} \quad 5.5 = \quad \begin{array}{l} Sc_1 + Sv_1 \\ 4.4C + 1.1V \end{array}$$

$$S_2 \text{ set aside:} \quad 2 = \quad \begin{array}{l} 1.6C + 0.4V \\ Sc_2 + Sv_2 \end{array}$$

which gives us:

investments = 66

$$\begin{array}{lll} \text{accumulation} & = & C_1 + C_2 + Sc_1 + Sc_2 \\ & = & 44 + 16 + 4.4 + 1.6 \;=\; 66 \\ \text{So investments} & = & \text{accumulation} \end{array}$$

Similarly we have:

Supply of consumer goods = 24

Demand for consumer goods =
$V_1 + V_2 + Sv_1 + Sv_2 + R_1 + R_2 =$
$11 + 4 + 1.1 + 0.4 + 5.5 + 2 \quad = \quad 24$

Hence supply of consumer goods = demand for consumer goods.

If we now introduce the effect of technical progress, in the form of an increase in C/V such that C/V goes up from 4 to 7, the surplus value will be differently allocated.

We get:

S_1 set aside: $5.5 = 4.8C + 0.7V$

S_2 set aside: $2 = 1.75C + 0.25V$

So:

investments = 66

accumulation $= C_1 + C_2 + Sc_1 + Sc_2$
$= 44 + 16 + 4.8 + 1.75 = 66.55$

In other words: Accumulation > Investment

Furthermore we have :

Supply of consumer goods = 24

Demand for consumer goods =

$V_1 + V_2 + Sv_1 + Sv_2 + R_1 + R_2 =$
$11 + 4 + 0.7 + 0.25 + 5.5 + 2 = 23.45$

So the supply of consumer goods > demand for consumer goods.

The above is the direct result of introducing technical progress and the concomitant increase of C/V as factors in Marx's schema: 'The introduction of technical progress as a factor in the system of production produces a relative shortage of capital goods or investments and an excess of consumer goods.' The outcome is the new contradiction which has been developing in the U.S. since early 1964, as the capitalist economy is *forced* to find outlets for its unsaleable surplus abroad. The future expansion of the capitalist system is thus necessarily linked to imperialist expansion. The West's prosperity is organically associated with the impoverishment of the Third World, as a direct consequence of fundamental mechanisms in the capitalist economy. Any increase in the prices of raw materials produced by these countries is 'soaked up' by a steeper increase in the price of industrial products and by the continuous devaluation of the dollar. The next stage is the growth of mechanisms whereby capital allocated for investment in the industrialized world is creamed off. Petro-dollars are a typical example, in which European capital (40 billion dollars in 1974) is shunted off into U.S. investments by Arab capitalist intermediaries.

Many of the current international struggles revolve around sources of technical and scientific knowledge instead of around sources of raw materials. Commercial relations are going through a new type of upheaval: thanks to their scientific potential, American firms which set up shop in Europe only bring 10% of the necessary capital with them; they find the remaining 90% on the spot.

The final point is that if one examines the sources and beneficiaries of research and development credits, it becomes apparent that the scientific revolution reinforces certain fundamental tendencies in capitalism and modifies others. For instance, let us take the role of the state. State research credits play a more important role in the United States than in any other capitalist country. In 1956, for the first time, federal credits were as significant as private capital – which shows that some aspects of the scientific revolution have developed only recently. By 1964 more than 60% of research credits were state-allocated. U.S. state credits for research in the chemicals industry amounted to almost as much as the sum allocated by the French Government for research in every branch of industry. But it is also worth noting that it is in the U.S. that most research by privately owned industry takes place. The development of scientific research completely shatters the 'liberal' myth of free enterprise. The interpenetration of the big companies and the state is constantly on the increase as the scientific revolution accelerates tendencies towards concentration in business. A recent study showed that in the electronics industry a firm had to have a fairly high level of material, financial and human resources if it was to operate competitively. This observation is just as applicable to all the new branches of industry, including aerospace, aeronautics and computers, in which research plays a key role. Any firm which cannot keep up with the pace of research either goes under or is absorbed by a bigger firm. The National Science Foundation estimates that, in 1964, 300 firms with more than 1,000 employees absorbed 97% of state R and D credits and 83% of private research investments: the remainder went to 10,000 smaller firms, out of a grand total of 262,000. The small U.S. firms, representing 80% of the total number, accounted for only 5 to 6% of the value of U.S. government research contracts. It is not difficult to understand why the accent is very definitely on 'big science'. But this type of development of research has repercussions, such as accelerated urbanization, which accentuate certain problems in the U.S., the question of Black Americans for example, or raises new ones such as the breakdown of communication between different age groups. The current mode of development of research, characterized as it is by the predominance of 'big science' and the need for massive investments, comes down essentially to the question of maintaining the marginal efficacity of capital. 'Gigantism' does, of course, have limits – for instance the Mohole project, which set out to pierce through the terrestrial crust, was eventually abandoned – but it is nonetheless characteristic. It is because 'big science' offered such great opportunities for investment that it continued to develop long after the invention of the atomic bomb. By launching into the space race, the Soviet Union merely reinforced this tendency within the capitalist system.[9] This gigantism, which is partly responsible for the technological gap between the U.S. and other countries, is unlikely to be reversed under capitalism, since it is an essential component of investment policy.

The economic and political effects of the scientific and technical revolution on the evolution of the rate of profit can be summed up in a few essential points:

Figure III.1 Profits in the Post-War Period

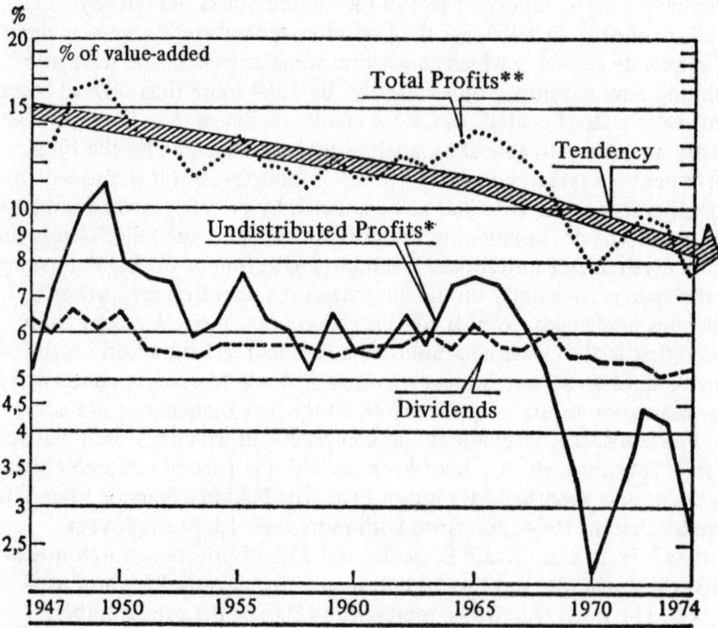

*After adjustment for stock evaluation.
**In billion.

1. The development of scientific and technical methods has not modified the tendency of the rate of profit to fall; it merely reversed this tendency temporarily, from 1945 to 1960. Since then, the fall has continued and is accelerating before our very eyes. Table III.1 illustrates this evolution in the

U.S, economy.

2. For a while, the scientific and technical revolution enabled the major industrial states to increase the mass of absolute surplus value produced. However, this increase, which fostered the illusion that the system had definitely overcome its problems, did not mean that it had escaped from the deadly contradictions which are, in the long term, implicit in the private appropriation of the means of production.

3. The revolution was used to stem the tendency of the rate of profit to fall in three main ways. The relative importance of V in the organic composition of capital was increased – for instance, in the electronics and computer industry, where 'software' is still far more significant than 'hardware'. The productivity of labour was improved, thereby increasing S/V. Finally, constant capital was renewed at shorter and shorter intervals, as outdated machinery had to be replaced. All these changes threw the economy into a very shaky equilibrium, which made it more and more vulnerable.

4. The efforts described above were negated by the steady growth of constant capital (nearly 5% in the U.S.) which is only economically acceptable if industrial production increases at a greater rate. This eventually led to a renewed wave of exported U.S. crisis when the dollar fell sharply in December 1974.

5. The revolution engenders an acceleration in the concentration of capital, both nationally and internationally. As the cost of research rises only the major firms can hold their position in the market. The crisis is not catastrophic for everybody. The big U.S. and Western trusts see it as an opportunity to restructure industry with a view to an eventual upturn in the economy.

6. The revolution also introduces the ever-increasing likelihood that the international division of labour will be permanently altered. The strong strive to keep certain key sectors, and the associated high profits, entirely to themselves. This is the basis for Gulf Oil's transformation into Gulf Atomic, and for the U.S.'s desire, expressed by Ford and Kissinger in Brussels in May 1975, for a monopoly in satellite communication, supersonic flight, nuclear energy and computers.

Historically speaking, the scientific and technical revolution has thus profoundly modified the mechanisms of capital accumulation. During the nineteenth century 'scientific revolution', the dominant type of accumulation relied essentially on the production of 'absolute surplus value', in other words on a general increase in the hours of work without any concomitant increase in real wages. Nowadays scientific and technical development favours another mechanism, described by Marx as the 'production of relative surplus value'. This means that the growth of profits is based on the fact that the quantity of goods consumed by the workers does not increase as fast as their capacity to produce them. *From now on, the survival of capitalism requires the existence of a permanent gap between increases in the consumption of the masses and increases in the productivity of labour.* In other words, it rests on the hypothesis of an uninterrupted development of the means of production and a steadily rising productivity of labour.

Of course, both types of exploitation have always existed. Before the scientific and technical revolution, the production of relative surplus value was far less significant and limited both in time and space. Indeed it is the production of relative surplus value, based essentially on 'Taylorism' and assembly line labour, which explains the relative ascendancy achieved by U.S. capitalism over its rivals who drew the essential part of their profits from colonial exploitation and did not bother to increase the productivity of their national industries. After the Second World War the mechanism of relative surplus value gradually extended its hegemony, first in the U.S. and then throughout the economies of the capitalist world. It forms the economic foundation of the 'consumer society'. Since then the expanded reproduction of capital has become ever more reliant upon a growing subordination of people to machines and on constant increases in productivity which are from now on absolutely essential to the system's chances of survival.

The Scientific and Technical Revolution and the Extension of the Capitalist Market

The time is long gone when the reproduction of capital was based mainly on the creation of new means of production. Thanks to the scientific and technical revolution, the capitalist system is developing new forms of exploitation and can broaden the economic base of capital reproduction to include mass consumption and whole new sectors of production, such as electronics, petro-chemicals, etc., which result directly from scientific development. It brutally eliminates all pre-capitalist forms of production, notably in agriculture. It extends its hegemony over every aspect of human economic activity. From leisure to transport, every human activity is henceforth integrated into the market economy. The process of 'reification' described by Marx is practically complete in the more developed parts of the world. As a first step, this capitalist market expanded internally, within the industrialized countries themselves, by extending mass consumption to include the majority of wage earners. But this was not enough for its development. As a result, a new contradiction is now emerging before our very eyes, corresponding to the latest stage of capitalism's evolution.

New social structures are born within the previous structures. They grow at the expense of the latter. Capitalism arose and developed historically within pre-capitalist socities. It emerged from the feudal system and embarked upon the conquest of the world. Having brutally eliminated the outdated pre-capitalist structures, it undertook a programme of colonial pillage during the seventeenth century, thereby providing itself with an essential element for the 'take-off' stage of capital accumulation.

During a later stage, in the nineteenth century, this pillage continued to provide the capital and the markets necessary to capital accumulation. The growth of capitalism implies continuous extension, especially now, after the scientific revolution, when the accelerated reproduction of capital has become absolutely essential. Capitalism's very nature is hegemonic; it cannot tolerate the survival of other systems for very long. Once the home market had been developed, the U.S. capitalists necessarily embarked upon the conquest of Third World markets, at the expense of their European and Japanese competitors. U.S. industrial and agricultural products also continue to force their way into the markets of the E.E.C. and the socialist world. The system in the era of scientific revolution only survives because of the dynamic of its own development. It is condemned to expand endlessly or die.

Inflation

The preceding analysis sheds some light on the problem of inflation. Inflation originally became a permanent element in the system as a result of increases in public spending linked to the continuous renewal of more and more costly military and civil equipment. It was given a further boost as modern banks began using mechanization and electronics, which speeded up the circulation of money in a way which was effectively equivalent to the issue of new banknotes.

Two key factors underlie the growing inability of governments to cope with the acceleration of inflation. Firstly, the extension of the home market to include the working class as a whole shattered one of the most important means of control. For obvious political and economic reasons, capitalism can no longer afford to allow unemployment to climb too steeply, since such a contraction of a now indispensable market might bring the whole machine to a grinding halt. Secondly, capitalism can no longer use the elimination of pre-capitalist sectors of production in its struggle against the tendency of the rate of profit to fall as constant capital grows. The only field left for such operations is the Third World, where this sort of policy is very likely to lead to political explosions which could easily get out of control.

In its struggle against falls in the rate of profit, the capitalist system has always sought to put pressure on wages, through the industrial reserve army, thereby diminishing variable capital's share in the production process. To the extent that this army is no longer available, *inflation becomes essential to maintain the rate of profit and to provide the investment capacity which is crucial to the reproduction of capital.* Figure III.2 and Table III.2 illustrate how it now affects all products.

Inflation is now essential to the system's 'high wire' equilibrium act. As we shall see later, even the last two economic recessions in the U.S. did not put a brake on it.

One figure in particular highlights this necessity. The U.S. economy alone will need about $5,000 billion between 1974 and 1985 to maintain a growth rate of 2%. As individual savings and total business profits will at best amount to slightly less than $4,000 billion, U.S. capital will have to find some other source of funds for investment at home and abroad. Since the exploitation of the Third World cannot fill the gap, inflation must now be considered as a

Table III. 2
Prices Shift in the 6 Main Capitalist Countries, 1970-74* (Inflation is by now the main means of capital accumulation)

	France		*Germany*		*U.K.*		*Italy*		*Japan*		*U.S.*	
	1973	*July 1974*	*1973*	*June 1974*	*1973*	*July 1974*	*1973*	*May 1974*	*1973*	*July 1974*	*1974*	*July 1974*
Retail Prices	119.9	137.5	118.8	127.2	126.7	148.6	122.4	140.6	124.5	154.3	114.4	127.5
Production Prices												
Manufactured Products **	109.5	148.8	114.9	126.0	124.5	152.4	127.2	177.8	105.5	130.3	144.5	143.5
Foodstuffs	135.5	140.5	114.4	120.1	132.6	163.2	127.6	147.0	113.6	144.6	142.6	154.3
Oil Products	–	–	125.3	205.6	–	–	110.4	210.5	120.2	226.7	127.3	236.8

* Index 100 = 1970; 1973 average, 1974 latest established figures.
** Refers to machine tools and other capital goods except for France (Metallurgy) and U.K. (Mechanical Industries).

Source: O.E.C.D., September 1974.

permanent element in the very structure of the system.

Figure III.2 Comparative Price Increases since 1971

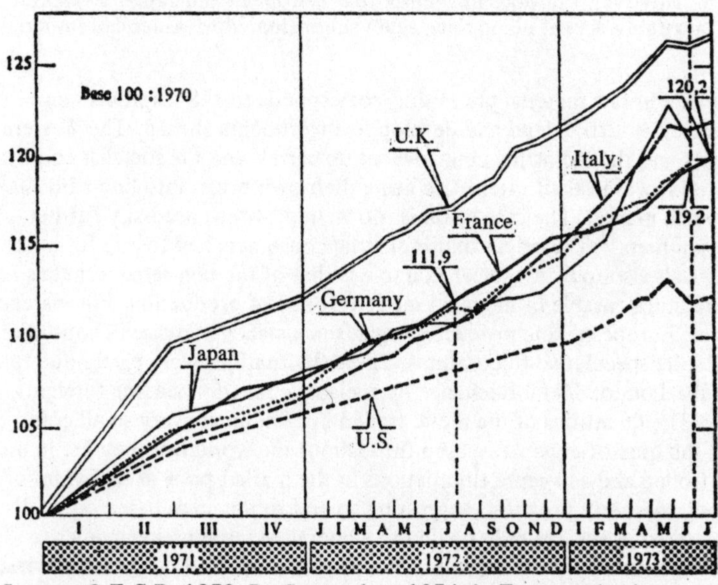

Source: O.E.C.D. 1973. By September, 1974, in France price increases over the previous year had reached 14.8%, as against 7.3% in Germany, 10.3% in the Netherlands, 10.6% in Luxembourg, 23.7% in Italy, and 17.1% in the U.K.

As Granou[10] puts it:

> Even though the hike in oil prices was the oil exporting countries' own decision, there can be no doubt that it was 'organized' by the oil consortiums, who drew fantastic profits from it. In the case of raw materials, domination by international companies was even more apparent, in that the price rises were almost entirely the result of international speculation; the exporting countries themselves saw very little of the extra revenue generated by the price hikes – but they did bear the full weight of the increases in the price of manufactured products imported from the capitalist countries. Worldwide inflation in raw material prices thus allowed U.S. companies to increase their profits enormously and to secure important financial resouces . . . It benefited U.S. capital as a whole, by giving a boost to the eight U.S. financial organizations which effectively control most of the main U.S. industrial companies and their subsidiaries abroad. The profits centralized

> by these organizations provide the funds for an international restructuring of production, and give U.S. capital a considerable lead over European and Japanese capital which is financially far less centralized. So far the new world war triggered off by the American offensive is restricted to economic and political fronts, but it may at any moment turn into a military confrontation. However, this does not imply that European and Japanese capital will inevitably accept being once again subordinated to American imperialism.

The increase in raw material prices thus corresponds to U.S. capital's long-term needs if it is to defend and develop its investments abroad. The Western companies and the exporting countries set up cartels and the socialist countries found that it was in their interest to bring their own prices into line with those of the world market. The case of oil is too well known to need any further elaboration here.[11] The prices that industrial consumers had to pay for most raw materials also rose. A typical example is that of the non-ferrous metals which are indispensable in the most modern forms of production. For instance, a cartel of 'European' zinc producers organized a steady increase in consumer prices despite speculative fluctuations. These fluctuations were partly due to sales on the London Metal Exchange by socialist countries needing foreign currency. The quantities of the metal traded in London are very small compared to the quantities actually used throughout the world but they are in no way controlled and can cause fluctuations in the market price at the whim of a few operators. Any prognosis suggesting an end to the crisis based on a fall in raw material prices can only be due to a complete misapprehension as to the deep motivations of the capitalist companies which produce these materials.

There are three further causes of the price increases, and these are permanent features linked to the impact of technological progress on the capitalist economy.

The first stems from the extension of the capitalist mode of production's hegemony over most pre-capitalist sectors of production, such as agriculture. In the system's ascendent phase, the capitalists forced a drop in the price of agricultural products, wheat for example, in order to lower the cost of reproducing the work force and to maximize the unpaid part of their workers' labour (surplus value). In a more recent phase, which culminated after the Second World War, the capitalist system penetrated the countryside in forcę, eliminated archaic forms of production and integrated cereals, soya and meat into the circuit of capitalist production and distribution.

From then on, agricultural products played an increasing role in international trade, and agricultural prices followed market laws and the movement of industrial prices. As the leading agricultural exporter in a world threatened by famine, the U.S. started to make full use of the resulting new method of blackmail. The U.S.S.R.'s massive purchase of 20 million metric tons of U.S. wheat in 1972, which liquidated existing stocks, triggered off a hike in wheat prices which contributed to the development of the crisis.

The second cause stems from the rapid decline in the lifespan of industrial products. This has evidently been organized with the aim of accelerating the rotation of capital. A growing part of the research effort – nearly 20% according to some estimates – goes into finding ways of making products less durable.

The third of these supplementary causes is the extraordinary growth of the tertiary sector and the disproportionate multiplication of non-productive services which occupy an increasing section of the active population. The constant rise of agricultural retail prices, at a time when the producer prices for the same goods are falling, clearly illustrates the parasitic character of publicity and the distribution circuits.

Finally, it is worth stressing that inflation has become an international phenomenon and a weapon in inter-imperialist confrontation. Capitalist governments can no longer hope to contain inflation on a national scale because they can no longer really control the international movements of capital organized by imperialist multinationals. No government has the means to prevent the Americans continuously exporting their crisis.

Since January 1974, by using oil as a weapon to the full, the U.S. has forced Japan and Europe to capitulate on one key point: they have had to recognize the paper dollar rather than gold as an international means of payment. In the context of the system, the Europeans and Japanese had no choice but to give in to this blackmail. There were only two ways of meeting deficits: liquidating already inadequate gold reserves (Germany $5 billion; France $4 billion; Switzerland $3½ billion) or short-term borrowing based on reserves evaluated at the real free market price. In the short term, American agreement to the latter operation saved the West, but in the long run it condemned it. To accept the paper dollar as a means of payment meant accepting that America's immense liquid debts (more than 100 billion paper dollars) would be increased by massive purchases of real goods and services, all paid for in paper. In fact, this amounted to an appropriation of the debtor countries' real wealth by the U.S.

What all this comes down to is that the essential motor of inflation is linked to the recognition of the paper dollar as an international means of payment, which cannot be challenged without a break with the international market dominated by the U.S. In other words, the only way out of the crisis is to change one's foreign policy and to stand up to the Americans.

12. The Scientific and Technical Revolution and Imperialism

Lenin's pamphlet, *Imperialism, the Highest Stage of Capitalism,* dominates the whole question of imperialism. What he had in mind when he wrote this work is perfectly straightforward: the point was to forge a weapon for the struggle and hence to provide a precise analysis which eliminated all the generalities which obscured the mechanisms of imperialist domination. Lenin wrote: ' "General" disquisitions on imperialism, which ignore or put into the background the fundamental difference between social-economic formations, inevitably turn into the most vapid banality or bragging, like the comparison between "Greater Rome and Greater Britain". Even the capitalist colonial policy of previous stages of capitalism is essentially different from the colonial policy of finance capital.' He suggested that imperialism was characterized by five essential traits:

1. Concentration of production and capital becomes so intense that it leads to the creation of monopolies whose role in economic life is decisive.
2. There is a fusion of bank capital and industrial capital, and a financial oligarchy emerges to control the resulting 'finance capital'.
3. Export of capital, as opposed to export of goods, becomes particularly important.
4. Capitalists form international monopolist groups which divide the world between themselves.
5. The major capitalist powers have already divided up the whole world amongst themselves.[12]

We shall take up each of these points and see how it fits into the context of the scientific and technical revolution. But this revolution itself has engendered two new phenomena which dominate the contemporary organization of capital.

State Capitalism

The first of these new phenomena is the state's growing economic role in the workings of the capitalist economy. The major firms henceforth live in a sort of symbiosis with the state apparatus. By monopolizing certain state contracts, these companies benefit directly from public funds. This is the stage of 'state capitalism', analysed at length by John Maynard Keynes, the greatest economist thrown up by the bourgeoisie since Adam Smith and Ricardo. He was the first non-Marxist economist to grasp the possible consequences of the use of modern state economic power for the overall development of the capitalist economy, and he managed to define the financial and economic mechanisms which would influence its course. He recommended the use of changes in the bank rate and public expenditure as economic regulators. As applied by Roosevelt, these conceptions saved U.S. capitalism at the time of the 'New Deal'. After the Second World War, state-financed investments, in areas like armaments and atomic research, reverted to the private sector and increased the value of 'private' industrial plant from $40 billion to $60 billion.

The International Organization of Capital

One of the main consequences of the scientific and technical revolution was a qualitative leap forward in the international organization of capitalist companies. It is doubtful that the organization of capital could have gone beyond the stage described by Lenin without modern means of communication and considerable progress in electronics and computer science. Since the 1950s the organization of capitalist companies has clearly reached a new level: the appearance on the world scene of so-called 'multinational' companies is a definite manifestation of the most advanced form of capital organization.

The Scientific and Technical Revolution and the 'Multinationals'

The existence of these companies poses new theoretical problems. Most Marxist economists and left-wing politicians have moved somewhat uncritically from a purely descriptive approach, concentrating on the growth of subsidiaries, to a theoretical position suggesting that capitalism has now transcended the national stage which gave it birth, and that it is now ready to organize itself trans-nationally. Each of the different tendencies in the socialist movement has drawn its own conclusions about how to respond to this development. For instance, the Social Democrats have justified their participation in a Europe dominated by Monnet, Pompidou, Schmidt and Giscard on the grounds that one must organize 'a workers' Europe' to stand up to the international organization of capital. The Communist Parties have gone even further; they have adopted a broad front tactic, the 'historic compromise' which 'unites' the workers, the middle classes and 'national' capitalists against the 'rootless' international trusts.

Of course, this vocabulary has nothing in common with that of Marxist analysis. If the question is 'has the organization of capital broken away from national structures?', the answer is that clearly it has done nothing of the sort. Ever since the 1929 Crisis the link between big capital and the state apparatus has steadily become closer. Following in the footsteps of the financial oligarchy, the major 'multinationals' now live in close symbiosis with the bourgeois states. The state is in fact both a source of economic support and a useful instrument for these companies. They monopolize military and civil contracts, turn the politicians into their messenger boys and act as the main motor of inter-imperialist conflict.

What we are seeing today is certainly not the internationalization of capital; on the contrary, we are witnessing the birth of an organization of capital which reflects contemporary inter-imperialist rivalries, as foreign subsidiaries compete for the remains of the international market. It is this new post-scientific revolution form of organization, the imperialist company, which explains and conditions the evolution of the balance of forces between imperialist states.

Over the last ten years the 'multinationals' have grown so fast that their collective global sales now exceed the G.N.P. of every country in the world except the U.S. and the U.S.S.R. Imperialist companies control assets of more than $200 billion and account for 20% of world production. Since 1950 their growth rate has been two or three times higher than that of the most advanced industrial countries, including the United States. For instance, General Motors' annual sales exceeded $28 billion, $2 billion more than the national product of a country like Switzerland.

These companies are one of modern imperialism's key features. In 1970, 298 U.S. imperialist 'multinationals' drew more than a third of their overall profit from their investments abroad. In 1971 the 122 principal U.S. companies were getting a much higher return from their foreign investments than from their U.S. based assets – 26% as opposed to 9%. The U.S. Department of Trade's statistics show a growing tendency towards the export of capital to the industrialized countries.

In 1971, both the U.S. chemicals and consumer durables industries held 25% of their assets abroad. The corresponding figures for the electrical industry and the pharmaceutical industry are 40% and 50% respectively. During the last ten years, the imperialist companies have accounted for 60% of U.S. exports and 35% of U.S. exports.

But of course, the U.S. has no monopoly on this sort of organization. Major multinationals such as Royal Dutch Shell and Unilever represent Dutch and British capital. European imperialist companies own more than 700 major factories in the U.S. itself. The new organization of capital has, in fact, established a new international division of labour and new financial methods which transcend national frontiers.

Multinational Financing

The first stage in the internationalization of finance was associated with the imperialist companies' ability to borrow on all the main capitalist money markets.

Like the pound sterling during the nineteenth century, the dollar no longer has a homeland. During the 1960s, the Euro-dollar market – which now amounts to over $160 billion – grew steadily larger. This market in U.S. currency, held in banks outside the U.S., was originally organized by a Soviet bank, the Bank of Northern Europe, which was created especially to finance the Russian state's purchases abroad. Internationally organized American banks then set up a system of multinational lending, through banking groups such as Orion (created in 1970 by Chase Manhattan), National Westminster, the Royal Bank of Canada and the Westdeutsche Landesbank. From then on, U.S. banks engaged in more and more foreign operations. In 1972 the First National City Bank of New York had as many branches abroad as it had at home. And more recently the imperialist trusts have taken to setting up their own credit establishments, such as the Dow Banking Corporation which was established in Switzerland in 1965 by the U.S. chemicals combine and which is now the second largest Swiss bank. Using computers and modern methods of gathering information, these organizations engage in permanent speculation on international financial markets (immediately exploiting fluctuations in the exchange rates and provoking enormous movements of capital outside the control of local governments) and they contribute to the ruin of the Third World. It is clearly far more profitable for Latin American capitalists or oil producers to engage in short-term speculation on the Euro-dollar market than to invest at home and run the risk of inflation and revolution.

The International Division of Labour

The imperialist companies have now organized production on an international scale. Components for a whole variety of goods are manufactured in one country and assembled in another. In many cases a firm will sell components to another subsidiary of the same parent company and the transaction will appear in their accounts in whatever manner best serves the overall interests of the multinationals involved.

Top management is always recruited from the parent company's country of origin, whereas the workers are mainly drawn from low wage areas. This is a perfect combination for U.S. imperialist companies. As technical progress continues to increase productivity, it becomes more and more essential to use cheap labour if the rate of profit is to be maintained at a competitive level. This is the underlying reason for the massive employment of Blacks and Mexicans in the U.S. itself, and of immigrant workers in Europe, as well as for the increasing tendency amongst imperialist companies to seek out low wage areas abroad. For example, Fairchild Camero and Texas Instruments have both set up factories in Hong Kong, where they can exploit a labour market in which 60% of adults work a seven-day week, and which also includes 34,000 children below the age of fourteen, half of whom work a ten-hour day.

It is worth noting that the imperialist companies are increasingly coming to international agreements whereby they share out the market amongst themselves and co-ordinate the rhythm at which new scientific innovations are introduced, thereby ensuring that all of them recoup their investments in new technology. After a breakthrough has been made with a new product, there usually follows an 'advertising war' which in fact corresponds to a temporary equilibrium between the economic forces involved in a specific sector.

Another aspect of the activity of the imperialist company is the development of trade between various subsidiaries of the same company which happen to be located in different countries. This is quite a long step from the situation described in Ricardo's famous early nineteenth century example, explaining that it was better for the English to exchange wool and cloth for Portuguese wines than to try to grow vines themselves. Nowadays the imperialist companies own the equivalents of both factories *and* vineyards. For instance, General Electric produces parts for computers which it sells 'at a loss' to its subsidiaries in Singapore, where they are assembled for 30 cents an hour, rather than pay $3.40 an hour to workers at the parent company's plant in Ashland, Massachusetts. One subsidiary's deficit is compensated for by the profits of the others; according to official figures, General Electric set up more than 60 subsidiaries between 1959 and 1969. The big U.S. watchmaking companies, Timex and Bulova, manufacture more than half of their products in Taiwan, alongside European companies such as R.C.A., Admiral and Zenith. The European imperialist companies definitely share the U.S. imperialist companies' enthusiasm for South-East Asia. The Rollei Company recently announced to its shareholders that, as wages were accounting for 60% of the cost of its cameras, it was going to invest in Singapore where wages were six times lower . . . and where the government provides big investors with a water-tight guarantee against any trade union agitation for a given number of years. There can be no doubt that the imperialist companies' ability to shift production from one country to another will have qualitative repercussions upon the activity of trade unions internationally.

Because of the falling rate of profit, U.S. capitalism cannot content itself with accumulating relative surplus value at home, so it is hardly surprising that it seeks out forms of exploitation based on the accumulation of absolute surplus value abroad. To understand why, one only has to compare the average hourly wages at home and abroad for similar tasks in various typical sectors of industry (see Table III.3).

During the last few years, the exports of multinational subsidiaries have gone up steadily. But this in no way implies any real economic development for the countries involved. Table III.4 should give some idea of the dynamic of this new type of 'neo-colonial' exploitation. It shows the growth in exports from the underdeveloped countries which are particularly 'favoured' by the U.S. multinationals. Finally, the following tables illustrate:

1. The growing dependence of U.S. imperialist companies on the Third World (see Table III.5).

2. The seriousness of the conflict between the U.S. and the other industrial powers over the exploitation of Third World raw materials (see Table III.6).

3. The growing dependence on imported sources of energy on the part of the U.S. and other industrialized countries (see Table III.7).

Table III.3
Average Hourly Rates of Pay: U.D.C.s and U.S.A. (in U.S. $)

Sector	*Underdeveloped Countries Country Rate of Pay*	*U.S.A.*
Electronics		
Hong Kong	0.27	3.13
Mexico	0.53	2.31
Formosa	0.14	2.56
Office Equipment		
Hong Kong	0.30	2.92
Formosa	0.38	3.67
Mexico	0.48	2.97
Semi-Conductors		
Korea	0.33	3.32
Singapore	0.29	3.36
Jamaica	0.30	2.23
Textiles		
Mexico	0.53	2.29
British Honduras	0.28	2.11
Costa Rica	0.34	2.28
Honduras	0.45	2.27
Trinidad	0.40	2.49

Table III.4
Industrial Exports from Underdeveloped Countries

	Value ($millions)			*Annual Growth Rate*
	1960	*1965*	*1971*	*1960 – 71*
Brazil	23	109	424	30%
Hong Kong	434	788	2,936	18%
Mexico	61	156	484	21%
Portugal	171	355	1,172	19%
South Korea	5	107	873	60%
Spain	221	380	1,771	21%
Formosa	59	228	1,588	35%

Table III.5
Raw Material Imports by Imperialist Countries

	Percentage from all foreign sources				*Percentage from under developed countries*
	1950	*1970*	*1985*	*2000*	*1971*
Bauxite	64%	85%	96%	98%	95%
Chrome	n.a.	100	100	100	25
Copper	31	17	34	56	44
Iron	8	30	55	67	32
Lead	39	31	61	67	32
Manganese	88	95	100	100	57
Nickel	94	90	88	89	71
Potassium	13	42	47	61	n.a.
Sulphur	2	15	28	52	31
Tin	77	98	100	100	94
Tungsten	37	50	87	97	37
Vanadium	24	21	32	58	40
Zinc	38	59	73	84	21

Source: I.L.O.

Table III.6
Developed Countries' Consumption of Third World Resources (as a %age of 1971 total world production)

	Produced by Under-developed Countries	*Consumed by all Industrialized Countries*	*Consumed by the U.S.A.*
Antimony	54.1%	59.8%	19.5%
Bauxite	55.6	75.5	24.6
Copper	41.0	75.23	24.8
Fluorine	46.4	80.7	26.3
Graphite	67.3	69.4	22.6
Lead	26.3	72.8	23.5
Manganese	41.5	33.7	11.0
Tin	80.5	83.8	28.5

Source: I.L.O.

Table III.7
Growing Dependence on Imported Sources of Energy (as a %age of total domestic consumption)

	1960	*1965*	*1970*	*1971*
Total Energy				
U.S.A.	6.2%	10.55%	8.4%	10.2%
West Germany	7.9	44.5	58.9	60.6
Japan	46.6	74.9	94.5	98.5
Oil				
U.S.A.	16.3	21.5	21.5	24.0
West Germany	83.8	90.4	94.4	94.7
Japan	100.0	98.2	100.0	100.0
Natural Gas				
U.S.A.	1.2	2.79	3.5	3.8
West Germany	0.0	29.3	22.7	29.3
Japan	0.0	0.0	32.3	34.5
Coal and other Fuels				
U.S.A.	0.0	0.0	0.0	0.0
West Germany	6.5	7.6	8.8	7.7
Japan	13.3	26.5	56.3	58.7

The Export of Capital

The export of capital was one of the main characteristics of pre-Second World War capitalism as described by Lenin. There was a reversal of these capital flows in the immediate post-war period. By the export of capital we mean investment in the colonies aimed at reaping profits from capital which can no longer be used in the imperialist metropolitan centres. As Lenin explains, the need for this arises when capitalism has matured excessively in these independent metropolitan centres.

The creation of monopolies in the advanced countries produced a surplus of capital at the beginning of the twentieth century, but in these same countries agriculture was backward and the masses impoverished. There was a danger that the gap between the newly multiplied capital's capacity for production and the masses' capacity for consumption would create a serious distortion. The only way to avoid the crisis was to export capital. Money flowed out to the colonies or to Russia, where it could be 'put to work'. This was no half-hearted effort: colonial settlements were established, especially by France after the 1870 Franco-Prussian War. When Germany seized the Eastern territories of what is now modern France, the French Government responded by sending the expatriated Alsatians off to work in Algeria. As Lenin points out repeatedly, the export of capital was the crucial factor. As he put it, 'the main characteristic of the old competitive capitalism was the export of goods: modern capitalism, under the monopolies, is essentially characterized by the export of capital.'[13]

But Lenin does not just explain why this is the criterion for differentiating the two stages of capitalism. He also shows all the consequences of this shift in emphasis. As capital investment in the monopolies declines, there emerges a tendency towards stagnation. The bourgeoisie becomes a purely parasitic 'coupon-clipping' class living off its shareholdings.

Examining the situation in Britain, at that time the most powerful of the capitalist countries, Lenin found that the export of capital had reached such a high level that production was already suffering seriously. As the number of shareholders reached a million, the proportion of people actively engaged in productive work dropped. From 1851 to 1901, the population grew from 17.9 million to 32.5 million but the number of workers in the main industries only went from 4.1 million to 4.9 million. In fifty years the proportion of productive workers had dropped by more than 30%. It had fallen from 23% to 15% of the total population.

Imperialism was the shareholders' apogee, and Marxist critiques took this very much into account. When, in 1919, Bukharin set out to write a 'critique of marginalist economy' as an answer to the works of the Vienna School,[14] he naturally called it 'The Political Economy of the Shareholder'.[15] Parts of this work (which was dedicated to Lenin) are unintelligible today if one does not bear in mind the very strong contemporary correlation between shareholding as a mass phenomenon and the export of capital so characteristic of imperialism. An analysis of imperialism therefore requires an examination of how capital reproduces itself.

The United States is the best example: only 5% of all U.S. investments are placed abroad. In 1963 less than $2 billion left the U.S., at a time when new investment in factories and plant reached almost $40 billion. This in itself should be enough to show that the situation is very different from that of the victorious Britain of the past. But this does not mean that these foreign investments are unimportant; on the contrary, they are an expression of the domination exercised by U.S. monopolies. However, these foreign investments are distributed very differently from those of early twentieth century British capital. The flow of investment capital today is directed mainly towards the developed capitalist countries rather than towards the 'economically backward' countries.

Since 1929 the percentage of U.S. investments abroad, as a proportion of the G.N.P., only exceeded 1% during two periods, 1938-40, when it reached 2.2%, and 1946-47, when it reached 3.8%. The former period corresponds to the preparation for the War, the latter to the launching of the Marshall Plan in Europe – both cases quite exceptional. If one looks at the scale of investments placed abroad today, one soon sees that it is no longer an essential stablizing element for the system.

The fact is that, nowadays, capital flows mostly in the opposite direction, from the poor countries to the rich countries. Imperialism is practising a new form of exploitation. For instance in 1975, Latin America paid out $15 billion to the U.S., $5 billion more than in 1974.

The main reason for all this is that the scientific and technical revolution allows a temporary attenuation of the contradiction between productive capacity and the capacity for consumption in the developed capitalist countries. The scientific revolution has made it possible to partly control the rate of investment, the structure of the market, and public and military expenditure. So the production/consumption contradiction is no longer so acute, and it is normal for the capitalist countries to import capital.This 'tendency' is not only reinforced by the fact that production and consumption can be adjusted; under conditions of international competition, technological and scientific advances are themselves a means of establishing hegemony. They make possible increases in the rate of profit on investments abroad and hence an even greater repatriation of capital.

As we have mentioned, when a U.S. firm seeks to set itself up in Western Europe, it only needs on average to bring in 10% of the necessary capital, since it can obtain the remaining 90% on the spot. To maintain this tendency there has to be a constant 'technological gap'; hence the necessity to continue investing in the U.S. itself. The growth associated with the scientific revolution has made investment in the imperialist metropolitan centres essential. Woe to anyone who does not respect this imperative: post-war Britain is a good example of what can happen. After the Second World War, British imperialism was faced with a choice. It could either continue with a modified version of its traditional colonialist policy or, on the contrary, break off from the Commonwealth and rejuvenate its particularly out-dated industrial apparatus. Britain chose the first alternative and as a result was eventually forced to devalue the pound. The turnabout in French capitalism, in 1958, also reflects the acuteness of the problem of how to assimilate the technological revolution and the concomitant need to invest in the metropolitan centre. The importance of investments in the imperialist countries explains why the underdeveloped countries' share of world industrial production has remained almost static despite the 2-3% per annum growth rate in these countries.

This reversal in the direction of capital flows is no temporary coincidental phenomenon; it is a fundamental characteristic of contemporary imperialism. As the after-effects of the Second World War wear off, and as the scientific revolution is increasingly integrated into the production process, this movement of capital is in fact accelerating.

How does this come about? The main mechanism is the return on foreign investments. Harry Magdoff's study of the U.S. balance of payments[16] shows that, during the period 1950-65, U.S. foreign investments amounted to $23.9 billion, and that the return on these investments repatriated to the U.S. amounted to $37 billions! So when one talks about the scale of foreign investment, it is worth noting that they make an important contribution to the flow of U.S. investment capital. It is no longer appropriate to see imperialism as a monster thrashing about in its death-throes; the monster has a hearty appetite and is constantly absorbing more in order to ensure its domination over the planet.

Formal political independence is thus no guarantee of having broken away from the grip of imperialism. On the contrary, imperialism has shown itself to be perfectly capable of adapting to the new situation created by the achievement of formal political independence in many countries. Through aid, loans and technical 'co-operation', new chains have been forged.

For the countries which are its victims, the export of capital means not only the renewal of exploitative relations but also a net loss of substance and the frustration of any efforts to accumulate the surplus which is so essential for development.[17] So the exploitation of the poor countries has been reinforced. Their labour contributes to a part of the capital which makes accumulation of wealth in the imperialist countries possible.

Table III.8
Investments Repatriated by the U.S. ($ billion)

	Europe	*Canada*	*Latin America*	*Others*
Investments brought in from the U.S.	8.8	6.8	3.8	5.2
Investment revenue repatriated to the U.S.	5.5	5.9	11.3	14.3
Resulting net flow (+ indicates flows into the U.S.)	–2.6	–0.9	+ 7.5	+ 9.1

Let us briefly examine the consequences of this new imperialism, and see if we can highlight aspects of its relation to the scientific revolution.

Firstly, there is the problem of unequal exchange; the prices of the products produced by the poor countries tend to fall in absolute terms (with some exceptions, as in the case of oil), whilst the products of the rich countries tend to become more and more expensive. Planned obsolescence is consistently used by capitalist management as part of a strategy to create more and more elaborate products, a strategy in which research plays an increasingly important role. The very rules of the game demand that prices rise. And of course, in the case of a new product, innovation also becomes a reason for price rises.

New forms of pillage now supplement classical exploitation. New and old exploitative practices go on side by side. Just as one can say that in the European countries the rulers are trying to restore market mechanisms, so it is fair to say that the contemporary operation of imperialism runs counter to the evolution described by Lenin, in that the use of the technological gap promotes the export of *goods.* One of the most novel aspects of this pillage is undoubtedly the 'brain drain', a feature which is clearly linked to the new importance capitalism gives to control over scientific and technical advances.

As Dr. Parkins, President Johnson's adviser on Third World affairs, once put it in an offical report: 'We no longer say "give me your poor, your hopeless masses"; what we say now is "give me your most brilliant, learned and talented citizens and let our machines do the manual labour".' The U.S. drains off precisely the sort of people who are most needed in the Third World. Out of 43,000 engineers and scientists who emigrated to the U.S. between 1949 and 1961, more than 60% came from underdeveloped countries. Out of the 11,200 immigrants who came from Argentina between 1951 and 1963, for example, more than 50% were qualified engineers, and 15% were skilled administrators.

The main consequence of all this is the acceleration of underdevelopment. The poor countries get poorer and the rich countries get richer. The growth of technical progress means that 'the scissors' separating those countries which have embarked on the technical revolution from the old colonies which are still struggling to get there are opening wider and wider. It is becoming more and more difficult for the latter countries to achieve their goal. There has been a dramatic drop in *per capita* production of foodstuffs in the Third World. The trade of these countries has not grown as fast as that of the developed countries and it is to be expected that it will be one of the first things to suffer from the slowing down of growth in the industrialized countries.

According to the bourgeois economists the problem is to get a country to a certain threshold, from which it can then 'take off'. We are told that everything comes down to introducing changes in a country's customs, agricultural structure and cultural level, by means of appropriate technical aid. If so, one wonders how it is that 'aid has not even prevented the situation in these countries from deteriorating.' The real issues are in fact quite different. However true it may be that the so-called underdeveloped countries need to reach a certain technical threshold in order to 'take off', this would require a complete reversal in investment policy, involving an attack on the international accumulation process and hence on capitalist structures themselves. Political independence in itself no longer has the value it used to.

For both analysts and observers it should be clear that contemporary imperialism has integrated the scientific revolution and is using it to maintain its domination. Underdevelopment cannot be understood as a delay, a historical late start, as suggested by W. Rostow who distinguishes five phases of social and economic evolution supposedly applicable to every part of the world, as if each area had the same social history. The reality is that the current situation of the underdeveloped countries has nothing in common with previous phases of industrial development in the developed capitalist countries. Unlike nineteenth century Europe, the underdeveloped countries of today have to cope with the pressures exercised by big international firms which enslave their labour force, exploit their raw materials and export the profits. The sheer scale of these firms enables them to exert enormous pressure. General Motors' annual turnover is equivalent to the total budget of thirty-five underdeveloped countries.

There is a second reason why underdevelopment cannot be assimilated to historical delay, even if such a delay were the original basis for the phenomenon. The demographic explosion in the underdeveloped countries is the direct consequence of disequilibriums introduced by imperialism at the beginning of the century. Industrialization in Europe did not shatter the balance between the European rate of demographic growth and available resources. Underdevelopment is not a hangover from the nineteenth century in a world of plenty; it is an integral part of modern reality. There is a cause and effect relationship between the situation of the developed capitalist countries and that of the underdeveloped countries. Both the demographic explosion and the export of capital contribute to the fact that the productive potential of the underdeveloped countries is under-utilized. On the surface, the statistics for *per capita* G.N.P. show a slight increase in several countries. But one should remember that these figures only apply to a modern sector of the economies in question, whose activities centre around exporting to the rich countries. The other economic sector, geared to the internal market, hardly ever appears in these statistics, since generalized under-employment and subsistence living mean that exchange and production within this sector do not usually involve money at all. Furthermore, progress in the modern economic sector often actually determines the regression of the sector geared to the domestic market. One could add that, by definition, statistics of *per capita* income do not tell us anything about inequalities in income (in the case of Kuwait for example). The very slight increases in *per capita* revenue indicated in these statistics (less than 2% in most underdeveloped countries) give a very one-sided picture of the evolution of these countries.

The export of economic surplus (due amongst other things to the weakness of the home market) and the demographic explosion together result in the paradox that underdeveloped countries cannot even fully use what productive capacity they do have. So the gap between rich and poor countries can only grow wider. Imperialist policy has reached a dead end: in maintaining its dynamism, the capitalist economy engenders growing disparities between rich and poor countries and increasingly between the developed capitalist countries themselves. The size of these disparities will be the essential theme of the coming 'explosions'. And the existence of 'aid' certainly does nothing to remove the problem. To begin with, there is no point in talking about 'aid' when one gives with one hand and takes back more with the other. Secondly, so-called 'aid' covers a wide range of expenditure, including military expenditure – which is often very extensive. Military aid to Latin America alone represents 6% of all military aid to foreign countries. It is well known that such aid enables the U.S. to unload out-dated surplus. 'Aid' also covers expenditure on common interests, expenditure involved in various forms of representation, and pensions.

When these categories are discounted, 'aid' dwindles spectacularly. In 1960 the U.N. expressed the hope that the rich countries would set aside 1% of their resources for aid to the underdeveloped countries. At the moment, 'aid' falls far short of this figure; expressed as a percentage of national income it is in fact falling constantly. Between 1963 and 1973 the real *per capita* income in the developed countries rose by 50%. During the same period the real value of official development aid fell by about 7%. In 1976, each inhabitant of the Third World received 30% less aid than in 1963.

The most obvious aspect of aid is that the recipient always has to buy from the donor. What is perhaps less apparent is that, even when aid does not come with specific economic and political strings attached, as it often does, it nonetheless contributes explicitly to maintaining existing social structures in the underdeveloped countries where capitalist relations of production rub shoulders with feudalism – one only has to think of the sort of working day put in by the peasants in Latin America. Powerful minorities draw off most of the country's wealth and further impoverish it by placing their capital abroad and by importing luxury goods. It is these minorities who benefit from 'disinterested aid'. It is hardly surprising, then, that the way the socialist countries distribute their aid has rather baffled the left.

As far as relations between rich and poor countries are concerned, the problem is not whether aid comes from a socialist or a capitalist country, but whether it reinforces an exploitative system or contributes to a socialist experience. The aid's country of origin has nothing to do with the matter. If it is given to a country controlled by a minority, aid only serves to bolster the *status quo.*

Like it or not, the fact remains that today the question of underdevelopment involves a very specific struggle. The way the imperialist system operates offers no hope that the underdeveloped countries will ever escape from their problems as long as they stay in the capitalist world market. As we have seen, what is happening today is a move in the opposite direction. A new period is beginning in the old colonial countries still under the neo-colonialist yoke. If there is anything to be learnt from an analysis of contemporary imperialism, it is that the struggle of the masses against the local bourgeoisie and bureaucracies will inevitably be renewed.

13. The Crisis

The preceding analysis should enable us to understand the new characteristics in the dynamic of the world crisis which is developing before our eyes. The strength of Marx's analysis is that it sought the origins of crises in deep contradictions in the capitalist mode of production and provided a dynamic explanation based on the progress of technology and the corresponding development of the forces of production. For Marx, 'the underlying reason for all crises is always the poverty and opposition between the restricted consumption of the masses on the one hand, and capitalism's method of developing the forces of production as if there were no limits to them other than society's absolute capacity to consume, on the other.'

Nature of the U.S. Crisis

The 'Crisis of 1929' was a crisis of overproduction linked to the tendency of the rate of profit to fall. It fits into the classical pattern. First, there was a surplus of goods and a generalized underemployment of human and material productive capacity; then, after a brief period of stops and starts, trade became paralysed and the circuits of capitalist production gradually ceased to function.

As Marx puts it in *Capital:*

> As the capitalist mode of production develops, along with the importance and durability of the fixed capital employed, so the life of industry and industrial capital lengthens, extending up to an average of ten years. But although its life is in some ways prolonged by the growth of fixed capital, it is also shortened by the constant revolution of the means of production, a revolution which intensifies as the capitalist mode of production extends itself. The resulting depreciation of the existing means of production means that they have to be replaced long before they are physically worn out.
>
> For the most important branches of industry this cycle may be said to be ten years long on average. But the precise figures need not concern us here. The point is that this cycle of rotation which extends over several years, during which capital is retained in its fixed form, is the material

Table III.9
Recessions in the U.S. since 1945

Periods affected	*Measured in*	*Nov'73 Nov'74*	*Nov'69 Nov'70*	*May'60 Feb'61*	*Jul'57 Apr'58*	*Jul'53 Aug'54*	*Nov'48 Oct'49*
a) Drop in GNP (in $ contemporary values)	months	0	0	6	6	12	12
b) Drop in GNP (in $ constant values)	months	9	6	12	6	12	6
c) Drop in industrial employment	months	0	8	10	14	14	13
d) Increase in rate of unemployment	months	12	30	15	16	15	21
Depth of effect							
a) variation in GNP (in $, contemporary values)	%	+ 5.0	+ 4.5	– 0.3	–2.6	– 1.9	– 3.4
b) variation in GNP (in $, constant values)	%	–2.9	–1.1	–1.6	–3.9	–3.4	–1.9
c) variation in rate of unemployment	%	+ 1.4	+ 2.8	+ 2.3	+ 3.8	+ 3.6	+ 4.5
d) maximum rate of unemployment	%	+ 6.0	+ 6.0	+ 7.1	+ 7.5	+ 6.1	+ 7.9
e) variation in industrial employment	%	+ 1.0	–1.6	–2.2	–4.3	–3.4	–5.2
f) variation in retail price index	%	+11.3	+5.6	0	–1.0	–1.0	–4.2
g) variation in industrial price index	%	+26.7	+3.6	–1.3	–0.5	–0.5	–5.5
Extent of effect							
a) % of expanding industries	%	42.4	19.2	19.9	11.7	13.3	10.0
b) consecutive months when the above % fell below 25%	months	0	4	6	12	10	8

Source: U.S. Bureau of Labor Statistics.

Table III.10
Industrial Production, 1950-73

	G.N.P. ($ billion)			Steel (million metric tons)			Cars (millions)		
	1950	1960	1973	1950	1960	1973	1950	1960	1973
U.S.	288.	511	1,289	88	90	136.4	8	7.9	9.7
Japan	12	43	418	5	22	119.3	–	0.5	4.5
Western Europe	152	330	1,150	50	106	150.0	1.5	5.5	10.4
Germany	23	71	357	12	34	49.5	0.3	2	3.6
France	29	61	253	9	17	25.3	0.3	1.4	3.2
U.K.	37	72	145	16	25	26.6	0.8	1.5	1.7

Table III.11
U.S. Profits ($billion) 1966-74

	Undistributed Profits				
	1966	1968	1970	1972	1974 est
Finance companies (Banks, oil majors, etc.)	4.3	4.3	4.0	7.7	10.9
Other companies (Steel, auto, building, etc.)	23.0	17.5	0.2	18.1	28.2
Adjustment for stock depletion	– 1.8	– 3.3	– 4.8	– 6.9	– 31.2
Total	21.2	14.2	3.4	11.2	– 3.0
Rest of market	1.8	2.4	2.4	3.5	11.6
Grand Total	27.3	20.9	9.8	22.4	19.5

Table III.12
U.S. Company Cash-Flow* ($billion), 1950-74

	Finance Companies	Other Companies	Rest of the World**	Total
1950	1.9	22.4	0.5	24.8
1960	3.8	33.3	1.0	38.1
1966	5.4	61.4	1.8	68.6
1970	6.0	62.2	2.4	70.6
1973	11.4	99.4	3.7	114.5
1974	11.7	104.4	11.5	127.4

* Cash-flow includes net pre-tax undistributed profits and amortization. Undistributed profits include the effects of stock revaluation.
** Cash-flow of U.S. companies abroad. Column 2 shows the cash-flow of companies within the U.S.
Source: *Survey of Current Business.*

Table III.13
Domestic Cash-Flow of U.S. Non-Finance Companies ($billion)

	Profits*	Stock Revaluation	Amortization	Total
1950	8.8	5.0	8.6	22.4
1960	9.2	– 0.2	24.3	33.3
1966	21.2	1.8	38.4	61.4
1970	3.4	4.8	54.0	62.2
1973	13.7	17.6	68.1	99.4
1974 (est.)	1.7	32.0	70.7	104.4

* Undistributed pre-tax profits less stock revaluation.

Source: *Survey of Current Business.*

> basis for the periodic crises which plunge business into successive phases of stagnation, normal activity and acceleration. The actual periods of capital investment are quite dissimilar and different from each other but the crisis nonetheless is always the starting point for the major enterprises, and when we look at society as a whole, we can see that it more or less provides the new material basis for the next cycle of rotation.[18]

The contradiction between the dynamic of technical progress and the private ownership of the means of production had not disappeared between 1945 and 1965. Its effects had merely been delayed as it took on a new form. The break in the cycle of crises forecast by Marx was only temporary. Table III.10 enables us to make the necessary comparisons.

When technical progress was slower, overall oscillations in the various sectors of industrial production accounted for the six to ten year cycles between crises. Later, as scientific progress increased, it brought with it a new, incoherent and accelerated rhythm linked to advances in the different branches of technology. The jagged oscillations which have characterized the overall movement of the economy since the Second World War replaced the old pattern. The incoherence of the new pattern slowed capitalist production's rate of growth and gave rise to the illusion that crises were a thing of the past. In fact, this phenomenon was the build-up to the generalized economic stagnation which has prevailed since 1965 in the world's most developed country, the U.S.

Even in periods when the system as a whole was expanding, cyclical crises did not disappear altogether. Apart from the present crisis, there have been four major depressions in the U.S. economy since 1945. Table III.9 illustrates their length, scale and seriousness.

From 1965 onwards, the scientific and technical revolution amplified two phenomena which began seriously to undermine the system. To begin with, a falling rate of profit and the growing saturation of the domestic market accentuated a tendency to concentrate on high technology industries at home while pushing for economic expansion abroad. As domestic profits fell so did investments. The U.S.A. had embarked on the course the British Empire had adopted some years before, with fatal consequences: neglect of domestic development in favour of foreign expansion. The U.S.'s share of the Western market fell from 70% in 1950 to 57% in 1965 and 49% in 1973.

The banks and foreign trade became the essential centres of profit. Tables III.11, III.12 and III.13 provide data to back up this proposition quantitatively revealing the intensity of the new Cold War launched by the U.S.

The History of the Crisis

To really understand the impact and dynamic of the crisis in the American economy today, we must put it into its historical context. With hindsight, we can distinguish three periods in the evolution of the U.S. since the end of the Second World War.

The Cold War and the American Empire 1945-58

The War which came to an end in 1945 was historically unique, in that, when peace finally came, nearly all the antagonists were broken and exhausted. The United States was the only exception. Its strength had more than doubled. Then having contributed to the overthrow of the old British and French colonial empires, the U.S. quickly set about filling the power vacuum. In the end, the U.S. replaced the old colonial system based on export of capital by a new neo-colonial system based on new technology and the pillage of the energy and mineral resources the system needed for its development.

With 6% of the world's population, the U.S. was using 60% of the world's mineral resources. By broadening the gap between industrial product prices and raw material prices, it created a flow of capital from the poor countries to the rich ones, and thereby methodically reduced two-thirds of humanity to ruin. The Latin American deficit went from $10 billion to $60 billion in a few years.

On another level, the U.S. was faced with the consequences of the sudden expansion of the socialist camp. The Chinese Revolution had pulled a quarter of humanity out of the capitalist system. The emergence of the People's Democracies (whatever one may think of their eventual evolution) threatened the stability of capitalist Europe. The revolts in the old colonies and the gradual march towards formal independence presented a long-term threat to a system which was ever more avid for cheap raw materials and labour.

So the U.S. embarked upon the Cold War. With the self-confidence conferred by atomic weaponry, the U.S. set about repairing the breaches in capitalism's defences made by the development of revolutionary ideas throughout the world. The Marshall Plan swung into operation, allowing the U.S. to make the most of the new markets opened up by the mass destruction during the War. It helped its vanquished opponents to recover economically, but at a price: U.S. imperialist companies seized control of whole areas of Japanese and European industry. The dollar reigned supreme; the Bretton Woods Agreements provided the legal back-up for American imperialism's domination in financial affairs. At the same time the European workers' movement fragmented. The Social Democratic Parties went over to the Americans *en bloc.* The Communist Parties were thrown out of several governments; as they became politically isolated, their line began to harden.

In a few years the U.S. had emerged as the greatest power the world had ever known. The real secret of its strength was the new life injected into capitalism by the technical and scientific revolution following the Second World War. However, as we have seen, there were inherent long-term limits to the economic stability of the American Empire.

The U.S. had no choice but to 'go along' with the economic trends towards foreign expansion. It set itself up as the 'policeman of the world' and covered the planet with strategic bases. Then it began to export its economic difficulties by dumping an increasing number of dollars on the international market – a solution which in fact only aggravated the balance of payments deficit.

From Cold War to Peaceful Coexistence, 1958-71

The war in Vietnam was a turning point in the American Empire's evolution. The United States was forced to send in its own troops, as opposed to getting the local fascists to fight its battles for it. The military intervention launched by Kennedy and intensified by Johnson failed to achieve its essential object, as defined by MacNamara, 'to demonstrate to the peoples of Africa and Latin America that guerilla warfare does not pay' and that the poorer countries can have no real hope of contesting the periodic redistributions of world wealth amongst the developed countries.

Relieved of part of the burden of military defence by the presence of American troops, the leaders of Europe and Japan began to assert themselves on the economic front. In Europe they organized the E.E.C. to protect themselves. They attacked the American market and penetrated it massively, especially with cars. The American balance of payments deficit got worse. First the pound, then the dollar came under threat, for similar reasons. De Gaulle went so far as to criticize the dollar's role as an international means of payment.

On the political level, the Atlantic Alliance, a product of the Cold War, gradually lost all content. Fuelled by the Vietnam War, unrest grew amongst the Blacks and the young. The American Empire was clearly overstretched and unstable, and there was only one thing in its favour. Khruschev's Russia, having proved incapable of eliminating the after-effects of the Stalinist era, weighed down by the cost of the arms race and weakened by the secession of China, was ready to compromise.

To get their country out of its difficulties, first Khruschev, then Brezhnev embarked on a political operation unprecedented in the history of the U.S.S.R. since the New Economic Policy of the early twenties. They purchased massive quantities of wheat. They accepted billions of dollars in loans, thereby hitching their waggon to the American star. In order to catch up economically, they did not hesitate to sell raw materials in exchange for the factories delivered by the American and European capitalists. The U.S.S.R. and the U.S. moved from the Cold War to Peaceful Coexistence. Eventually, however, America's leaders realized that this policy would not resolve all their problems. The fall in the domestic rate of profit continued: adjusted for inflation, the rate fell from 15% in 1955 to 10% in 1963 to 5% in 1973. Freed from the crushing burden of military expenditure, the U.S.'s Japanese and European competitors accelerated an expansion based on the super-exploitation of their workers; Japan had cheap labour and Europe was using a mass of immigrant workers to keep up. The U.S. balance of payments deficit got worse; by 1971, it had reached $7 billion. Inflation was at 5%. Some new policy was essential.

Towards a Third World War?

Lenin's prediction of the First World War in his work on imperialism was based on Marx's suggestion that in its ultimate stage the capitalist system would lead inevitably to world confrontations aimed at a periodic redistribution of markets and raw materials. These conflicts would develop into wars as an extension of normal politico-economic antagonisms. Two World Wars in a span of twenty-five years have confirmed the acuity of his analysis.

Now that both sides are equipped with hydrogen bombs and inter-continental ballistic missiles, a 'hot' war is obviously highly undesirable. Neither side would survive. But if one extends the analysis of Lenin to the period 1965-71, it is clear that World War Three has already started on the economic and political planes.

The diplomatic offensive of the U.S. opened with the spectacular about-turn in the line pursued hitherto by American imperialism in the Pacific. Taking a leaf out of Hitler and Ribbentrop's book (at the time of the German-Soviet Treaty) first Kissinger, then Nixon, went to China to conclude a treaty, thus isolating the Vietnamese who were eventually forced to accept the truce which came to an end in Autumn 1974. In the second place, the U.S. also developed its political and economic agreements with the U.S.S.R. (notably the massive sale of cereals) and began to confront its Japanese and European allies on the economic level. At first, Nixon and Kissinger accepted a fall in the dollar and its eventual devaluation. Then in 1971 they suspended its convertibility into gold and took draconian control measures which triggered off a panic. The political and economic risks were enormous, but so were the stakes. By brutally reducing imports and promoting exports, the deficit was stabilized and the haemorrhage of capital was staunched.

On the whole, the operation was successful. Analysis of Figure III.3 illustrates the correlation between the fall in the dollar and the increase in U.S. exports. It is more difficult (or perhaps all too easy) to understand why the Europeans, be it Giscard, Schmidt, Mitterand or Marchais, made efforts

Figure III.3 U.S. Industrial Exports ($ billion)

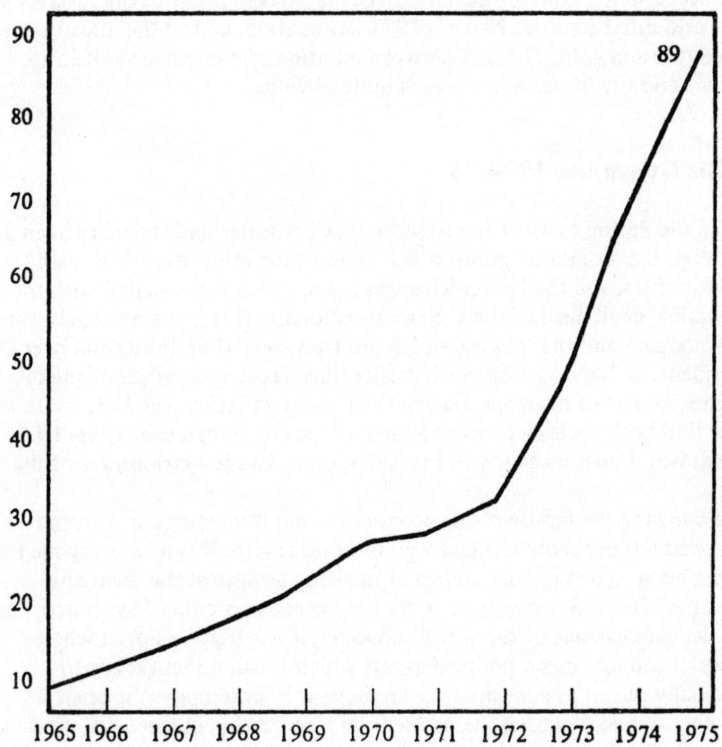

to revalue the mark and the franc, efforts which suited Kissinger's plans perfectly. This is the real context of the recent acceleration of inflation. After some significant early successes, such as the stabilizing of its balance of payments, the political re-conquest of the Middle East and the consecration of the dollar as the international means of payment, the U.S. ran into some fairly serious resistance from Japan. The latter even launched a counter-offensive. It began to trade directly with the oil producers, rejecting the dollar as a means of payment. It extended its economic influence in Brazil, Indonesia, Canada and even in the U.S. itself. Despite galloping inflation (more than 27% in 1974) it has just managed to re-equilibrate its balance of payments. The U.S. balance of payments, on the other hand, has begun to deteriorate again. U.S. exports of capital have been growing since the end of Summer 1974.

From then on, the crisis took the form of a growing disruption of the international financial system, which is characterized today by fluctuations in the exchange rates and uncontrolled movements of speculative capital (Euro-dollars and petro-dollars). To illustrate this argument, and to highlight the irreversible nature of the crisis, one only has to point to the feverish pace of world inflation since Nixon's 1971 devaluation, and to the 'uncoupling' of the dollar and gold. The link between inflation, the circulation of Euro-dollars and the increase in prices is quite obvious.

Crisis Dynamics, 1974-75

Since the Spring of 1974 the situation has got worse and there has been a split between the 'domestic' group which defends the interests of U.S.-based industrialists, and the Nixon-Kissinger team, which is associated with the 'outgoing' capitalism of the U.S. multinationals. This is the real background of Watergate and the removal of Nixon. However, when Ford took over as president, he had to accept Rockefeller, the classic spokesman of the oil majors, as part of his team. Having been hit by inflation, the U.S. consumers now find both their incomes and their jobs being threatened. Table III.14 which was drawn up at the end of 1974, illustrates the seriousness of the crisis.

Following the failure of the economic summit meetings of Autumn 1974, the crisis has probably reached a point of no return. It is now everyone (or rather every state) for themselves in the struggle against the crisis and inflation. The U.S. has proved to be a sorcerer's apprentice. By destroying the delicate balance of the world economy, it has triggered off a whole series of economic and political events which it can no longer control. Originally meant as a means to re-establish U.S. hegemony, the crisis is growing and accelerating. Its momentum is increasing in three different but mutually reinforcing ways.

The actual process is quite simple: the balance of payments deficits[19] caused by the price increases in oil and raw materials result in rising prices.[20] and accelerate inflation. As it is impossible for a country to export more unless it can find a country which is importing more, there is a general contraction of production, associated with credit restrictions and increases in the interest rate.[21]

All this results in growing unemployment. As the immigrant workforce is reduced, the crisis is exported to the home countries of the foreign workers. The economy then begins to choke up: increased interest rates squeeze the life out of small and medium firms, to the greater benefit of big capital which can still draw on the international money market. In the Summer of 1974 there was even an excessive accumulation of stock and a partial paralysis in industries, such as the car industry, which had been amongst the main driving forces of expansion from 1950 to 1970. The crisis has assumed the appearance of a classical crisis of overproduction.

Table III.14
Components of the Acceleration of the Crisis

	Gross National Product ($billions)	Cost of Living (1967=100)	Industrial Production (1967=100)	Unemployment (% of Labour force)	Personal Incomes ($ billions)	Industrial Profits ($ billion)	Retail Sales ($ billion)	House Building ($ billion)
1974	1,393	148	125.2	5.5%	1,150	88	544.9	1,371
1975	1,515	161	126.0	6.8%	1,246	79	599.0	1,200
Change	(–1% adjusted for inflation)	+8.8%	+0.6%	+23.6%	+8.4% (–3% adjusted for inflation)	–10%	+10% (–5% adjusted for inflation)	(–20% adjusted for inflation)

Table III.15
The Crisis, 1973-76

	Gross G.N.P. (% change)				Retail Prices (% increase)				Balance of Payment ($billion)				Unemployment** (000s of people)	
	1973	1974	1975*	1st half 1976* (est.)	1973	1974	1975	1st half 1976* (est.)	1973	1974	1975*	1st half 1976* (est.)	1974	1975*
United States	5.9	–2.1	–4	5	5.6	11.5	8.5	8.5	0.34	–0.87	3	–1.5	5,076	9,000
Japan	9.9	–1.8	1.5	6	11.8	21.7	11	6	–0.14	–4.69	–0.5	–1.25	720	900
West Germany	5.3	0.6	–3.5	4	7.1	7.3	6	5.5	4.31	9.34	8	3	582	1,060
France	6.5	3.8	–2	5	7.1	13.7	11.6	9	–0.69	–5.90	–1.75	–1.5	501	850
U.K.	5.2	–0.7	–0.7	0	8.5	15.2	21.5	15.5	–2.88	–9	–3.75	–2	637	860
Italy	6.3	3.4	–3	3	10.8	19.6	17	12	–2.67	–7.92	–1.75	2	560	700
Average for above countries	6.5	–0.6	–2.25	4.5	7.4	14	10	8	–1.73	–19.04	3.25	–4.25	8,076 *	13,370 *

* Total.
** Figures for different countries not strictly comparable.

Source: O.E.C.D. and E.E.C. (23 July and 21 October, 1975).

A comparison between the present recession and previous recessions shows that the crisis is no longer moderating inflation but is even tending to accelerate it. The Ford-Kissinger-Rockefeller government found itself condemned to simultaneous application of the brakes and of the accelerators provided by Keynesian economics. For each dollar's worth of goods sold in Department 2, 1.77 dollars' worth of unsold goods piles up in the warehouses. The ensuing contraction obviously has a deleterious effect on Department 1.

By the end of Summer 1974 the U.S. economy was in serious difficulty. The collapse of the New York Stock Exchange (the Black September of the new crisis) threatened the equilibrium of the whole country. For, as opposed to what happens in Europe where the stock exchanges play only a marginal role in the financing of businesses, shareholdings in the U.S. are a vital ingredient in the financing of new investments, and a considerable source of profit to the insurance companies, pension funds and various other foundations; shareholding also makes a sizeable contribution to the incomes of the U.S. middle classes at large.

In Autumn 1974 the deficit in the trade balance, which had been cancelled out during the Spring, started to grow again. The crisis in the car industry spread to other areas. Falling sales actually resulted in more redundancies outside the industry than within it. Calculations based on Leontieff matrices show that for every 250,000 car sales lost (worth say one billion dollars at constant values) one can expect 22,900 redundancies in the car industry, which implies 4,600 redundancies in the steel sector, 4,420 in the sales sector, 4,170 in metallurgy, 2,650 in machine tools, 2,200 in publicity and administration, 2,050 in transport and warehousing, 1,900 in textiles, 1,840 in electricity, 1,340 in rubber, 1,060 in maintenance and 760 in the glass industry. For every $billion in lost sales, there would thus be 22,900 redundancies in the car industry and 34,000 outside it. If one compares the car industry's 1973 sales figure of $57.5 billion with the 1974 result, $45 billion, the rise in unemployment due simply to the decline of the car industry is probably in the region of 250,000.

There were 4.3 million unemployed in the U.S. in November 1973. By December 1974 the figure had reached 7 million. The Blacks, Puerto Ricans and Mexicans were the first to suffer: 60% of Detroit's unemployed are Blacks. More detailed study reveals that the most badly hit industries are those in the forefront of technological advance. The relative inertia of the U.S. authorities was clearly due to their fear of putting the economy into an uncontrollable skid. Instead, they tried to export their crisis as much as possible, so as to attenuate its effects at home.[22] Kissinger's survival in office after Nixon's fall, and the arrival of Rockefeller were integral elements in this new policy. In fact, the U.S. re-adopted its 1971 policy of not supporting the dollar; its fall was even deliberately accelerated, when gold was put on sale again. The idea was to give a big boost to exports. The authorities had definitely rejected the attempt to bring oil prices down, thereby opening a new round in the cold war with Europe and Japan.

The difference between this crisis and previous ones was that it was genuinely international. The world economy can be compared to a network in which any specific upheaval triggers off a chain reaction, produces feedback and upsets the whole structure.

The Second Stage of the Crisis, 1975-?

The forecasts made in Spring 1975 by capitalist leaders and economists, predicting that the crisis would soon be over, merely illustrates how little they have understood what is going on and why. The crisis of overproduction in the American economy is not over. The first round in the economic battle triggered off by the U.S. did not produce any definite result. The Japanese economy has pulled itself together and since January 1975 has even succeeded in increasing its sales on the U.S. domestic market, especially motor car sales.

Secondly, the American grip on Europe has not been stabilized, despite a few spectacular successes (the Americans managed to grab the 'market of the century' away from the French). The new international division of labour has not been consolidated, and the U.S. is far from having established complete hegemony over the distribution of essential raw materials.

Furthermore, the U.S. has recently suffered the worst political and military defeat of its history. The Vietnamese people's exemplary victory has provoked a renewal of American expansionism. Finding itself threatened in Asia, American efforts now turn to the most decisive area of inter-imperialist confrontation in the world, namely Western Europe. The U.S. is more than ever committed to maintain – or re-establish – its hegemony there, a hegemony which necessarily prolongs and aggravates the economic and social crisis in Western society.

Finally, the U.S. has drawn certain lessons from the first phase of the crisis. After some conflict between Kissinger, who supported a high floor price for oil ($11 a barrel), and Senator Jackson, the spokesman of the industrialists, who wanted it to drop to $7 a barrel, the U.S. has decided in favour of the oil interests. The American strategy now has two main themes. They are making efforts to end their dependence on OPEC by ensuring their own monopoly over oil discovered in Africa (Zaire, Nigeria and Angola), Alaska, Mexico, Indonesia, etc. And they are promoting a new increase in oil prices, in co-operation with Iran and Saudi Arabia, as a means of striking at Europe and Japan again, and protecting their Arab proteges from the deterioration in the value of their income. Kissinger's two main weapons against the U.S.'s economic rivals, the falling dollar and increased oil prices, are still very much in use – and will eventually result in another phase of crisis.

In fact, during 1975 the main aspects of the crisis continued to manifest themselves in inflation, recession, unemployment, and a deterioration in the Third World's economic position. The decline in industrial production (see Figure III.4) which began in the middle of 1974 actually accelerated in the

Figure III.4 The 'Slump' in Industrial Production

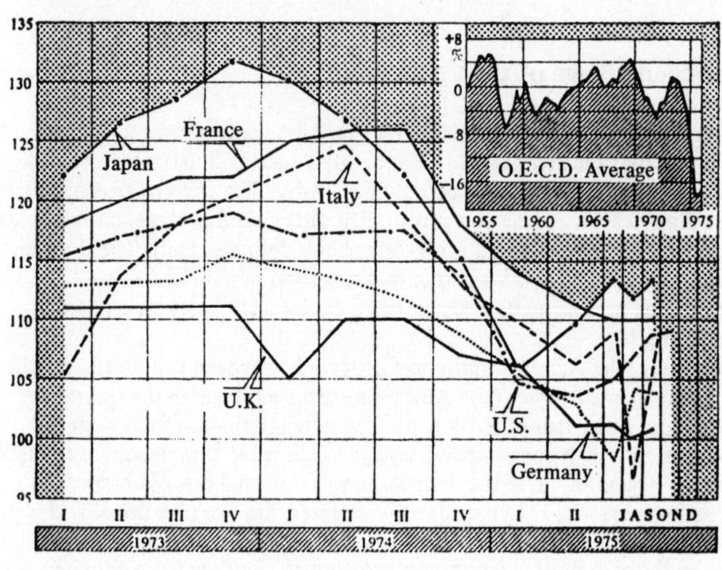

first half of 1975. Although it has now levelled off and production is increasing in the U.S., Germany and Japan, this slight improvement cannot be expected to compensate for the losses suffered during the first half of 1975 until well after 1976. G.N.P. fell in all the major industrialized countries: by 0.2% in Japan, 7.7% in the U.S., 7.2% in Germany, 5.8% in Italy and 5% in France. The results for 1976 look like this: +2% in France, +2.5% in the U.K., –3% in the U.S., –3.75% in Italy and +1.25% in Japan.

Unemployment has reached levels unseen since the War in most European countries, despite exceptional reductions in the working week (see Figure III.5). The most striking increases in unemployment occurred in Denmark (+103.5%), the U.K. (+81.9%), Belgium (+79%) and France (+77%). Seventeen million unemployed in the O.E.C.D. countries have just joined the thirty million unemployed in Latin America. World industrial production is still falling. Apart from local improvements which are essentially a matter of price changes (the French balance of payments is improving thanks to both the drop in imports due to the crisis and the increase in the prices of exported industrial goods), the capitalist market is contracting and the international monetary system is gradually falling to bits.

In the U.S. the main symptoms of the crisis continue to manifest themselves: contraction of trade, increased number of bankruptcies, etc. The number of companies going into liquidation in 1975 increased from 20% to

Figure III.5 Unemployment as a % of the Active Population, 1973-75

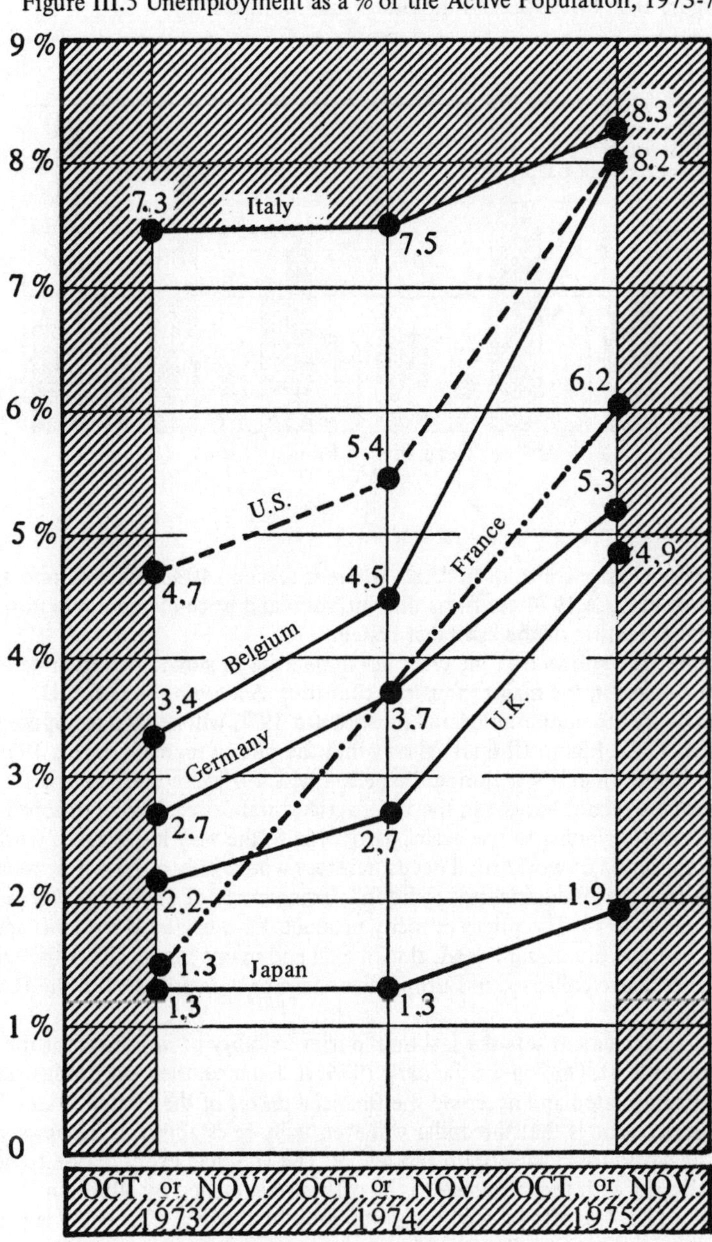

Figure III.6 Price Rises in the Industrial Countries (%)

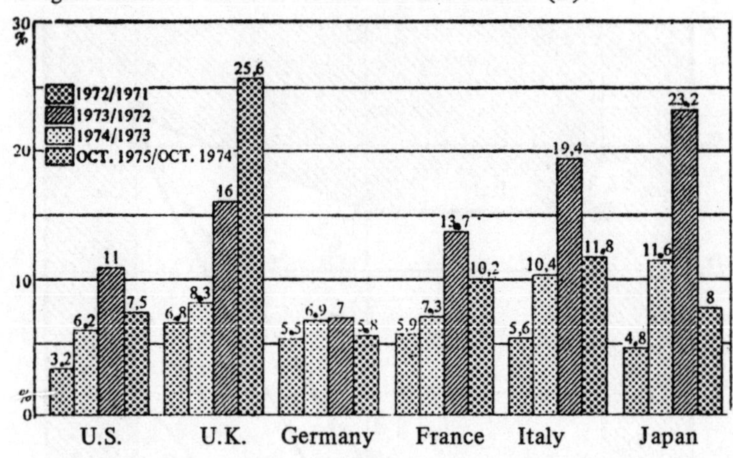

25% everywhere except in the U.K., where it reached 40%. The way prices have moved since 1974 confirms that inflation and price increases are now a permanent feature of the capitalist system.

Figure III.6 shows that the crisis has done little to slow down the rate of price increases in the major industrial countries. According to O.E.C.D. calculations, the minimum overall increase for 1976 will be 8%, as opposed to 9% in 1975. Figure III.6 also shows that the rate of increase during 1976 will be higher than it was during the period which triggered off the crisis.

Despite a record harvest in the U.S., agricultural prices, having dropped for a while, are beginning to rise again, partly due to the very low level of world stocks (in terms of world food needs, reserves would only cover a few weeks)

It is true that industrial prices did fall during much of 1974, but this came to an end in 1975. The prices of many products have begun to rise; this applie to oil, bauxite, aluminium, lead, zinc, nickel and many chemicals. Although steel prices have collapsed in Europe, they have been maintained in the U.S. and Japan.

One final element sets the seal on the irreversibility of inflation, for the moment at least. On 7 and 8 January 1976, in Jamaica, the major industrial powers capitulated and accepted the financial *diktat* of the United States. Th main implication is that the dollar will eventually re-establish its hegemony over the world financial system as a whole. The U.S. had every reason to be well satisfied with this outcome to the offensive launched by Nixon in August 1971. The official gold price was abolished, which effectively legalize the role of the paper dollar as international currency. Furthermore, the statutes of the I.M.F. were modified in such a way that the U.S.'s adversaries no longer have any recourse against the manipulation of their currencies, since the U.S. (supported by Britain and Italy) now commands enough votes (30%) to block any counter-measures. With the help of its clients, America can now force through the issue of sufficient quantities of S.D.R.s to prevent its economic adversaries struggling against the continued devaluation of the dollar.

The decisions taken in Jamaica are a reflection of how successfully the U.S. has exported its crisis. Since the end of 1975, the American balance of payments has improved. It is even running a surplus (nearly $10 billion) despite the $5 billion added to the deficit in 1974. Thanks to the crisis, imports have been reduced; the fall in the dollar, combined with increased sales of armaments and agricultural goods, has boosted exports, especially to the Asian countries and the oil states. By the end of the first stage of the crisis, the United States has clearly managed to redress its position in relation to its European and Japanese rivals.

The other major industrial countries, plunged into crisis a little later than the U.S., have now also taken steps in the same direction. France's trade balance improved, from being $4 billion in the red in 1974 to $2 billion in the black by 1975. Japan's surplus went up from $1.5 billion to $5 billion during the same period. Meanwhile, Germany's surplus fell from $22 billion to $18 billion. Figure III.7 illustrates how the main O.E.C.D. countries turned a $27 billion deficit in 1974 into a $7 billion surplus in 1975.

The other half of the picture is the radical deterioration of the Third World's economic position. Apart from the oil producers, there are no longer any really 'developing' countries; certain countries may be expanding industrially but this expansion benefits mainly the big 'multinational' companies.

If one takes a closer look at what has happened to all the petro-dollars, it emerges that most of them have been reinvested in the wealthy countries ($40 billion out of $60 billion in 1974). The remainder has been issued as loans to cover the growing deficit of the poor countries, who have to buy the increasingly expensive but indispensable products they import on credit.

In 1976 the four essential characteristics of the crisis are as follows:

1. There is a general contraction of trade, linked to the contraction of the industrial economies.

2. Inflation continues as the scientific and technical revolution makes it increasingly possible to substitute relative surplus value for absolute surplus value.

3. There is an overall drop in G.N.P., linked to the impact on the capitalist system as a whole of the U.S. crisis of overproduction. This expresses itself as underemployment of the apparatus of production and a general increase in world unemployment.

4. The Third World's problems are getting worse, as the terms of exchange continue to deteriorate, as the price of industrial products rises and as their raw material exports diminish.

Obsessed as they are with their own problems, Westerners do not realize

Figure III.7 Changes in the Trade Balance, 1973-75

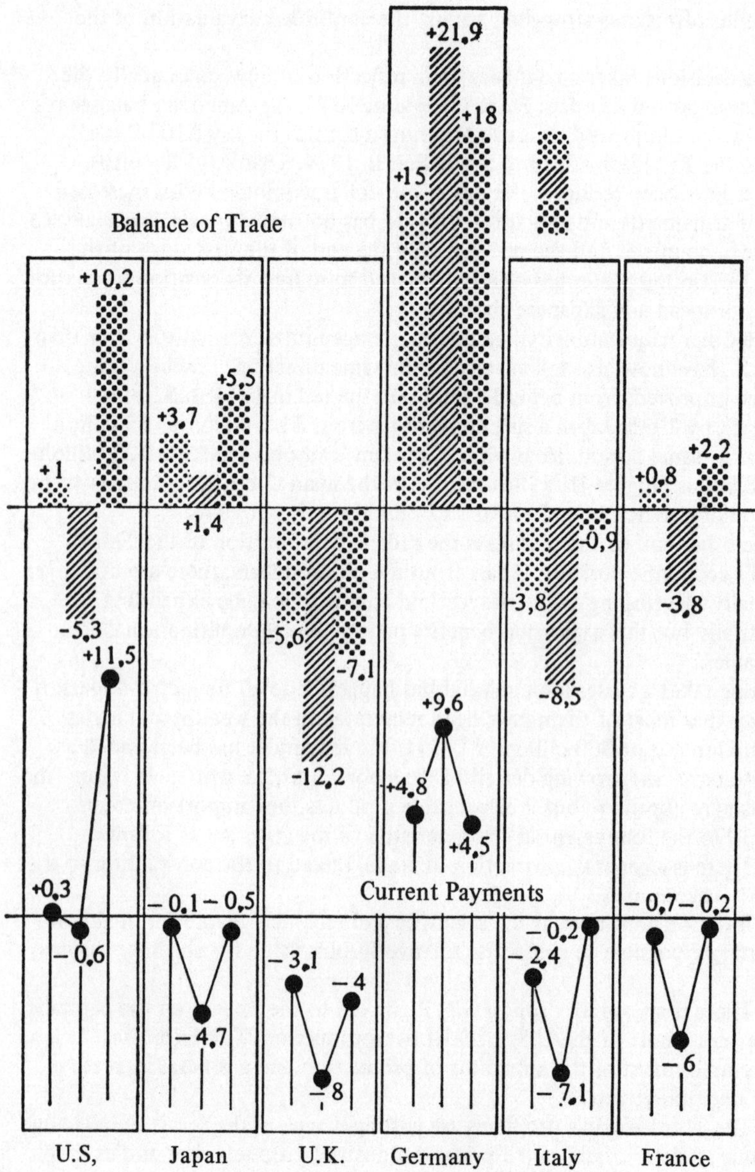

how serious the situation in the Third World has become. Since 1972, when the 'developing' countries accounted for 70% of the world population, 20% of total production and 7% of industrial production, things have got steadily worse. Since 1973, for example, the gap between the *per capita* annual income of people in the rich countries and the poor countries ($3,841 as against $202 in 1973) has widened by 10% a year. In the light of all this, it is hardly surprising that Mr. Giscard d'Estaing was 'successful' in organizing the North-South confrontation in December 1975. Between Spring 1975, when Kissinger rejected the idea of talks, and the Autumn, the situation of the Third World countries (including the Arab countries) had got so bad that they had to accept many of the conditions laid down by the Americans, the Germans and the French. For example, the income of the oil countries has dropped in absolute value since the beginning of 1975 as a direct result of the fall in the gross volume of oil exported, the fall in the dollar, inflation and the corresponding deterioration in the terms of trade. Countries like Algeria which had launched long-term industrialization schemes found themselves running into the sort of difficulties which pushed them back into subjection to U.S. imperialism. Paradoxically, the one thing which saved them was the U.S. oil multinationals' desire to keep the price of oil as high as possible.

Dr. Kissinger's diplomatic successes in the Middle East have nothing to do with a desire for peace. They are merely the expression of the U.S.S.R.'s failure in Egypt and should be seen as part of the attempt to re-establish the American Empire in the Mediterranean. This is also where Spain comes in. Kissinger and Ford have just paid out $750 million to Spain in order to consolidate the U.S.'s military bases there. Juan Carlos' fascist Spain is one of the key strategic 'padlocks' in the American *Mare Nostrum*.

Since the middle of 1974 industrial production in the developed countries as a whole has been poor compared to 1973, even if in some countries, Japan, for instance, certain sectors seem to be improving. In the E.E.C. one can extrapolate that in 1976 there will be a weak upturn or even economic stagnation, with rising unemployment, increased inflation (10 to 12%) and deteriorating trade balances. The results for 1975 are themselves less good than the experts predicted: the gross domestic product of the Western countries is down 2.4% on average, as opposed to a 2% increase in 1974. In the most seriously hit countries such as Britain and Italy, there are no signs that the decline in G.N.P. is slowing down. Britain, where the index has fallen by 10% since 1974, is worse off economically than in 1970. In Italy, economic deterioration is even leading to disintegration of the state's political and economic apparatus.

National idiosyncrasies are not the only explanation for the fact that different countries are experiencing the crisis in very different ways. The more powerful states can use one of two methods to attenuate the effects of the crisis, at least for a while. The first method consists of forcing weaker and dependent partners to pay for one's own crisis. Just as the U.S. tried to export its crisis to Europe and Japan, so Germany and then France have exported theirs to the weaker E.E.C. and Mediterranean countries. For example, the increase in unemployment is 'slowed down' by expelling foreign workers.

The crisis has accentuated the disparity in economic strength between the major industrial countries, to the considerable advantage of West Germany. The control exercised over Europe by the U.S. through Germany is intensifying constantly. Schmidt is increasingly assuming a dominant leadership role in Europe. On 14 October 1975 he issued a stern warning to the other eight European heads of state that Germany was no longer prepared to tolerate new expenditure aimed at promoting Third World development. He then went on to criticize E.E.C. agricultural expenditure as an impediment to the import of American agricultural produce. And he declared his opposition to any future long-term contracts with Third World countries.

Three years after the first wave of the U.S.'s counter-offensive against its European and Japanese rivals, Europe is further than ever from a return to the prosperity of 1958-73. The breakdown of the E.E.C. monetary 'snake', the beginnings of economic and political collapse in Italy, Britain and Spain, the catastrophic decline of the Third World, the surge of political and social tension in Europe and the revival of Cold War hostility between the U.S. and the U.S.S.R. all indicate that there is no reason to hope that the present stirrings of an upturn in the U.S. will lead to a generalized phase of expansion throughout the system.

Political Implications of the Crisis

It is obviously too early to analyse the eventual consequences of the battle at hand. What we can say is that the equilibrium established between the major powers at the end of the Second World War has been broken once and for all. In the first place, the crisis is going to make the gap between rich and poor countries irreversible. New inequalities will appear, between overpopulated countries who do not have any raw materials, such as India, and underpopulated countries who do, such as the Arab states.

On the international level, the U.S. intends to use the crisis in order to re-establish its hegemony over Europe and Japan, thereby emerging as the greatest power in the history of the world. Of course, if the Americans can help it, they will not push the pressure they can exert through oil to the point where Europe and Japan succumb to revolutionary crises. The U.S. only intends to keep its rivals in their place – alongside Latin America – even if this means supporting authoritarian or even military regimes so as to maintain order amongst the population.

Having established a firm grip on the Japanese and European economies, the U.S. will be in a very different position in its negotiations with the U.S.S.R China and the Third World. How the rest of the world will react to such a threat is difficult to foresee. The U.S.'s adversaries can still join together, but they may also adopt the sort of individualistic approach which Europe has just demonstrated so pathetically. It is also quite possible that *'detente'* and the present forms of 'co-existence' between the Russians and the Americans will evaporate far more rapidly than the supporters of the U.S.-U.S.S.R. condominium expect. Since early 1974, it has been clear that relations between the Russians and the Americans are definitely going to 'cool', as a necessary by-product of the new inter-imperialist confrontation and the resulting disequilibrium in the balance of forces between the two superpowers.

The U.S. has come a long way since De Gaulle forced them to pull their military bases out of France. The impact of the crisis has definitely brought Europe to heel – not long ago Giscard authorized U.S. marines to conduct manoeuvres in the South of France. The U.S. probably contributed to Brandt's downfall, and had no reason to be displeased by Wilson's victory over Heath. The fiasco of Cyprus was amply compensated for by the consolidation of the Karamanlis regime in Greece.

Kissinger was able to use the economic upheaval in another area as well. The pro-American Arab rulers are now afraid of losing the economic advantages obtained from the oil 'crisis'. They dread the possible revolutionary consequences a new war might have, both in Europe and in their own countries. They therefore pretend to believe America's promises that Israel will restore the conquered territories. By Spring 1974 the position that Britain once occupied in the Middle East had been taken over by the U.S. The U.S.S.R. had lost all influence in the area except in Iraq (threatened by the Kurdish revolt) and Syria. Kissinger must surely have read Machiavelli; he needs Israel far too much to force it to hand back anything except a few square miles of desert in Sinai.

In the face of the intensifying crisis, Ford has now opted for a resurgence of inflation as a means to halt the decline in the American G.N.P. The way has been paved for a return to the 'Cold War', which will boost military expenditure and ensure U.S. control over Europe. The U.S. is well aware that the exporting of its crisis to Europe will put severe strains on the Atlantic Alliance. A renewal of international tension would contribute considerably to the consolidation of an empire previously undermined by *'detente'*.

This is why Washington has recently been provoking the U.S.S.R. The conflict between Jackson and Kissinger was pure sham. Ford and Kissinger were fully aware that, by suspending the 1972 trade agreement, they were opting out of the main commitment made to the U.S.S.R. in exchange for promoting a favourable resolution of the Vietnam problem.

The consequences of such a policy are obvious. The U.S.S.R. cannot accept the loss of its influence in Europe and the Middle East without reacting in some way. Furthermore, it seems likely that the crisis will soon affect the people's democracies, whose economies are too closely linked with that of the West to escape unscathed – already prices on their parallel markets are increasing. Insignificant technical improvements are being used to justify substantial price rises. The sale of housing to individuals is no longer sufficient to re-absorb the considerable liquidities accumulated in deposit accounts. As a result, improvements in the standard of living and the introduction of the consumer society have been postponed indefinitely. The fact that the U.S. is re-establishing its hold on Europe and the Mediterranean, and freezing out the U.S.S.R., has inevitably resulted in a shift in policy, for instance the recent hardening of the U.S.S.R.'s line on Africa. The new line makes it easier to consolidate the people's democracies and to justify economic sacrifices in the name of defending the Motherland.

The threat may even become concrete; in the long term the European crisis raises once again the whole problem of German imperialism. The Federal Republic of Germany is the U.S.'s main ally in Europe, suffering far less from the crisis than its E.E.C. partners. Such a situation must eventually find some sort of political expression. The dynamic of the crisis impels the ruling classes towards the type of regime which is strong enough to defend their privileges, so that Strauss may well be the man of the future in West Germany.

Indeed, on the domestic level, the end of abundance is likely to result in profound changes in the vanquished capitalist countries. Whole sectors of industry, such as the Concorde programme or the Italian petrochemical industry, are on the verge of collapse. Inflation and prices will soar and permanent trade deficits will become the order of the day. In terms of profitability, the only way to preserve an acceptable minimum level of capital reproduction and competitiveness on the world market is to reduce the rate of improvement in the standard of living and to freeze salaries; in other words, to get the working class to accept sacrifices significant enough to preserve capitalism in Western Europe and Japan. This will not be easy, since a continued improvement in living standards has been promised for a long time now the whole vocabulary will have to change. It would certainly prove very difficult to push through the classic solutions to times of crisis, namely the war economy and the development of state capitalism.

The crisis has also changed the European political scene. The Moscow-Washington *detente* had enabled the Western Socialist and Communist Parties to move closer together, since foreign policy differences could be shelved. The revival of the 'Cold War' has forced the partners to choose which camp they support. This is part of the reason for the growing quarrel between Socialists and Communists in France and Portugal. Apart from the Swedes, none of the European Socialist leaders has ever publicly condemned U.S. policy, Mitterand included. Formally, Marchais' accusations against Mitterand are absurd, but they do express a profound underlying truth: European social democracy has definitely been the accomplice of a certain type of U.S. policy, a complicity it has hidden behind empty phrases about the 'multinational' character of capital.

The suspicions which animate the quarrel are quite understandable. The crisis implies that the 'historic compromise' elaborated by the Italian Communist Party, and effectively adopted by the European Communist movement will eventually break down. Kissinger has already stated quite plainly, and with explicit reference to Italy, that the U.S. would take steps to prevent the Western Communist Parties from participating in government. As a result, the prospective bourgeois partners in the new alliance have back-tracked. Agnelli in Italy and Chirac's U.D.R. in France have rejoined the ranks. The Italian C.P. has therefore drastically moderated its pretensions. In exchange for its support for the Christian Democrats, it merely demands that it should be consulted. And in France, too, the legal parliamentary road to power is henceforth closed to any alliances between the Socialist and Communist Parties.

Because of the crisis, there has been a great resurgence of class warfare. Linked to an empire which is all too willing to sacrifice its allies in order to preserve its own leadership position, the various bourgeoisies are in for a difficult period. And the effects of the crisis show no signs of wearing off; it has now spread from the U.S. to the capitalist world as a whole. The economy of the Third World is collapsing before our very eyes. Countries which were painfully labouring towards 'take off' have crashed to the ground again. There are thirty million unemployed in Latin America, and throughout the world millions of people are starving. A new phase in revolts against imperialism is in the offing. Following the brilliant victory of the Vietnamese, revolution is on the march again in South-East Asia. In Asia as in the Middle East, the time for truces and compromises is over.

American 'Recovery' and the German Viceroy of Europe

There are no definite signs of a general economic recovery in Western Europe, although a few illusory hopes rest on the oversimplification that the present situation is comparable to the 1950s, when U.S. expansion did give a very large boost to the capitalist economy of Europe. But the post-1945 expansion was based on conditions which are no longer present. In 1945 the upturn provided by the need to rebuild Europe, the flood of technical innovations and the widening out of the capitalist market to include the masses provided the system with the tonic it needed to overcome the after-effects of 1929. But it was not enough to prevent a new drop in the rate of profit and a new crisis of overproduction, starting in the U.S. in 1965. 1945 has long since passed.

Even superficial analysis will show that the partial recovery of the U.S. economy is based on two different factors, which do not alter the essential contradictions afflicting the American system since 1965 – the very contradictions which led to the worldwide export of the U.S. crisis. The first factor is the sudden upturn in armaments expenditure. In just one year the U.S. military budget jumped from $90 billion to $115 billion, to which one should add the 20% increase in research and development expenditure, amounting to over $24 billion. The second factor is the growth of U.S. exports due to the continued fall of the dollar (as against the overvalued European currencies) and to the consolidation of the new international division of labour. The U.S. now dominates all the most advanced industrial sectors, such as electronics, chemicals, etc., and has routed its economic rivals in those sectors in which it felt threatened, such as aeronautics.

The fact remains, however, that U.S. industry is still only operating at 75%

capacity and that the official figures show a 15% drop in investment. A recent study by McGraw Hill, comparing the first thirteen weeks of 1976 with the same period in 1975, even indicates that the number of factory construction projects has fallen by 44%. Finally, the U.S. balance of trade is in the red for the second month running (falling from –$72.6 million in January 1976 to –$140.8 million in February), after having been in the black (+$11,050 million) from January to December 1975.

Housing and consumer goods, and the other economic sectors linked to mass consumption, are still stagnating. It is now clear that this type of 'recovery' will not solve the unemployment problem in the U.S. Government experts admit that, even according to the most optimistic estimates, the rate of unemployment will still be over 7% during the presidential elections. To bring it down to 5% by 1980, one would have to create twelve million jobs, which would imply the sort of 'Japanese style' growth unseen since the War. Henceforth a high rate of unemployment will thus be a permanent feature of the capitalist economy as a whole. This is particularly problematical in the U.S. where unemployment affects mostly the young and the Blacks. It reaches 19.2% amongst the under-20s and 35.2% amongst Blacks under 20. As the *New York Times* cheerfully pointed out in February 1976, the Ford Government will spend $18 billion on unemployment benefit during 1976, so as to keep the unemployed off the streets.

So we see that the lull in the crisis in the U.S. is based not on a broadening out of the market, but mainly on economic and political victories over its Japanese and European rivals, who finally capitulated on 19 January 1976 in Jamaica. The European governments are completely paralysed and do not even dare denounce what is happening, for fear of triggering off uncontrollable upheavals. Like unemployment, inflation is now one of the system's permanent features. It epitomizes the defeat of Europe and the emergence of a new balance of forces, reassuring the Americans that the time when their supremacy was threatened by the recovery of rival imperialisms (1935-73) is over once and for all. So what the U.S. 'recovery' really means is that the U.S. has managed to pull out of it to some extent, by the simple expedient of exporting it, by plunging relatively 'healthy' capitalist economies right into it.

The U.S.'s leaders have learnt their lesson from Vietnam. Their support now goes to political agents whose corruption is somewhat less blatant than Thieu's. European social democracy is one of their main trump cards. After Schmidt, Wilson and Soares, Kissinger is now wooing Mitterand. In short, the Socialist International is now the left-wing of the American party in Western Europe. In the class war, words count for nothing: the only thing that matters is one's attitude to the concrete economic measures which ensure American big capital's domination over Europe.

The new U.S. strategy involves a return to large-scale arms production and export. This old method of fighting crises is becoming increasingly important now that the remedies proposed by Keynes have been found wanting. But the military budget ($90 billion) has not been enough to revive the U.S. economy. American arms exports have gone up from about $4 billion in 1973 to $11 billion in 1975, easily overtaking agricultural exports. They were one of the key factors in the improvement in the U.S. balance of payments during 1975. France has adopted the same course. It recently displaced Britain as the third largest exporter of arms after the U.S. and the U.S.S.R. The value of French arms exports – mainly to the most reactionary regimes in Africa and Latin America – quadrupled in 1972 and doubled again in 1973. In 1975 they reached $5 billion. Without arms sales, the French balance of payments situation would be one of the worst in Europe.

Since 1973 West Germany has also joined in. In order to side-step the treaties, the German Socialist leaders, encouraged by the U.S., have set up armaments factories in Algeria, Burma, Ghana, Indonesia, Nigeria and the Sudan, as well as shipyards in Singapore and tank factories in Argentina. Finally, Germany has now embarked on building nuclear factories and atomic weapons in Brazil and South Africa. The 1973 crisis, just like the one in 1929, has forced the major industrial powers into an arms race, and the possibility of a revival of autonomous German imperialism is beginning to worry its neighbours.

The way the U.S. has chosen to deal with its problems implies in itself a shift in American foreign policy. The dynamic underlying the decline of *detente* policies and the return to a new 'populist' form of Cold War favoured by Schlesinger, Jackson, Carter and Reagan is a direct reflection of the balance of forces within big U.S. capital.

Kissinger's policy was mainly based on the growing importance of U.S. multinationals in the U.S. economy. One can easily show that every stage of the Nixon-Kissinger foreign policy (including the approaches to China and *detente* with the U.S.S.R.) corresponded exactly with the essential interests of the big U.S. banks and multinationals. However, this policy was not accepted by the entire ruling class of the United States; indeed it clashed head on with some very important interests, thereby engendering new internal contradictions which eventually resulted in Nixon's downfall.

Supported by the most dynamic sections of U.S. capital, the policy was strongly resisted by the old 'national' industrial capital, especially steel and automobile interests, who found it particularly difficult to cope with the penetration of their home market by Japanese and European competitors. Later on, other interests joined the opposition to the Kissinger line; the new industries of the military-industrial complex (nuclear, missiles, electronics, etc.) found that *detente* and the concomitant arms limitations did not suit them at all. Finally, there were the big unions. Class collaborators from way back, and since 1949 staunch opponents of any agreements with the socialist states, these unions naturally fought against a policy which led to the creation of jobs outside the U.S. and which in the long term threatened the privileges derived from the American workers' participation in the super-exploitation of the Third World ever since the end of the Second World War. In their own terms, the opponents of the Kissinger line are quite consistent. They have evolved a new policy which has already found many spokesmen, such as Jackson, Carter and the U.S. Senate, who are pressing for a return to a somewhat modified version of the Cold War. This would justify constantly expanding the U.S. military budget which, in association with a mini New Deal should do something to stimulate mass consumption, at home at least.

Kissinger's opponents also hope to consolidate the new international division of labour by cutting down American commitments abroad and concentrating American resources on a few key sectors, while trusting a few reliable allies to keep the 'Pax Americana'. This new policy has nothing in common with the 'isolationism' of the 1930s. The U.S. has merely appointed its proconsuls: West Germany in Europe, Iran in the Middle East and Brazil in Latin America.

The new policy is on the verge of triumphing in the U.S. Its opponents are constantly making concessions to it. The present paralysis of U.S. foreign policy reflects the transition. The antagonism between the multinationals and the military-industrial complex underlies both the Watergate scandal and the Senate investigation into corruption financed by the multinationals. The Watergate affair does indeed do honour to certain democratic features of the U.S. press and public opinion, but it is also very much a reflection of the split in the American ruling class and of the extensive support which Mr. Nixon's adversaries in the state apparatus and the White House have enjoyed.

The American and German veto on any participation in government by the Western Communist Parties concretizes the dilemma which faces the advocates of the 'historic compromise', a dilemma which reflects the inadequacy of their leaders' political analysis and understanding of the balance of forces which determines U.S. policy. Berlinguer, Carrillo and Marchais are quite mistaken if they believe that they will overcome the suspicions of their bourgeoisies and obtain even tacit consent from the U.S. to their participation in government merely by launching a polemic against the U.S.S.R. and adopting all the fundamental theoretical positions of social democracy. The Italian Communist Party is learning this lesson at the moment. Despite the fact that the Italian state is falling apart, that the economy is collapsing and that the regime is at least as corrupt as Thieu's, the U.S. has not conceded one inch. For several weeks now, the U.S. has stopped supporting the lira, to ensure that Italy will toe the line. Amendola and Segre have shown themselves willing to offer Kissinger any guarantees he likes, but all in vain. The U.S. would not go back on a decision which rests on a now irreversible feature of the new American policy. *Domination and control over Europe is essential to the future of U.S. power.*

Ford, Kissinger and Haig have issued a warning which must be taken seriously: they represent a thoroughgoing shift to the right in U.S. public opinion. Whoever wins the U.S. elections, it seems clear that *detente* is dead and that no American government will ever tolerate Communists holding high office until the European C.P.s have broken irreversibly with Moscow. Mitterand is wrong: the U.S. will not eventually reconcile themselves to part-Communist governments in Europe, and he too has come to a crossroads. If he accepts U.S. guardianship over Europe, if he recognises the West Germans as viceroys, if he continues to defend an American and German dominated

Europe, he will have to come to some compromise with the French C.P., in order to ensure that the latter does not participate directly in government. This solution is not altogether inconceivable. Marchais has even mentioned the possibility of a government similar to the Popular Front, in which the Socialists and Radicals enjoyed the support of the Communists under the banner of the anti-Fascist cause. But the problem is that in the long term such a strategy implies dropping the Party's national line. Europe is the only subject on which the French C.P. has so far not followed the lead given by the Italian C.P. in adopting an essentially social democratic approach. The Party will find the pill hard to swallow. Already at the 22nd Congress, there were nationalist rumblings.

The working classes of the Western countries have a long history of struggle behind them. They are not prepared to accept being cast out of the consumer society and ruled over by German viceroys, even in the name of the 'Western', 'democratic' and 'liberal' values of the Atlantic Alliance.

As Germany slips to the right, so Southern Europe slips to the left. Things have got so bad that we are now witnessing the astonishing spectacle of a great working class party (the Italian Communist Party) making strenuous efforts *to avoid being put in power,* since power would bring it into a headlong clash with Europe's German and American masters. As Marx pointed out, crises are not bad for everybody. Until 1929, the successive jolts could even be said to have promoted the organization of industrial concentration, by eliminating the less competitive firms in each capitalist country. Since 1929 they have also had an international impact. Now that the dust of inter-imperialist confrontation has settled, the new balance of forces coming out of the 1973 crisis is discernible. From 1973 to 1976 the economies of Southern Europe collapsed to a greater or lesser extent while West Germany emerged as the main economic, political and military power of the capitalist West.

While Northern Europe moves to the right, the bourgeoisies of Southern Europe are battling with growing economic and political difficulties. In France, in Italy, and in Spain, the government no longer reflects a majority of public opinion, and the Italian state, faced with regional and municipal bodies controlled by Communists and revolutionaries, is even on the way to disappearing completely. Britain continues to sink deeper and deeper into the crisis.

The outcome is twofold. In the first place, the Western capitalists put their money away in Germany or the U.S., for safekeeping. The drain of liquid capital from Europe to the U.S. went up from $2 billion to $4 billion between 1974 and 1975, and the U.S.-bound flow of investment capital rose from $15 billion to $32 billion. Agnelli, for instance, has made extensive purchases in Montana. One should also bear in mind the recent outflow of Italian, British, Portuguese and French capital into the German Federal Republic. (In just one day in March 1976, foreign buyers invested 275 million marks on the German stock exchange.) This exodus is combined with a political surrender. Even the 'Gaullist' U.D.R. has accepted the Germans as viceroys over Europe. The balance of forces which made possible the Europe of the Treaty of Rome no longer exists; German Europe is on the horizon. The Western ruling classes are either resigned to it or actively desire it. In a recent speech, Agnelli even envisaged the possibility of 'resolving' the Italian crisis within the supra-national framework of a European government. Whenever the European social democrats (including the Italian and French C.P.s) go on about a 'Workers' Europe', they play straight into the hands of American imperialism.

But there is a more serious effect. In such a context, even the most democratically obtained successes of the left are unlikely to lead to changes in power acceptable to the U.S. and the German Federal Republic. The bourgeoisies of Southern Europe are well aware of the fact and are making appropriate preparations. The example of France during March 1976 illustrates the point: the authorities shelved most of their proposed tax reforms and business legislation; the government linked arms with the most reactionary wing of the employers and formalised the symbiotic relationship between businessmen and politicians institutionalized by the Fifth Republic.

The conclusions one can draw from this analysis are obviously at odds with the general orientation of social democratic forces in Europe. The rise of the German-American Empire in Europe, the threat it poses to democratic liberties, the 'Latin Americanization' of the peoples of Southern Europe all indicate that the near future is going to be very difficult. Left-wingers or revolutionaries who expect change to spring automatically from the development of the crisis are merely repeating in 1976 the errors of the Third International following 1929. It is the immediate political side-effects of the crisis which carry the most direct dangers, since there is no guarantee that the economic upheaval of 1973-75 will necessarily lead to new economic catastrophies. Minor upturns and short periods of stability are perfectly possible, in the context of a structural crisis which may go on for years.

The essential task of today is primarily political, to prevent the U.S. and its German allies from organizing the counter-revolution in Europe. One must therefore do what one can to block the building up of a Europe dominated by big American or German-American monopolies. This is perfectly feasible. Recent experience has shown that the struggle for socialism gains irresistible strength when it is linked to the fight for national independence. The Vietnamese example is particularly striking. The only way open to the peoples of Southern Europe, their only hope of avoiding the consequences of the crisis and their only means of defending their liberties is to launch an implacable struggle against the aims and political ambitions of the U.S. and the German Federal Republic.

The Struggles Ahead

The impact of the scientific and technical revolution on the socialist system is beyond the scope of this work. The working class movement is far from having fully analysed the nature and consequences of this new factor.

Following the Second World War, Stalin's successors, faced with the revival of capitalism as well as U.S. hegemony over the capitalist world and the growth of neo-colonialism, have merely continued his policies, with a few 'liberal' modifications. Their whole strategy relies on the use of market mechanisms, on the assimilation of technology and American social values, on the massive use of material incentives and on the stabilization of social differentiation, as means of catching up and even over-taking the U.S. They hoped that the policies of Yalta could be developed into a Russo-American partnership which would stabilize the international situation, promote the growth of international trade and facilitate the import of foreign capital which they mistakenly still believe is essential to Russia's development. As we have seen, the outcome of such policies is at the expense of the majority of humanity.

This strategy means that the U.S.S.R. has given up the idea of promoting revolution in Europe and in the underdeveloped countries. Instead the stabilization of the status quo implies giving support to national bourgeoisies and bureaucratic compradors in the underdeveloped countries.

This policy is now discredited. Experience has shown that the material basis of socialism cannot be built by playing on economic mechanisms and motivations which promote social differentiation. Socialism has an irreducibly moral dimension. Che Guevara's famous warning applies to the developed countries as well as to the Third World:

> In these countries, the people have still not been completely educated towards social labour, and the system of appropriation makes it impossible for all to have access to wealth. Given underdevelopment and the usual exodus of capital towards the 'civilized' countries, there can be no hope for a rapid change, and sacrifices will be necessary. We still have a long way to go before we achieve an adequate level of economic development and it is all too tempting to tread well beaten paths and to use material self-interest as a lever to accelerate development. The danger is that one can lose sight of the wood for trees. One can easily run into a dead end if one pursues the chimera of achieving socialism by employing the rotten methods inherited from capitalism, such as treating profit as a value in itself, merchandise as the economic unit, or material self-interest as an incentive. And one gets to this dead end after having back-tracked and shifted course so many times that afterwards it is often difficult to decide where one went wrong. Meanwhile the economic basis one has adopted has been at work, steadily sapping the growth of men's consciousness. To build socialism, one must change both man and the economic base at the same time.
>
> Hence the great importance of choosing the correct instrument to mobilize the masses. This instrument must be fundamentally an ethical one, although material incentives, especially social ones, do have a role to play.[23]

Stalin and his successors have reduced and impoverished the Marxist dialectic until it has become a self-caricature, a model condemned by history in terms of both humanity and efficiency. In the field of science, the U.S.S.R. is increasingly falling behind the U.S., while the crisis in agriculture due to exorbitant exactions is getting worse. Work is becoming more and more hierarchical and mechanical. Education is constantly growing more selective and technicist, the bureaucracy grows stronger, inequalities deepen and the depoliticization of the masses becomes more generalized. In terms of foreign policy, the failures of the U.S.S.R. are manifest; the U.S. also has difficulties but the Soviet Union does little to aggravate them.

The 'national' bourgeoisies are disintegrating. Following Asia and Latin America, Africa has in its turn suffered a series of military coups. Neo-colonialism continues to widen the gap between the rich and poor countries. Clearly the end of the twentieth century will be marked by overpopulation, famine and the growth of revolutionary struggles which may well lead to brutal retaliation on the part of the 'national' bourgeoisies of Europe and the U.S.

In an almost completely integrated society, where economic and political mechanisms fit together as intricately, and hence as delicately as clockwork, social battles are not completely economic. A major strike or a period of prolonged agitation can threaten the whole structure of established authority. But what direction will struggles take? This is the key issue. Those who hope to improve the system will strive to limit their scope and channel them into 'reasonable' economic demands, thereby preventing them from breaking out into the field of politics. The French C.P. adopted this reformist course during May 1968, and the Italian C.P. followed suit in Autumn 1970.

The development of the crisis will eventually force all the working class organizations to make a decisive choice. They will have to decide whether they will fight within the system as reformists, or outside it as revolutionaries. The latter course presumes a critique of the aspirations with which bourgois ideology and propaganda has imbued the masses – it involves the presentation of an egalitarian alternative based on qualitatively different human relations. In this context, the 'Manifesto' theorists are quite right to suggest that the realization of communism is a contemporary issue:

> The abolition of the capitalist division of labour is becoming a real necessity for a growing mass of workers; for those who carry out the most unpleasant and repetitive tasks, but also for those who are highly skilled but can find no way of expressing themselves in their work. The need for a different sort of urban life, for a different approach to health and to democratic participation in the making of decisions is increasingly apparent. As a result there develops an implicit critique of the individualist model of social life, of production oriented economic structures, and of the absence of any collective planning. But if we are to abandon the present absurd pattern of consumption based on the pursuit of the false needs created by economic growth itself, there will have to be a change in the nature of work itself, leading to an explosion of free activity and the overthrow of the present individualist model of social organization. A critique of authoritarianism and concentrated power is also necessarily a critique of their economic

> roots, of the pattern of economic and social organization, of the mystification implicit in representative democracy and of the separation between the social and the political. The struggle against inequalities of culture, function, power and income, the struggle against arbitrary hierarchy, the struggle to give everybody the right to self-expression is directly linked to the principle 'from each according to his ability, to each according to his needs.'[24]

For the first time in history, it is possible to envisage the abolition of industrial labour, the transformation of the pattern of consumption and the inauguration of a different pattern of international economic relations. The scientific revolution is not just a symptom of the evolution of the capitalist system. It opens up new possibilities for revolutionary struggle. But its side-effects pose formidable problems for the workers' movement throughout the industrial West. It is essential that we grasp its implications for the labour force and for the development of inequalities amongst the advanced capitalist countries themselves.

Since Spring 1974, Kissinger has laid his cards on the table. He is quite simply proposing that Europe accept an 'Organization of American States' type of status. He is openly laying claim to the leadership of the capitalist world as a whole and is even suggesting that trade with the Third World and the distribution of raw materials should be organized under U.S. supervision. All pretence has been cast aside so that the real nature of America's aims is quite apparent. Everybody else must now make up their minds as to how they stand *vis-a-vis* U.S. policy as it really is. It is increasingly important to define a working class international strategy, since it is no longer possible to separate the struggle within the advanced countries from the problems posed by the international organization of capital. One of Marx's and Lenin's most significant contributions to the history of modern revolutionary ideas is undoubtedly the concept of proletarian internationalism. Faced with the recent evolution of the 'multinationals', the European working class has no choice but to apply this solidarity to its economic struggles and to fight back on a European scale. Of course, this does not mean that it should adopt the European ideology of the bourgeoisie or defend the 'Europe of Nations' beloved of Pompidou, Giscard and Franco.

Without some radical change in the system, the 'institutional' notion of a 'Workers' Europe', as outlined during the most recent meeting of the Communist Parties, is pure metaphysics. Its only effect is to sidetrack analysis and struggle in a way which both obscures the real nature of the danger (the extension of U.S. hegemony over the whole capitalist system) and tells us nothing about the form this danger is taking, namely the growth of the U.S. multinationals. The real problem for socialists is to define an overall policy which will enable the working class everywhere to lead the struggle against the social forces and political organizations which serve U.S. imperialism.

References to Part III

1. The U.S. G.N.P., which has been falling for two years, fell again, by 5%, during 1975. U.S. unemployment has now reached 9%.
2. On 1 January 1974 the U.S. alone had twice as many computers as Japan, Germany, France, the U.K. and Italy put together. This should give some idea of the weight of the U.S. market. I.B.M. completely dominates the market: it accounts for 50% of world sales; its profits are fifteen times those of the second largest company (Honeywell) and three times those of all the other computer firms in the world as a whole.
3. This rhythm of acceleration is beginning to stabilize. By the end of the century about 20% of the population of the developed countries will consist of scientists, 99% of all scientists in human history will be living at the same time.
4. The terms 'old' and 'new' merely refer to previous stages in the organization of production, stages which may have lasted only one year or a dozen.
5. In the *Grundrisse,* Marx wrote: 'The exchange of living labour for objectified labour – i.e. the positioning of social labour in the form of the contradiction of capital and wage labour – is the ultimate development of the *value relation* and of production resting on value. Its presupposition is – and remains – the mass of direct labour time, the quantity of labour employed, as the determinant factor in the production of wealth. But to the degree that large industry develops, the creation of real wealth comes to depend less on labour time and on the amount of labour employed than on the power of the agencies set in motion during labour time, whose "powerful effectiveness" is itself in turn out of all proportion to the direct labour time spent on their production, but depends rather on the general state of science and on the progress of technology, or the application of this science to production.' K. Marx, *Grundrisse,* (Pelican, 1973), p.704.
6. *Ibid.,* p.22.
7. R. Luxemburg, *The Accumulation of Capital,* various editions.
8. Cf. S. Vannier, *Les Temps Modernes.*
9. Socialism denies itself and limits its own ability to make a critique and intervene when it accepts this type of scientific development.
10. *Le Monde Diplomatique,* (November 1974).
11. Cf. P. Pean, *Petrole, La troisieme guerre mondiale,* (Calmann-Levy, 1974).
12. Lenin, *Imperialism, the Highest Stage of Capitalism,* Chapter 7, various editions.
13. *Ibid.,* Chapter 4.
14. Dominated by Bohm-Bawerk and counting Schumpeter as one of its junior members.
15. At the time, the state of capitalist society gave little reason to believe that marginalism, which was then in its very early stages, had much future as a serious ideology.
16. Harry Magdoff, 'Les Aspects economiques de l'imperialisme americain', *Les Temps Modernes* (March 1967).
17. Estimates suggest that for centuries demographic growth remained at

about 0.1% per annum, on average. Around 1900 it rose to 0.5%, reaching 1% in 1940 and 2% in 1960.

18. *Le Capital,* Vol.6, p.61.
19. $10.5 billion for the U.K. and $6.5 billion for France in 1974, for example. All in all, the industrial countries lost more than $40 billion, most of which was reinvested in the U.S.
20. 12% in Britain, 15% in France.
21. 20% in Britain, 18% in France, 10% in the U.S., more than 25% in Italy and Japan.
22. One can expect the Republicans to boost inflation throughout 1976, in order to slow down the development of the crisis.
23. *Textes Politiques* (Maspero, 1968).
24. *Manifesto, These* (Seuil).

Index